CAMPAIGNS IN
THE NEWS

Recent Titles in
Contributions in Political Science
Series Editor: Bernard K. Johnpoll

The Unfulfilled Promise of Synthetic Fuels: Technological Failure, Policy Immobilism, or Commercial Illusion
Ernest J. Yanarella and William C. Green, editors

The French Socialists in Power, 1981–1986
Patrick McCarthy, editor

Dwight D. Eisenhower: Soldier, President, Statesman
Joann P. Krieg, editor

Irrationality in International Confrontation
Robert Mandel

The European Community and the Management of International Cooperation
Leon Hurwitz

Terrorism, U.S. Strategy, and Reagan Policies
Marc A. Celmer

Franklin D. Roosevelt: The Man, the Myth, the Era, 1882–1945
Herbert D. Rosenbaum and Elizabeth Bartelme, editors

Ethnic Groups and U.S. Foreign Policy
Mohammed E. Ahrari, editor

Referendum Voting: Social Status and Policy Preferences
Harlan Hahn and Sheldon Kamieniecki

Ordered Liberty and the Constitutional Framework: The Political Thought of Friedrich A. Hayek
Barbara M. Rowland

Policy Evaluation for Local Government
Terry Busson and Philip Coulter, editors

New Tides in the Pacific: Pacific Basin Cooperation and the Big Four (Japan, PRC, USA, USSR)
Roy Kim and Hilary Conroy, editors

Campaigns in the News

MASS MEDIA AND CONGRESSIONAL ELECTIONS

EDITED BY

Jan Pons Vermeer

CONTRIBUTIONS IN POLITICAL SCIENCE,
NUMBER 187

GREENWOOD PRESS
NEW YORK · WESTPORT, CONNECTICUT · LONDON

Library of Congress Cataloging-in-Publication Data

Campaigns in the news.

(Contributions in political science, ISSN 0147-1066 ;
no. 187)
  Bibliography: p.
  Includes index.
  1. Electioneering—United States. 2. United States.
Congress—Elections. 3. Mass media—Political aspects—
United States. I. Vermeer, Jan Pons. II. Series.
JK2281.C36   1987   324.7'3'0973   87-8423
ISBN 0-313-25187-8 (lib. bdg. : alk. paper)

Library of Congress Catalog Card Number: 87-8423
ISBN: 0-313-25187-8
ISSN: 0147-1066

First published in 1987

Greenwood Press, Inc.
88 Post Road West, Westport, Connecticut 06881

Printed in the United States of America

The paper used in this book complies with the
Permanent Paper Standard issued by the National
Information Standards Organization (Z39.48-1984).

10 9 8 7 6 5 4 3 2 1

Copyright Acknowledgment
Grateful acknowledgment is hereby given for permission to quote from the
following source: Lyn Ragsdale and Timothy E. Cook, "Representatives'
Actions and Challengers' Reactions: Limits to Candidate Connections in the
House," *American Journal of Political Science* 31 (1987): 55, 58, and 75.
Reproduced by permission of the authors and The University of Texas Press.

For Kathy

Contents

TABLES   ix
PREFACE   xi

1. Introduction   1
   Jan P. Vermeer

2. Shaping the News: An Analysis of House Candidates'
   Campaign Communications   13
   Paul Bradford Raymond

3. Liberal Campaign Rhetoric in 1984   31
   Richard A. Joslyn

4. Why Some Constituencies Are Better Informed Than
   Most About the Positions of House Incumbents   51
   Robert O. Simmons, Jr.

5. Congressional Campaign Coverage in Rural Districts   77
   Jan P. Vermeer

6. The Scribes of Texas: Newspaper Coverage of the 1984
   U.S. Senate Campaign   91
   Jon F. Hale

7. Mass Media Effects on Recognizing and Rating Candidates
   in U.S. Senate Elections   109
   Edie N. Goldenberg and Michael W. Traugott

8. Exploiting Televised Coverage of National Party
   Conventions on Behalf of Congressional Candidates:
   The Case of 1984   133
   Dan Nimmo and Larry Smith

9. Show Horses in House Elections: The Advantages
   and Disadvantages of National Media Visibility   161
   Timothy E. Cook

10. Media Coverage of Congressional Elections:
    An Ethical Perspective   183
    Bruce Jennings

11. Future Research on the News Media and
    Congressional Elections   199
    Paul Bradford Raymond

   BIBLIOGRAPHY   207

   INDEX   219

   ABOUT THE CONTRIBUTORS   227

Tables

2.1 Percentage of Candidates Offering No Solutions, Nonspecific Solutions, and Specific Solutions   16

2.2 Percentage of Candidates Offering Specific Solutions, by Candidate Status   19

2.3 Percentage of Similar Problems   20

2.4 Percentage of Candidates Mentioning Problems, by Candidates' Partisan Affiliation   21

2.5 Predictors of the Number of Problems   22

3.1 Liberal Congressmen Included in Study   39

3.2 Ideological Content of Televised Advertisements   45

4.1 Mean Amounts of Issue-Oriented Media by Level of Incumbent Representativeness   58

4.2 Mean Amounts of Issue-Oriented Media by Level of Visibility of Incumbent's Issue Positions   60

4.3 Regression of Incumbent's Issue-Position Visibility on Incumbent's Television Advertising and Challenger's Television Advertising: Results for Discrepants and Representative Incumbents   61

4.4 Regression of Incumbent's Issue-Position Visibility on Newspaper Content, Controlling for Incumbent's Television Advertising: Results for Discrepants and Representative Incumbents   63

4.5   Regression of Incumbent's Issue Coverage on Race Closeness,
      Newspaper Efficiency, and Challenger and Incumbent
      Issue Emphasis   65

6.1   Thematic Focus of Articles   96

6.2   Issue Content of Articles   99

6.3   Issue Content in "Contest" Articles   100

6.4   Issue Content in "Issue" Articles   101

6.5   Wire Service Coverage   104

7.1   The Relationship between Media Exposure and Candidate
      Recognition in the 1984 Senatorial Campaign in Michigan   113

7.2   The Relationship between Media Exposure and Ability to Recognize
      and Rate Candidates in the 1984 Senatorial Campaign in Michigan   115

7.3   The Relationship between Exposure to Ads and Ability to
      Recognize and Rate Candidates in the 1984 Senatorial Campaign
      in Michigan   116

7.4   Coverage of the 1984 Michigan Campaign for U.S. Senate
      in Twenty-Nine Newspapers   118

7.5   The Relationship between Media Content and Ability to Recognize
      and Rate Candidates, Controlling on Media Exposure,
      1984 Michigan Senate Campaign   122

7.6   Television Advertising Placements in Minutes by Candidates in the
      1984 Michigan Campaign for U.S. Senate in Eight Markets   124

7.7   Exposure to Candidates' Television Advertising as a Function of
      TV Viewing Habits, October, 1984   125

7.8   The Relationship between Exposure to Candidates' Television
      Advertising and Candidate Evaluations, 1984 Senatorial Campaign
      in Michigan   126

7.9   Dichotomous Regressions of Candidate Recognition and
      Evaluation on Media Exposure and Party Identification,
      October, 1984   128

8.1   C-SPAN Coverage of Democratic and Republican
      National Conventions   147

8.2   Network Coverage of the Democratic National Convention   150

8.3   Network Coverage of the Republican National Convention   155

9.1   Determinants of the Congressional Vote—Regression Estimates   165

9.2   The Effects of Incumbent Resources on Challenger Strength—
      Regression Estimates   167

9.3   Determinants of Challenger Money—Regression Estimates   169

9.4   Democratic Press Secretaries' Evaluation of Media Outlets
      and Strategies   172

9.5   Democratic Press Secretaries' Attitudes on Local vs. National Media   173

9.6   Correlates of Democratic Press Secretaries' Perceived Value of
      National Media   177

Preface

This book grew out of a conjunction of research interests I have had for a number of years in media and politics and in congressional elections. Because more scholars have recently been concerned with the impact of the mass media on elections for Congress, the time seemed ripe to bring together a number of essays addressing the topic from various perspectives. The range of issues examined here, from ethics and ideology to newspaper and television exposure to policy information and advertisements, brings to mind as well the topics still to be explored, such as media's role in candidate recruitment and differences in coverage between midterm and presidential election year elections. Many more contributions to our understanding of the relationship of mass media and congressional elections can be expected in the near future.

Although the general focus of attention in this volume is patterns of news coverage of congressional elections, elements that closely relate to that concern are also covered here. Specifically, some space is devoted to the content of campaign materials, such as candidate brochures and television advertising, as well as to what voters can be expected to know about incumbent House members during the campaign. The rationale for including these studies is simply that campaign news coverage reflects what the candidates are doing; the media's choices are in many ways limited by what candidates make available. But the bulk of the work deals directly with news coverage of congressional elections.

The list of people and organizations to whom I owe thanks is long; not all can be acknowledged here. Walter F. Murphy suggested hosting a conference at which the essays in this volume could first be presented. John W. White, Jr., and Paul Laursen of Nebraska Wesleyan University agreed with the suggestion, leading to the Dwight P. Griswold–E. C. Ames Conference on Mass Media and Congressional Elections on March 7 and 8, 1986. Thanks go to Nebraska Wesleyan University for support in the form of an E. C. Ames grant, to the Department of Political Science for use of the Dwight P. Griswold funds, to the Convocations Committee of NWU for their support, and to the Don W. Stewart Family Fund for a special grant. To the participants in the conference goes special recognition.

Thanks, too, to Mildred Vasan, Bernard K. Johnpoll, Arlene Belzer, and Barbara Hodgson at Greenwood Press for their encouragement (and patience). To Ron and Gretchen Naugle, Trudy Selleck, and Hans Brisch, my gratitude for their moral support and guidance along the way. To my parents, Cornelis and Helena Maria Vermeer, my appreciation for the many spoken and unspoken ways they have helped over the years. And to Kathryn S. Gonnerman, typist *extraordinaire* and so much more, words cannot express what I owe.

The usual *mea culpa* applies for the errors that remain, despite the efforts of all those who have helped, for which they bear no responsibility.

1

Introduction

Jan P. Vermeer

Congress was supposed to be the branch of government most directly responsive to the people. The intentions of the framers were, as closely as we can reconstruct them, that members of Congress, especially of the lower House, should reflect the wishes of the citizenry. Popularly elected legislators would hold their seats if their constituents thought they took correct positions on the issues and if the constituents trusted their judgment. Representatives who lost the confidence of the people back home would face defeat at the next election, while those who maintained continued support among the voters would fare well at the polls. Shifts in the preferences of the electorate would then be reflected in corresponding changes in the positions taken by the legislators, as representatives worked to merit voters' continued confidence.

This representative relationship, whether played out in a delegate role or in a trustee role (Wahlke et al., 1962), is at the basis of any discussion of Congress or congressional elections. And even though the framers did not have representative democracy in mind, constitutional development since 1787 points to the increasing importance of the constituent-representative relationship. Any description of the functions of Congress must take into account its representational role. Unavoidably, Congress' performance in its other tasks, whether budgeting, lawmaking, or oversight, is evaluated in the light of its success in representing the views of the citizenry.

It is not necessary to delve into theories of representation to make this point (for discussions of representation generally, see Pitkin, 1969). Suffice it to say that democratic theory justifies the people's delegation of power to representatives, given the right to choose freely and meaningfully. When citizens freely and intelligently choose others to act on their behalf in the halls of Congress, basic presuppositions of representative democracy are met.

Describing such a representative relationship in the abstract is easy. What is of greater interest—and quite a bit more difficult—is to decide whether the practices and customs that have grown up around congressional elections in the United States approximate these ideals. The representational mechanisms in use in the United States (individualistic, through personal contacts with government officials; functional, through action by groups of citizens with similar interests; and electoral, by choosing between competing aspirants for office) may or may not result in the adoption of governmental policies consistent with the preferences of a majority of citizens.

Studies of elections as representational mechanisms are not new—Charles Merriam in the 1920s (e.g., Merriam and Gosnell, 1924) conducted several. What is relatively new, however, is concern with congressional elections. In a field dominated by studies of presidential elections, comparatively little research has been done on elections for members of the House of Representatives and even less for members of the Senate. The reader will find references to many of the most important studies in the chapters in this volume, conveniently listed in the bibliography at the end of the volume.

Results from research on presidential elections cannot be readily generalized to congressional elections. Incumbency is a much more important factor in congressional elections (Erikson, 1971; Mayhew, 1974b; Cover, 1977; and Nelson, 1978/79) than in presidential elections. Voter information levels are substantially higher in presidential elections. Party identification plays a different role for voters in congressional elections than in presidential elections. The strength of the challenger to an incumbent seeking reelection to the presidency is usually greater than in congressional elections. Further, the patterns of media coverage of presidential elections are markedly different than the patterns of media coverage of congressional elections.

In recent years, congressional elections have received increasing attention from scholars, in part because beginning in 1978, the National Election Study (NES) included questions about elections to the House and Senate. It became possible to draw conclusions about the responses of voters to candidates and issues, to determine levels of name familiarity, and to weigh the impact of party affiliation on election outcomes. Much of what we know about congressional elections can be traced to studies using NES data, and questions raised by the first research papers using those data are still being addressed (cf. Mann and Wolfinger, 1980; Abramowitz, 1980; and Hinckley, 1980a).

Early results supported David Mayhew's (1974b) conclusion that incumbents were (increasingly) more likely to win. Hinckley (1981) noted that the advantage enjoyed by incumbents was primarily due to voters' greater familiarity with their names and the greater likelihood of positive voter evaluations. Jacobson (1983), on the other hand, argued that the strength of incumbents was primarily the result of their greater success in attracting the kinds of campaign resources necessary to withstand challenges. A great deal of succeeding work has centered on explaining the incumbency advantage.

But incumbents sometimes lost. Occasionally a challenger would become well known, and voters would respond positively. Sometimes a challenger would amass the campaign resources (usually financial) necessary to run a formidable campaign. It did not happen frequently enough to warrant throwing out the notion of incumbent strength (although perhaps incumbent invulnerability had been overstated [Vermeer, 1984]), but there were enough such upsets for political scientists to examine the factors that transform incumbency from a general asset to a specific campaign resource.

Further, patterns earlier discovered in the defeat of incumbents, and analyzed first by Campbell (1966), by Kramer (1971), and by Tufte (1975) were reexamined in the light of the NES data. Midterm elections and economic downturns were associated quite consistently with defeat of incumbents of the president's party, but survey data seldom indicated that voters responded to congressional candidates on the basis of either the president's program or the state of the economy. Jacobson and Kernell (1981) presented one theory to account for this anomalous finding. They argued that an intermediate factor was involved: the decisions by "strategic politicians" to encourage strong candidates to run and to finance strong challengers liberally. Jacobson and Kernell argued that when national tides, whether indicated by presidential popularity or by economic events, were running against one party, strategic politicians associated with that party would discourage strong challengers and keep their campaign contributions low; when national tides were favorable, the opposite responses would occur.

Jacobson and Kernell's theory has its critics (e.g., Uslaner and Conway, 1985). But it points out a factor that deserves emphasis. Reelection is not caused by incumbency per se. Rather, it comes from an incumbent's ability to gather the campaign resources necessary to run a hard campaign and the absence of a similar effort by a well-qualified challenger. It is, in other words, the product of a campaign. What happens in the November congressional elections is not predetermined by the

outcome of the election two years before. It is the result of the candidates' efforts during the summer and fall.

The activities of political action committees (PACs) over the past de-
cade and a half raise a different perspective. On the one hand, they are
a source of campaign funds, most abundantly for incumbents, but also
significantly for congressional challengers deemed to have a good chance
of winning. In contests for open seats, especially, PAC financing has
been important. But the impact of PACs on the campaign itself is limited. Acceptance of PAC money may become an issue in a particular
campaign, and candidates may find it necessary to make the rounds of
fund-raising cocktail parties with PAC representatives, but the day-to-
day activities of the campaign are not directly affected. Even in Senate
campaigns, the amount of money donated by any one PAC constitutes
only a relatively minor percentage of the total funds necessary to wage
a viable campaign. Decisions about how to run the campaign, how to
use the media in the election period, and how to reach voters are not
likely to be directly affected by PAC money. PACs are concerned about
access to officeholders, not about the conduct of campaigns per se. It is
PAC money, undoubtedly, that makes sophisticated use of media—an
expensive campaign tool indeed—possible, but PACs do not dictate how
the campaign is conducted.

On the other hand, some PACs have waged virtually independent
campaigns for Congress on behalf of candidates whose stands they approve. The National Conservative Political Action Committee (NCPAC)
is a prime example, having "targeted" a number of incumbents in the
Senate in 1978 and having spent a great deal of money on behalf of
their opponents without involving itself directly in their campaigns. They
purchased media time and placed advertisements, winning a great deal
of attention for their efforts and name recognition for the challengers.
Marjorie Randon Hershey's study of learning in campaigns has dealt
admirably with this sort of PAC activity (see Hershey, 1984, chapter 6).
On the whole, this kind of PAC activity is still an exception; few PACs
are large enough and well-financed enough to be able to conduct such
efforts. Although the authors of the chapters in this volume are aware
of these groups' participation in modern congressional elections, PAC
involvement is generally too marginal to the nexus between congressional campaigns and the mass media to receive extensive attention in
their contributions.

The campaign activities of candidates for Congress have become increasingly sophisticated in recent years, in part because of greater access to campaign funds and in part because of the spread of modern
campaign techniques from the presidential level to lower-level campaigns (Agranoff, 1976). Congressional candidates turned more and more
to mass media as a vehicle for reaching voters. Television advertise-

ments, radio spots, and attempts to generate news coverage became more and more prominent in campaigns, not replacing pamphlets, personal appearances, and shaking hands at shopping centers and factory gates, but supplementing them. Well-financed challengers could hope to overcome the edge in name familiarity that incumbents generally enjoyed by generating substantial news coverage and buying a great deal of media advertising.

Not much insight is required to note that the context for media use by congressional candidates is much different than that for presidential candidates. Generating news coverage on television newscasts is much more difficult for candidates for Congress; even Senate candidates are at a disadvantage compared with candidates for president. There are so many more of them than there are contenders for the nation's highest office; congressional candidates simply are not as newsworthy. Reporters are much less likely to generate news stories on campaigns for the House and the Senate on their own initiative. Whereas presidential candidates will have virtually every one of their campaign appearances chronicled in the press, congressional candidates have to work hard to stimulate coverage of even their most noteworthy campaign efforts.

The biggest difference is in the fit between media markets and congressional districts. Pointed out early by the participants in Clapp's Brookings Institution roundtable on serving in Congress (Clapp, 1963, pp. 382-83), the congruence between the areas served by television stations, newspapers, and radio stations and the boundaries of congressional districts presents the biggest hurdle to effective and (relatively) inexpensive use of mass media to reach voters. Goldenberg and Traugott (1984) devoted substantial attention to this factor in their attempts to account for the campaign patterns they found among candidates for the House in 1978. Campbell, Alford, and Henry (1982) similarly use the degree of congruence between media markets and congressional districts to account for the level of voter awareness of candidates' positions on the issues.

Some candidates are in an advantageous position, with media markets and congressional district boundaries virtually identical. But these contenders are in a decided minority. Most congressional candidates either have to generate news coverage and buy advertising time and space in several media markets or must pay to reach a lot of voters who live outside their districts. Further, candidates for Congress must often compete for news coverage with candidates for other seats in the same media market. If a newspaper or television station is going to run a news item on a congressional race, it is going to choose to feature the most notable one, not cover all races equally.

Ultimately the disjunctions in fit result in a lesser reliance by congressional candidates on the electronic media. The reason is simply cost.

Although candidates running for the House from New York City would dearly love to get substantial exposure on the city's television stations and would relish having the resources to buy extensive advertising time there, they must be realistic. That kind of exposure, in which television reaches twenty times the target constituency, is much too expensive for most campaigns. The burden is not as great for the print media, since the press news hole is elastic (given sufficient advertising) in a sense that television news broadcasts are not—adding five minutes to a newscast is virtually unheard of. Only where television markets fall completely or substantially within a congressional district and where candidates are well financed can we expect to see much emphasis on television exposure as a campaign technique. (Nevertheless, a number of the chapters that follow deal with television and congressional campaigns—the interested reader should consult the Cook, Nimmo and Smith, and Goldenberg and Traugott chapters in this volume specifically.)

It is therefore not an easy matter for candidates for Congress to get their messages across to the voters. Districts are too large for efficient personal campaigning. Voter interest generally is not high enough so that candidates can hope that voters will seek them out. Media advertising is expensive, and news coverage tends to be sporadic and thin, except where campaigners have the resources to generate the kind of media attention that can successfully penetrate voter consciousness. And the problem of reaching the electorate is greater for challengers than for incumbents.

Effective representation is thereby threatened. When campaigns are low-information affairs, with voters uninterested and uninformed, the choice between candidates is not instrumental. It is not the product of a preference about policies. It is not the result of a weighing of advantages and disadvantages, of strengths and weaknesses, of the candidates. It is frequently a response to rather shallow cues, such as name recognition. If representation implies a choice between candidates on some basis connected with performance in office, whether past or future, voters require at least a minimum amount of information.

Incumbents are better able to provide voters with information about themselves. As officeholders, they can attract news coverage through official activities. As victors in previous elections, they have built higher name familiarity among voters. As veterans of earlier campaigns, they have made contacts with members of the media. The information that voters have about incumbents and challengers is therefore asymmetric, with the advantage overwhelmingly in favor of incumbents.

It is difficult to argue, given this imbalance between incumbents and challengers, that congressional campaigns provide a meaningful choice for voters. Here we have representation in the sense that the member of Congress is chosen by the voters, but not representation in the sense that the views of the officeholder reflect the views of the constituents (see Pitkin, 1967, for a discussion of the different meanings of representation). Although voters choose their representatives, the dynamics of the electoral process presents them too frequently with a well-known incumbent and a weak, little-known challenger. The election outcome is more likely to reflect the relative vigor of the candidacies than voter preferences among the policy alternatives offered.

But incumbents cannot rely on name recognition alone when faced with strong challengers. They must generate sufficient news coverage and place enough advertisements to keep their names known and their evaluations positive. With strong challengers in the arena, incumbents cannot afford to have the media focus their attention on the vigorous campaign being waged against them. They must successfully apply their resources to stimulate news stories on their background, their accomplishments, and their qualifications. Incumbents cannot rest on their laurels.

But let us not jump from the recognition of an incumbent advantage in news coverage to a conclusion about media bias. The argument here, and in the chapters that follow, is implicitly that there is media selectivity, that there are patterns in journalistic practices, that media are not neutral reflectors of the political world, and that candidates in some situations benefit more from these facts than do others. The Hale chapter is a good example of such an approach. But saying so is completely different from asserting that the uneven distribution of the benefits (and, yes, the costs—if the publicity is unfavorable) of news coverage is the result of an intention on the part of the media to secure such an outcome.

Members of the media have preferences, they form stronger attachments to some political figures than to others, and they must make a multitude of daily choices that cannot help but be at least subtly influenced by some of these factors. But stronger influences are the norms and procedures of the journalistic profession and the needs and requirements of the various media themselves. The evidence marshaled in the chapters in this volume more clearly supports the notion of structural bias (see, for instance, Ranney, 1983, chapter 2) than that of political bias.

But it is because the patterns of reporters and the requirements of various media are well known that newsmakers, including candidates, can in fact manipulate the news media. By providing the kind of news that reporters and editors cannot resist, candidates can get publicity that is otherwise unavailable. Modern campaign techniques concern themselves extensively with manipulating the media to enable candidates to get their messages across to voters. Campaign strategies reflect the opportunities available to candidates to get news coverage (Arterton, 1984). It is not surprising that some contenders for office are more successful in this quest—they have a greater supply of the resources necessary to attract media attention, and incumbency is one of those resources. (Clarke and Evans spend a great deal of space discussing the journalistic practices that result in greater coverage for incumbents; see Clarke and Evans, 1983.) The fact of an advantage for some candidates over others is not necessarily the result of an *intent* to produce such an advantage. The "bias" one finds in media coverage of congressional elections overall tends to be structural, not political, a by-product of journalistic practices, not the result of reporter preferences.

Congressional candidates cannot ignore the media. Their campaigns are, of course, exercises in communication. They are essentially attempts by candidates to reach an audience, the electorate, with their names, messages, campaign themes, positions on the issues, and other such matters. Both incumbents and challengers engage in these communication activities in order to influence the perceptions and actions of the voters. Incumbents want to reinforce what is probably a favorable attitude in the absence of an opponent. Challengers want to introduce themselves to the electorate and persuade the electorate to identify them with the values it holds. These goals are attainable only through effective use of communication opportunities.

Campaigns are, then, attempts at education. Voters, left to their own devices, learn little about congressional campaigns, about the policy issues debated, or about the positions their current and future representatives hold. Neither, it seems, do the media supply a great deal of information on their own initiative. Candidates cannot evoke the responses they want from voters if the electorate is not exposed to information from and about the contenders.

But education through campaigns is not merely a question of volume of information; it is also a matter of content. Manipulation of political symbols and stress on superficial issues may attract votes, but they do not enlighten voters or strengthen the representational relationship between lawmaker and constituent. Campaigns educate when they make reasonable choices possible. Essentially, they are attempts by candidates to publicize their positions on campaign issues or remind voters of their ability to perform official duties. In either case, voters learn about the contenders.

The chapters in this volume address many of these concerns. Virtually all directly address some aspect of the news coverage accorded congressional campaigns, but although the conjunction between news and congressional elections is the subject of this volume, a worthwhile treatment of the subject encompasses some areas somewhat outside that relationship. For instance, an awareness of what candidates stress in their campaigns and an understanding of the factors that lead to voters knowing more about one candidate than the opponent provide a worthwhile context for more detailed examination of news coverage of congressional elections. As Hale argues, news media tend to pick up on the themes stressed by the candidates. And so we look here also at the content of congressional campaigns.

We begin with Paul Bradford Raymond's analysis of the content of the campaign brochures and pamphlets that congressional candidates produce. Not only do these materials provide a good indication of the emphases of the candidates during the campaign, but they are also a source of information for news media. Further, they parallel the campaign themes the candidates stress in other aspects of their campaigns. Raymond suggests that one cannot blame the news media for a dearth of substantive policy discussions; rather, he finds that news media coverage of candidate qualifications and issue positions is more the result of journalistic initiative than of campaign brochures and handouts.

Richard A. Joslyn takes the education theme further. His analysis, also based on examination of candidate-produced campaign material, but in his case television spot advertisements, focuses on their ideological content. His concern is that campaigners do not provide the kind of clear ideological information necessary for voters to place the candidates accurately along the liberal-conservative spectrum. He finds that these campaign commercials are not likely to make the electorate's ideological belief system more sophisticated and constrained.

Robert O. Simmons, Jr., suggests that the issue positions of unrepresentative incumbents are not always well known to their constituents. They may in fact be relatively invisible to their constituents, with their "out-of-step" policy positions virtually unknown in the district. But when a well-financed challenger enters the picture, one who can run a viable campaign against the incumbent, and when that challenger emphasizes issues, then newspapers become an important source of information for voters about the positions the incumbent has taken during his term in office. But these conditions are not often met; the upshot is that representatives who take issue positions their constituents oppose can frequently keep their public record obscure and out of the campaign limelight, with obvious impact on effectiveness of representation.

My study examines press coverage of congressional campaigns in rural districts. In areas where no one media market or newspaper can claim a proprietary interest in the incumbent ("He's our man, and no one else's!"), it would be expected that news coverage would be generally low and that challengers would experience greater difficulties than incumbents. Overall, that picture is accurate, but the advantage incumbents enjoyed in the columns of the press in these rural districts was not as great as one might have expected. Challengers do get space, but not nearly the amount they would need to mount a serious threat to most incumbents.

The 1984 Texas Senate race provides the setting for Jon F. Hale's analysis of the coverage provided by six of the state's major daily newspapers, which he examined in the context of the notion of media bias. He, too, found issue coverage to be sporadic at best, but he found a noticeable "Amarillo difference." Whereas the other dailies responded to the themes and issues stressed by the candidates, often in response to points raised by the television spot advertisements, the Amarillo paper successfully focused the candidates' comments on issues the paper considered relevant to its circulation area. Clearly the campaign agenda was set differently in the Texas Panhandle than elsewhere in the state. What one learned about the issues in the Senate campaign depended on where one lived.

Those differences in information environments were explored by Edie N. Goldenberg and Michael W. Traugott for the Michigan 1984 Senate race. Examining television and newspaper content for different media markets in the state, Goldenberg and Traugott conclude that opportunities for candidates to become well known vary across different information environments in the state. Their evidence strongly suggests that the news media are more important to campaigns for the Senate than they are to campaigns for the House of Representatives. They also conclude that the electorate's media exposure habits and the candidates' strategies in buying television advertising in different markets are significant news media effects in the campaign.

Dan Nimmo and Larry Smith consider how well the national political parties used their nominating conventions to showcase congressional candidates. Here is a clear opportunity for the parties to demonstrate support for candidates for the House and Senate and for the candidates to link themselves with the national parties. Nimmo and Smith discover that television exposure of congressional candidates is a minor factor in the drama that the networks cover. One might wonder whether the link between party organizations at the national level and party members in Congress is weaker than it need be. Certainly, ties between the national party and the state-level campaigns are not strengthened by the patterns found here, to the detriment of the development of well-identified party teams contesting elections.

National news media coverage turns out not to be significant to members of Congress in their reelection bids. Timothy E. Cook explores the efforts members make to generate coverage at the national level and finds they are connected to goals they have in Washington—policy leadership, for instance—rather than to reelection. He notes that there are much easier ways to generate local district coverage than by frequently appearing in the newscasts and news columns of the national media. The overall picture is one of representatives running for office in the national legislature from a local stance.

Bruce Jennings draws out the ethical implications of news media coverage of congressional campaigns. He points out the principles, autonomy, accountability, and responsibility, that lie behind ethical representation, arguing that journalists and legislators alike must recognize their roles in making effective representation possible. To the extent that reporters do not recognize the impact of their choices on effective representation, and to the extent that campaigners make realistic choices between candidates more difficult, they fall short of meeting the ethical demands to maintain the integrity of the electoral process.

The book concludes with a short essay by Paul Bradford Raymond drawing out future lines of research and pointing out some of the inherent difficulties in conducting research on mass media and congressional elections. Indeed, given the wide variety of contexts in which congressional campaigns occur, and the importance of local factors in the outcome of those elections, developing general propositions becomes a major undertaking. Well-selected case studies, small-scale investigations within the resources of a single researcher, and collaboration among two or more scholars may lead the way to further progress in this field. This book is itself an example of what can be done.

It is too late in the game to think of the media as external factors in politics. Whether merely as "linkage institutions" or as actors in their own rights, media play important roles in the political system.

It is no less so in congressional elections. Although it has long seemed that media are of only minor importance in congressional elections, a greater and greater body of evidence has been built up demonstrating the interaction between congressional campaigning and media coverage.

No complex argument is required to persuade most readers that communication from candidate to voter is essential to the democratic process—voters must choose among candidates on the information available to them, usually ultimately provided by the candidates themselves. If that communication process is to succeed, much of it must be conducted through the media. The possibility then exists of educating voters, about the candidates, about the issues, indeed, about the democratic process. Then representative government can function.

2

Shaping the News: An Analysis of House Candidates' Campaign Communications

Paul Bradford Raymond

INTRODUCTION

The traditional theory of democratic elections assumes that citizens are provided with information about candidates that results in informed voting decisions.[1] Yet a considerable body of empirical research suggests that most congressional voters are unaware of House candidates' qualifications and issue-orientations. For example, a study of the 1978 House elections found that only about 20 percent of the people who had a position on a policy issue were also capable of indicating where both their district's House candidates stood on that issue (Hinckley, 1981, p. 102).

Early voting studies attributed the electorate's ignorance to a lack of interest in election campaigns and an inability to assimilate political information (Lazarsfeld, Berelson, and Gaudet, 1944; Berelson, Lazarsfeld, and McPhee, 1954). More recently an accusing finger has been pointed at the news media. Journalists are criticized for exerting minimal effort in covering congressional campaigns, and for paying too little attention to officeseekers' policy proposals (Clarke and Evans, 1983, p. 33). The press is also said to have an "incumbency bias," since it devotes more attention to the issue positions and political attributes of incumbents than it does to those of challengers (Clarke and Evans, 1983, pp. 45-46). And finally, reporters are blamed for placing too much emphasis on campaign strategy and hoopla (Hale, 1987).

No doubt both voters and the news media must share some of the blame for the prevalence of uninformed voters. Citizens do not always enthusiastically absorb political information, and some of the news media's organizational routines and norms adversely influence coverage of congressional campaigns.[2] But this study focuses attention away from the limitations of the voter and the press in order to examine the content of candidate-controlled communications. It investigates whether House candidates provide substantive information about their issue positions and qualifications in the communications they control. For while the content of the news is partially influenced by journalistic work ways and norms, it is also shaped by the nature of candidates' campaigns.[3]

Specifically, this study seeks answers to the questions that follow: Do House candidates' communications emphasize issues? To what extent do officeseekers offer specific solutions to policy problems? Are candidates who are competing against each other talking about the same issues? What conditions motivate congressional hopefuls to run issue-oriented campaigns? And finally, to what extent do candidates' nonissue-oriented appeals supply voters with substantive information?

METHODOLOGY

The campaign brochures of 137 congressional hopefuls were analyzed (53 incumbents, 63 challengers, and 21 open seat candidates). These data were gathered as part of the 1978 American National Election Study conducted by the Center for Political Studies of the Institute for Social Research at the University of Michigan.[4]

Brochures are chosen as the unit of analysis for several reasons. First, brochures are designed to be distributed to a cross section of the electorate. Consequently their analysis provides an opportunity to judge how candidates wish to present themselves to the average voter rather than to a particular subgroup. Second, an analysis of the content of brochures provides a good measure of the relative attention candidates devote to issues and other types of appeals. Unlike other communication mediums, such as radio and television spots (where monetary and production constraints force candidates to make only a few brief appeals), the length of brochures allows candidates to make several types of appeals, and to discuss them in some detail. Finally, in order to compare candidates' communication styles, one needs to examine how officeseekers present themselves in the same mediums. It makes little sense, for example, to compare one candidate's TV ads (where time does not permit much attention to issue positions) with another officeseeker's position papers—where lengthy discussions of issues are the norm. Candidates' brochures were the only type of campaign material gathered from a sufficient number of candidates to allow meaningful comparisons to be made.

In order to determine what candidates are attempting to convey about themselves, their literature is analyzed through content analysis. The coding scheme measures the relative emphasis candidates place on issue, candidate, and constituency appeals; the number and type of issues discussed; and the specificity of the solutions offered.[5] Coders simultaneously weighed multiple factors (text, size of type, pictures, etc.) before making a judgment about the amount of emphasis placed on particular types of appeals.[6]

FINDINGS

Issue Emphasis

On the average, candidates devote more than half (52 percent) of their communications to issues.[7] This finding belies the conventional wisdom that modern-day officeseekers "ignore the issues" in favor of what are usually regarded as less divisive appeals, such as discussions of candidates' personal characteristics or constituency appeals.[8] But this is not to say that House candidates' campaign communications are educating the electorate about officeseekers' policy positions. While most candidates refer to a variety of issues, officeseekers often offer ambiguous solutions.[9]

The extent to which candidates avoid specifics is well illustrated by the data in Table 2.1. This table reports what candidates have to say about five frequently mentioned policy problems (government spending, inflation, taxes, social security, and energy).[10] Each candidate's solutions to these problems are classified into one of three categories. Solutions that refer to particular programs, services, reforms, legislation, or dollar amounts are classified as "specific solutions." Those that pertain to more generalized activities are coded as "nonspecific." If a candidate merely restates a problem, he or she is said to offer "no solution."

For example, in regard to the problem of government spending, a reference to a 20 percent cut in spending or the elimination of a specific government program is classified as a specific solution. Those candidates who propose to solve this problem by cutting the deficit without suggesting any particular course of action or dollar amount are coded as offering a nonspecific solution. Officeseekers who simply say they want a spending cut are said to offer no solution.

Even though the definition of what constitutes a specific solution is broad, the data in Table 2.1 offer support for the supposition that many

Table 2.1
Percentage of Candidates Offering No Solutions, Nonspecific Solutions, and Specific Solutions

	No Solution	Nonspecific Solution	Specific Solution	N
Government Spending	37	10	53	73*
Inflation	40	31	29	72
Taxes	37	8	55	84
Social Security	21	29	50	38
Energy	25	11	64	55

* Number of cases.

Source: Computed by author.

candidates offer ambiguous solutions to one or more problems. Less than a third of the officeseekers discuss one or more specific solutions to the problem of inflation. Only slightly more than half of the candidates cite a specific solution to government spending or taxes. Exactly 50 percent of the candidates suggest specific solutions to the social security issue. Energy is the only issue for which the percentage of candidates offering specific solutions approaches two-thirds.

Why is it that candidates take vague positions on issues? Page's (1978) emphasis allocation theory provides a partial explanation. This theory suggests that candidates avoid specifics because they believe that most voters have little interest in the means by which policy problems are solved. If officeseekers were to take specific stands, this theory suggests, they would reduce the time available to make more productive campaign appeals. Consequently candidates allocate little time to discussing the means by which policies will be solved and emphasize general goals, qualifications, and personal characteristics. Only the existence of a public norm (reinforced by the news media) that urges candidates to offer some policy proposals prevents candidates from entirely avoiding specifics. Politicians, Page suggests, offer specifics grudgingly, and only when they fear that their failure to do so will itself become an "issue" in the campaign.

Page's theory explains why some congressional hopefuls avoid specific pledges. But the number of candidates who offer specific solutions, although lower than advocates of the democratic theory of elections desire, is greater than the emphasis allocation theory predicts. In part, this is a consequence of the manner in which these data have been coded. The fact that any proposal that makes reference to a dollar amount is classified as a specific solution inflates the number of candidates who are said to offer specific solutions to the problems of government spending, inflation, and taxes. For example, 35 percent of the candidates who are classified as offering a specific solution to government spending simply note that they believe that the budget should be cut by a specific amount. None of these candidates pursued the more controversial strategy of mentioning a specific program or service that should be targeted for elimination.

The brochure of a Republican candidate from a midwestern district offers a good example of this practice. He calls for a big cut in spending, but his literature does not state what services will be eliminated as a consequence of budget reductions. In fact, like many other officeseekers seeking election in 1978, this candidate calls for deep cuts in government spending while simultaneously proclaiming his support for a number of specific programs that will benefit constituents in his district.

Another frequently mentioned solution to economic problems is the Kemp-Roth Bill. Although candidates who mentioned it are credited with offering a specific solution, most do not speculate on the effects this bill's huge tax cuts will have on government services. As one might expect, this solution is a particular favorite among the Republican candidates. But many Democrats also indicate their support for the key provision of this bill (a 30 percent tax cut), although they are careful not to mention the names of its Republican sponsors.

A second reason there is a bit more specificity than the emphasis allocation theory predicts is that candidates tend to offer noncontroversial specific solutions to problems. For example, unambiguous (but popular) solutions to problems related to social security include elimination of earnings limitations and the "marriage penalty." Only a handful of candidates indicate their support for more controversial proposals for changing the social security program, such as the idea of including federal employees in the system. Candidates also tend to supply noncontroversial specific solutions to the energy crisis. Many of these solutions do not go far toward increasing the availability of cheap energy, but they are likely to be warmly embraced by constituents. For example, several candidates note that they favor tax incentives to homeowners who install insulation. Another officeseeker says he is firm in his opposition to increases in gasoline taxes. And a candidate from Kentucky (a state that mines much of the nation's coal) suggests that "Kentucky coal" will help solve the energy crisis. None of these specific solutions will lose candidates many votes.[11]

Variations in Specificity

Of some interest is the finding that there is variation in the types of issues for which candidates offer specific solutions. If one looks at the percentage of candidates who offer no solution in Table 2.1, it is apparent that specificity is greater for problems relating to social security and energy than for those relating to government spending, inflation, and taxes. Only 21 and 25 percent of the candidates fail to offer a nonspecific or specific solution to the social security and the energy problem, respectively. Between 37 and 40 percent of the officeseekers do not discuss solutions to government spending, inflation, and taxes. This finding is consistent with previous research on politicians' campaign communications. Gerald Pomper (1980, pp. 139-45) found that, historically, party platforms have made rather specific pledges on issues relating to natural resources and social welfare policies. More ambiguous stands are taken on economic issues and problems related to the size of government. Politicians, he argues, are more likely to be specific on issues for which voters have some knowledge or interest, since ambiguous pledges will simply not satisfy them. So it is not too surprising that we find candidates a little more willing to offer specific solutions to social security and energy than to other issues. In 1978 the elderly were particularly concerned about reductions in the purchasing power of their social security checks, and the energy problem was of interest to virtually everyone.[12]

The level of specificity is also influenced by candidate status (whether or not an officeseeker is an incumbent, challenger, or open seat candidate). As the data in Table 2.2 indicate, incumbents are more likely than nonincumbents to offer specific solutions to all five problems. This finding explains, at least in part, why Clarke and Evans (1983, pp. 45-46) found that journalists tend to emphasize issues when they write about incumbents' campaigns, despite the fact that challengers devote slightly more attention than incumbents to policy problems.[13] Although challengers are more likely than incumbents to discuss issues (58 and 41 percent of challengers' and incumbents' communications are devoted to issues, respectively), many challengers do not provide the news media with enough specifics to make their issue appeals newsworthy. After all, there is limited news value in reporting that a candidate is simply "concerned" about a problem.

Why challengers do not offer more specific solutions is not clear. Perhaps many nonincumbents are not knowledgeable about policy prob-

Table 2.2

Percentage of Candidates Offering Specific Solutions, by Candidate Status

	Incumbents	Challengers	Open Seat
Government Spending	75	34	60
	(28)*	(35)	(10)
Inflation	43	26	17
	(21)	(39)	(12)
Taxes	72	45	46
	(29)	(42)	(13)
Social Security	68	40	50
	(19)	(15)	(4)
Energy	74	63	50
	(19)	(24)	(12)

* Number of candidates.

<u>Source:</u> Computed by author.

lems. Unlike incumbents, they are not regularly required to pass judgment on the merits of particular solutions as they come before Congress.[14] Another possibility is that representatives are more inclined than nonincumbents to talk about specifics, since incumbents have a record to run on. But what is clear is that nonincumbents' aversion to specificity does not encourage journalists to emphasize challengers' issue appeals.

Parallel Campaigns

In order for voters to compare and contrast politicians' issue positions, competing candidates must discuss the same policy problems. Table 2.3 reveals the percentage of races in which candidates competing against each other in the same district discussed the same policy problems. A glance at these data indicates that there are relatively few races in which voters are given the opportunity to compare and contrast competitors' stands on most campaign issues. In more than half of the races less than 26 percent of the problems mentioned are discussed by both candidates. In another fifth of the contests the percentage of issues addressed by both contestants is between 26 and 50 percent. Only in 22 percent of the contests is the voter given an opportunity to compare candidates' thoughts on more than 50 percent of the campaign issues.

It is clear, then, that competing candidates usually discuss different issues. They engage in what might be called parallel campaigning, each

Table 2.3
Percentage of Similar Problems*

Percentage of Similar Problems	Percentage of Races	N
0- 25	57	31
26- 50	21	11
51- 75	9	5
76-100	13	7
Total	100	54

*Calculated for races in which literature was collected from both candidates.

Source: Computed by author.

candidate attempting to communicate with the electorate along a different path by addressing issues on his or her own agenda and paying
little heed to an opponent's policy concerns.[15]

No doubt candidates' failure to discuss the same issues can be attributed, in part, to differences in opposing candidates' background.
One congressman devotes a large share of his brochure to foreign policy matters. No doubt this is a policy area he knows well, since he sits
on a House committee that deals with international relations. Unable
to claim any special knowledge or accomplishments in the foreign policy area, his opponent never alludes to this subject in his brochure.

In addition to background characteristics, candidates' partisan affiliations might be thought to be useful in explaining why competing candidates often avoid discussion of the same policy problems. Studies of
congressional roll call votes show that congresspersons' voting decisions
are often influenced by their party affiliation (Mayhew, 1966; Clausen,
1973; Sinclair, 1976). Based on the legislative history of the parties, one
might expect Democratic candidates to emphasize the social security
problem whereas Republicans would stress cuts in government spending, inflation, and taxes. Democratic politicians have been the strongest
advocates of social security legislation. And it has been under Democratically controlled Congresses and under Democratic presidents that
social security legislation has been passed. On the other hand, the Republican party has exhibited a long-standing interest in cutting government spending and taxes. And the public has viewed the Republican
party as best able to deal with the problem of inflation.[16]

Table 2.4
**Percentage of Candidates Mentioning Problems, by Candidates'
Partisan Affiliation***

	Democrats	Republicans
Government Spending	58	50
Inflation	24	32
Taxes	52	56
Social Security	38	59

* Calculated for 65 Democrats and 72 Republicans.

Source: Compuued by author.

However, the data reported in Table 2.4 indicate that there are no dramatic differences in the tendency for Democratic and Republican candidates to discuss four frequently mentioned problems. To be sure, the small sample size gives one less confidence in the reliability of the findings than one would like, but Democrats are about as likely as Republicans to discuss government spending and taxes, and Republicans are actually more likely than Democrats to mention social security.[17] And only a few more Republicans than Democrats allude to inflation, despite the fact that 1978 was an especially good year for Republicans to stress this issue. There was a Democratic president, a Democratically controlled Congress, and double-digit inflation. When it comes, then, to predicting what problems candidates will discuss, candidates' partisan identification has limited explanatory power. Evidently what issues candidates choose to discuss will be determined more by their perceptions of the electorate's policy concerns than by their party affiliations.[18]

Predictors of Issue Emphasis

It was expected that certain conditions would encourage candidates to emphasize policy problems. First, because challengers have not engaged in constituency service or pork barrel activities, and cannot compare favorably with incumbents in regard to leadership qualifications, it was hypothesized that challengers would be more likely than incumbents to make issue appeals. Second, because neither the Democratic president nor the Democratically controlled Congress was perceived by the public to have successfully dealt with major economic and social problems in 1978, Republican candidates were expected to be more likely than Democrats to remind voters of various policy problems. It was also anticipated that candidates in competitive races would be more likely than officeseekers in noncompetitive races to discuss issues. This hypothesis was inspired by previous research that argues that candidates feel pressure to discuss issues in close contests because competitive races catch the attention of an issue-conscious press (Page, 1978; Goldenberg and Traugott, 1984, p. 124). Finally, it was hypothesized that candidates in moralistic political subcultures would be more likely than candidates in individualistic or traditional cultures to discuss issues. Drawing on Elazar's (1972) conceptualization of political subcultures, Joslyn (1980) has argued that moralistic subcultures encourage candidates to discuss issues because the pattern of competition in such subcultures is over issues rather than between parties or factions within a dominant party.

The aforementioned hypotheses are tested by regressing the proportion of attention devoted to issues on candidate status (whether or not the candidate is a challenger), partisan affiliation, competitiveness, and political culture (whether or not the culture is moralistic).[19] The results of this analysis are reported in Table 2.5. The unstandardized coefficients measure the extent to which a one-unit change in an independent variable results in an increase in the proportion of issues discussed.

The data in Table 2.5 evidence support for some of the hypotheses. On the average, nonincumbents devote slightly more than 13 percent of their communications to issues than do incumbents. Republican officeseekers' brochures include about 8 percent more attention than

Table 2.5
Predictors of the Number of Problems*

Predictors	b	Standard Error	F
Challengers vs. Nonchallengers	13.4	4.3	9.3
Republicans vs. Democrats	8.4	4.3	3.7
Competitive vs. Noncompetitive	8.0	6.6	1.4
Moralistic vs. Nonmoralistic	1.9	4.3	0.2

$R^2 = .10$

*Calculated for 137 candidates.

Source: Computed by author.

Democrats' literature to issues. Officeseekers in competitive races give 8 percent more consideration to policy problems than do sure winners or sure losers, but the coefficient is not statistically significant by conventional standards. Candidates in moralistic political subcultures are only slightly more likely to discuss issues than are officeseekers in traditional or individualistic cultures, and the reliability of the coefficient is low.[20]

Nonissue-Oriented Appeals

Although issue-oriented appeals constitute the bulk of candidates' communications, officeseekers also address other themes. Congressional hopefuls discuss candidate characteristics (personality traits, background characteristics, and leadership experiences), constituency service (casework and pork barrel activities), group associations, and partisan affiliations. Unfortunately, many of these appeals provide little substantive information about a candidate's qualifications.

Theoretically, group appeals could provide cues to the electorate regarding the issues a candidate regards as important and might be good indicators of which constituencies a candidate will be likely to assist after the election.[21] Yet many congressional candidates appeal to such broadly defined groups that it is virtually impossible for voters to use these appeals to discern what sorts of issues or people the candidate is concerned about. For example, about a fifth of the Republicans and nearly one-fourth of the Democrats proclaim their support for the "American Family." Many other candidates note their association with "taxpayers," "homeowners," or "consumers." References to such diffuse groups do little to assist the voter in discerning which interests a candidate supports. Moreover, many candidates appeal to groups that have been traditionally associated with their opponent's political party. For example, the percentage of Republicans appealing to "the working man" is virtually identical to the percentage of Democrats mentioning this group, 26 percent and 23 percent, respectively. Consequently a voter has a difficult time discerning which candidates are most likely to act favorably toward the groups he or she identifies with by being exposed to candidates' group appeals.

Some of the candidate characteristics mentioned are relevant to the job of a congressperson. The personality traits alluded to most often are strength, intelligence, empathy, and honesty.[22] Clearly these are all desirable characteristics for a congressperson to possess. Several of the background characteristics mentioned also supply useful information about candidates' qualifications. Forty-five percent of the candidates discuss their education and almost half (48 percent) mention their job experiences, for example. And many of the incumbents discuss their leadership experience. However, the candidate characteristics mentioned also include a sampling of qualities that have little relevance for the job of a congressperson. Forty-four percent of the candidates mention their children and 47 percent allude to their marital status. One candidate's brochure includes no less than eight pictures of his wife and children.

As one might expect, incumbents make almost all of the constituency appeals. This is understandable, since incumbents have a record to run on and pay a great deal of attention to district needs. This finding helps to explain why Clarke and Evans (1983, pp. 43-46) found that the news media pay less attention to challengers' than incumbents' political attributes. If challengers do not emphasize constituency appeals, one cannot expect the press to stress them.

Most candidates avoid partisan appeals—a voting cue that is a reasonably good indicator of candidates' policy positions.[23] Indeed, a number of candidates make it quite clear that they do not want voters to consider partisan attachments. One asks his constituents to be "independently minded" enough to vote for him. Another states flatly that partisan factors should not be considered. Others say they are appealing to both Democrats and Republicans. Most of the candidates who do stress their party attachments make it clear that these feelings do not run too deep. One Democratic incumbent does make a number of partisan appeals. A picture of the candidate with President Carter takes up half of the first page of the brochure. Later in the pamphlet he is shown shaking hands with the president as another well-known Democrat looks on. There is also a request to "Vote Democratic." But this candidate's brochure also notes his independence from the party. He is "one of the few people who can say 'no' to President Carter," his brochure reads, "and still be reinvited to leadership breakfasts and policy planning sessions." So while this candidate emphasizes partisan ties, he also reminds voters that these bonds can be easily severed.[24]

Those candidates who place the most emphasis on partisan ties tend to be challengers. Only 38 percent of the incumbents make a reference to their party. Fifty-seven percent of the challengers do so. The fact that challengers are more likely than incumbents to emphasize partisan ties may explain why the news media pays so much attention to this characteristic (rather than to issues or political attributes) when reporting about challengers' campaigns. If challengers choose to dwell on this type of appeal, one should not be too surprised that the press also does so.

CONCLUSION

This chapter examined House candidates' campaign appeals. The analysis indicates that although most congressional hopefuls devote about half of their communications to a discussion of policy problems, office-seekers often avoid offering specific solutions, and the specific solutions that are discussed tend to be noncontroversial. There is some support for the hypothesis that candidates are more likely to offer specific solutions to issues in which voters have an interest. At least this is true regarding issues for which there are popular noncontroversial solutions, such as social security and energy.

The findings also indicate that incumbents are more likely than non-incumbents to offer unambiguous solutions. This is probably explained by the fact that incumbents have more knowledge than do challengers of policy issues and have a record to run on.

In most races, competing candidates tend to discuss different issues, giving voters little opportunity to compare one candidate's solutions with his or her opponent's proposals. The data examined in this study do not allow one to identify with certainty the factors that lead competing candidates to ignore each other's policy concerns, but this finding is not a function of differences in candidates' party affiliations.

In regard to the conditions under which candidates will emphasize issues, these data suggest that challengers are more likely than incumbents or open seat candidates to stress policy appeals. Republicans are more likely than Democrats to run issue-oriented campaigns. Less support was found for the hypotheses that candidates in competitive races are more willing to discuss policy proposals than are sure winners or sure losers, and that officeseekers running in moralistic political subcultures are more likely to discuss policy problems than are candidates in individualistic or traditional subcultures.

Finally, this study found that nonissue-oriented appeals often provide little substantive information about the candidates. There is a tendency to appeal to diffuse groups, and candidates often appeal to constituencies that have not always benefited much from their party's policy stands. Many of the background characteristics mentioned are not particularly relevant to the job of a congressperson, and challengers are reluctant to talk about what they would do for the district or to criticize the incumbent's case work and pork barrel activities. Candidates avoid making partisan appeals, although challengers are more likely to make them than are incumbents.

What, then, do these findings tell us about the manner in which the news media cover congressional campaigns? One conclusion is clear. The news media cannot be held completely at fault for failing to devote as much attention to the substantive aspects of congressional campaigns as proponents of the traditional democratic theory of elections desire. This is not to say that the work habits and norms of the journalism profession do not partially explain why more attention is not devoted to issues or candidates' qualifications. The limited amount of time that reporters devote to a congressional campaign makes it difficult for them to report on complex issues. And it is also the case that the urge to play to their readers' interest in the dramatic and conflictual aspects of the political process inclines reporters to devote more time to campaign strategy and hoopla than they should. But the findings reported here suggest that some of the blame must be shouldered by the candidates themselves. When candidates competing against each other do not offer specific solutions to policy problems, do not offer controversial solutions, and do not talk about the same problems, one cannot blame reporters for failing to write about substantive issues. Similarly, when candidates insist on appealing to broadly defined groups and discussing background characteristics that have little relevance to the job of a congressperson, one cannot be too critical of the news media for not devoting more time to discussing officeseekers' group appeals or political attributes.

This study's findings also explain, in part, why journalists are inclined to write about incumbents' issue positions and challengers' partisan appeals. Although challengers are slightly more likely than incumbents to discuss issues, they are less likely to offer specific solutions. And challengers are more likely than incumbents to stress party ties.

Given the limited resources of most newsgathering organizations (Epstein, 1974b) and pressures to write news copy that will catch the attention of the general public, journalists should be credited with devoting as much attention to issues and candidates' qualifications as they do. Were it not for the fact that many journalists believe that it is their duty to seek out and report about the substantive aspects of House campaigns,[25] the electorate would know even less about candidates' issue positions and qualifications.[26]

NOTES

1. For discussion of this theory see Weissberg (1976, pp. 170-72).

2. For a discussion of how news reporting is shaped by organizational processess and professional norms see Graber (1984, pp. 69-102).

3. For example, Graber (1970, p. 3) found that the source of most information appearing in newspaper stories about the 1968 presidential campaign was the presidential or vice-presidential candidates. And Vermeer (1982, pp. 87-120) supplies evidence that a congressional and gubernatorial campaign succeeded in influencing newspaper coverage through press releases.

4. Campaign materials were collected from 159 candidates in the 108 randomly sampled districts. However, brochures were only obtained from 137 candidates. These data were made available by the Inter-university Consortium for Political and Social Research (ICPSR). Neither the original collectors of the data nor the ICPSR bear any responsibility for the analysis or interpretations presented here.

5. Candidate appeals include references to background characteristics, lead-

ership experience, and personality traits. Constituency appeals concern case work and pork barrel activity. Candidates also made appeals to particular groups, but because most of these references were brief and linked to issue appeals, the relative emphasis devoted to groups is not included in calculating the proportion of communications devoted to issues. Candidates' partisan appeals (statements about a candidate's party affiliation, endorsements from party leaders, and direct appeals to partisans) are also excluded from the calculation because so few candidates emphasize them.

6. Although this coding strategy relies on the subjective judgment of coders, it is the only practical way to simultaneously weigh the multiple factors (size of type, pictures, headings, etc.) that convey the amount of attention candidates devote to particular types of appeals.

7. On the average, congressional hopefuls also devote 12 and 36 percent of their brochures to constituency and candidate appeals, respectively.

8. This finding is consistent, however, with systematic studies of the communication styles of politicians (Joslyn, 1980, pp. 92-98; Clarke and Evans, 1983, pp. 35-50; Goldenberg and Traugott, 1984, pp. 122-24). It is important to note that many incumbents attempt to link national issues (e.g., inflation) with their pork barrel activities, such as lobbying, to acquire federal money for local industries. Consequently many issue appeals reinforce constituency appeals.

9. On the average, candidates alluded to about eight issues. Only a handful of officeseekers engaged in single-issue campaigns. The lack of single-issue campaigns among congressional hopefuls has also been noted by Maisel (1982, p. 90) in his study of congressional primary campaigns.

10. Candidates who referred to government spending or inflation are coded as having mentioned these problems. Candidates who comment on the individual income tax (rather than on corporate or social security taxes) are said to discuss this issue. Any candidate who complained about the cost, financial stability, or benefits of the social security system is coded as having mentioned this problem. And congressional hopefuls who indicate concern with either the cost or the availability of energy are said to have addressed this issue.

11. Some candidates may also take specific issue positions in order to draw attention to particular candidate characteristics. For example, a candidate might take specific positions in order to project an image of "decisiveness" or "independence" (Fenno, 1978, pp. 80-91; Vermeer, 1982, p. 66). The extent to which this campaign strategy was adopted by House candidates cannot be determined without more information about House candidates' campaign strategies.

12. Pomper (1980, p. 140) also found that there tends to be low specificity in foreign defense and civil rights, and detailed pledges in labor and agricultural issues.

13. Clarke and Evans (1983, pp. 66-67) argue that this is a function of a "tandem effect" between the coverage of incumbents' political attributes (committee work, constituent services, etc.) and issues. They argue that coverage of representatives' official duties is often related to policy decisions. Thus stories about incumbents' often contain issue information.

There may be considerable variation among newspapers in the emphasis given to incumbents' and challengers' issue appeals. Goldenberg and Traugott (1984, pp. 127-29) find that newspapers covering the same congressional race some-times have radically differrent types of coverage.

14. Although Huckshorn and Spencer (1971, pp. 210-12) note that challeng-ers do not believe that a lack of knowledge about issues is one of their "greatest obstacles to victory," there are several theoretical reasons for believing that the typical incumbent is better versed in the details of public policy than is the average challenger. First, most incumbents have had more experience in public office than have challengers. In the 1978 House election 81 percent of the challengers had never even held an elective office (Hinckley, 1981, p. 26). Al-though holding a public office does not guarantee that one will become knowl-edgeable about public policies, it certainly encourages one to acquire such in-formation. Second, the legislative norm of specialization (the idea that a legislator should develop areas of policy expertise) forces incumbents to become knowl-edgeable of public policy issues (Hinckley, 1983). No such institutional con-straint encourages challengers to learn about the details of legislation. Finally, there is a large amount of literature detailing the ineptitude of congressional challengers (for example, see Huckshorn and Spencer, 1971; Maisel, 1982; Hinckley, 1981). Nothing in this literature suggests that the typical House chal-lengers are knowledgeable about the details of public policy, although one can find an occasional single-issue candidate (Maisel, 1981, pp. 91-92).

15. Brochures (the unit of analysis in this study) are typically printed early in the campaign, before a candidate can be sure what issues his or her oppo-nent will stress. Late in the campaign (when candidates have identified their opponent's issue stands and when negative appeals are most likely to be made) voters may have a better opportunity to compare and contrast candidates' issue positions.

16. Differences in the policy concerns of the parties and public attitudes toward the parties' ability to solve problems are discussed in Polsby and Wildavsky (1984, pp. 175-81).

17. In part, the tendency for Republicans to discuss social security is ex-plained by differences in how Democrats and Republicans define the problem. Democrats tend to focus on how to "save" social security. Many Republicans mention the problem only because they object to increasing social security taxes.

18. In the more sophisticated campaigns, candidates attempt to discuss issues that will reinforce basic campaign themes and appeal to segments of the elec-torate who are most inclined to support the candidate. Consequently, in some districts, a candidate's supportive coalition does not comprise issue-groups that have traditionally been members of the candidate's party's coalition. For ex-ample, Senator Chafee (a Republican) has attracted the support of many groups that are usually identified with the Democratic coalition, such as environmen-talists and feminists (Salmore and Salmore, 1985, pp. 126-27).

19. The variables in this OLS regression equation were coded as follows:

Candidate Status—Candidate status is measured with a dummy variable, coded 1 if the candidate is a challenger and 0 if the candidate is an incumbent or open seat candidate.

Candidate Party Affiliation—Candidates' party affiliation is measured with a dummy variable, coded 1 if Republican and 0 if Democrat.

Competitiveness—Races are classified as competitive if the victorious candidate received less than 55 percent of the two-party vote. Competitiveness is measured with a dummy variable, coded 1 if competitive and 0 if noncompetitive.

Political Subculture—Congressional districts are classified as predominantly moralistic, individualistic, or traditional on the basis of Elazer's (1972) analysis. This variable is coded 1 if the district is moralistic and 0 if the district is individualistic or traditional.

20. When the number (as opposed to the proportion) of issues is the dependent variable, political culture is the only statistically significant predictor of issue orientation. However, the proportion of communications devoted to issues is the preferred measure of issue orientation, since many candidates discuss only two or three issues but devote a considerable proportion of their brochure to them.

21. On the average, candidates make three different group appeals.

22. Fenno's (1978) participant observation study also found that House candidates emphasize empathy and honesty.

23. For evidence that a representative's party affiliation is related to his or her policy positions, see Hinckley, 1983, pp. 201-3; Mayhew, 1966; Clausen, 1973; Sinclair, 1976. Of course, party is not as good a predictor of congresspersons' roll call votes as it once was (Brady et al., 1979; Sinclair, 1977).

24. Although the emphasis candidates place on partisan appeals is low, almost half of the candidates (48 percent) make a partisan appeal. But most such appeals are brief references to a candidate's party affiliation that are not prominently displayed in the brochure.

25. For a discussion of the social responsibility theory of news gathering, see Peterson (1956).

26. Kristol' (1967) has placed the blame for superficial coverage of the news squarely on the shoulders of the journalism profession. He argues that reporters fail to provide enough contextual information and interpretation. The data reported here suggest that the superficiality of candidates' campaign communications makes it difficult for even the most informed reporter to provide in-depth coverage of campaign issues.

3

Liberal Campaign Rhetoric in 1984

Richard A. Joslyn

Politics is fundamentally a matter of speech, and in democracies, of public speech.

—Wilson Carey McWilliams[1]

Liberalism is widely perceived to be in total collapse, bereft of creative ideas and leaders, and unlikely to ever again mobilize popular support.

—Linda J. Medcalf and Kenneth M. Dolbeare[2]

The early 1980s have not been especially propitious ones for liberal causes and candidates. Electorally, liberals have seen the GOP seize, in 1980, and retain, in 1982 and 1984, control of the U.S. Senate for the first time since 1952, and have failed to elect a mainstream liberal to the presidency for at least twenty years. Programmatically, many of the liberal policy initiatives of the past five decades have been under attack and in danger of being systematically eliminated. And philosophically, the core values of New Deal Liberalism—egalitarianism, expansion of social and political rights, governmental assistance for the economically disadvantaged, and the general notion of positive government—seem to be much less aggressively articulated and defended by political elites and embraced by the populace than at any time in the past fifty years.

By 1984 conditions had become so grim for liberals that "the Democrats were brought face to face with the inadequacy of the public philosophy that succeeded the era of the New Deal."[3]

These developments suggest that the United States may be in the middle of one of its occasional realigning or transitional periods. During such times partisan loyalties and popular support are up for grabs and political discourse shows signs of confusion, creativity, and uncertainty. In the moment at hand, programmatic, rhetorical, and electoral developments suggest that New Deal Liberalism is undergoing its stiffest challenge in the past five decades, and that political analysts should be especially attentive to how its proponents respond to their various critics.

In order to further our understanding of contemporary U.S. elections, this study focuses on the campaign rhetoric of liberal candidates for the U.S. Congress. By analyzing how such politicians respond to the electoral context with which they are presented, it is hoped that we will learn something broader about the content of and prospects for New Deal Liberalism.

There are a number of good reasons to be interested in the rhetorical appeals made by liberal candidates in 1984. The most obvious is that studying these appeals may help us understand what Liberalism itself has become as a public philosophy. Many of the programmatic assumptions and philosophical tenets that have been the cornerstone of New Deal Liberalism since the 1930s seem no longer to be asserted with the same confidence and enthusiasm as they once were. The days when liberals spoke of equal opportunity, eliminating poverty, and combatting urban blight are gone; one senses that contemporary liberals are searching for programmatic ideas and electoral appeals that will strike a responsive chord with the electorate and remain true to more general liberal goals of equity and the role of government. As Gerald Pomper has put it, "the basic need for the Democrats . . . is not leadership, organization, or demographic advantage—it is intellectual."[4]

The presidential race in 1984 provided abundant testimony that New Deal Liberalism is a beleaguered public philosophy, at least on the presidential campaign trail. Walter Mondale, in many ways the complete New Deal Liberal, found his philosophy challenged not only by his Republican opponent, but also by his major challengers within the Democratic party. Given that Mondale's programmatic general election appeals boiled down to opposition to Star Wars, opposition to the Marine presence in Beirut, and a willingness to raise taxes to reduce the budget deficit, it became quite clear that Liberalism, by 1984, had taken on quite a different face than it had during the campaigns of Franklin Roosevelt, Harry Truman, John Kennedy, Lyndon Johnson, Hubert Humphrey, and (even) Jimmy Carter. In fact, according to one political observer, "the combination of fiscal responsibility and political restraint made Mondale sound vaguely like an old-line Taft Republican."[5]

There were, however, other liberal candidates running for public office in 1984. Perhaps Walter Mondale's campaign rhetoric was more a consequence of an inept and confused campaign than it was a reflection on Liberalism itself. It would be interesting to see, then, if other liberal candidates, at other electoral levels, have discovered more suitable and persuasive depictions of their ideology. In other words, one of the goals of this analysis is to discover what Liberalism has become at the sub-presidential level, when articulated on the campaign trail. Is New Deal Liberalism—the ideology of "those favoring governmental nationalism on behalf of a more equalitarian distribution of the fruits of industrial growth"[6]—still recognizable and used to advantage by some candidates, or has the ideology become thoroughly discredited and transformed?

A second, and related, reason to be curious about liberal rhetoric in 1984 is for what it may tell us about the processes of partisan and ideological realignments. The basic contours of a realigning period have by now become quite familiar and oft-discussed: the public policy crisis or dissatisfaction that leads to the advancement by the minority party of a novel public philosophy and programmatic agenda that alters, in turn, the voting behavior of significant segments of the electorate for a long period of time. Many aspects of this process are now pretty well understood. One that has not received much attention, however, is the process by which the then-prevailing public philosophy is discredited and eventually abandoned. How do its proponents typically respond to the ideological and rhetorical attacks made on it, and to what extent can the rhetorical adaptations of the then-dominant philosophy affect the pace and depth with which realignments occur?

If, in fact, we are living through one of our nation's few realigning periods—or even if, as many have suggested, we are experiencing a dealigning period—we might well be curious about how beleaguered liberals are responding to the prospects of losing their philosophical grip on the American electorate. Have liberals sensed the philosophical attacks made on their ideology and redoubled their efforts to articulate and defend that ideology in the hopes of regaining public approval? Or have liberals acknowledged the defects in their ideology that their opponents have brought to light and attempted to revise or present a new face to their ideology while remaining true to its basic tenets and goals? Or have liberals, fearful of being punished for their ideology, developed ways of disguising it from their constituents, either by adopting some of the rhetorical appeals and policy goals of their opponents or by eschewing programmatic appeals altogether?[7] Because the rhetorical responses made by liberals to their more telling and popular critics may influence, in turn, the locus and intensity of ideological debate, it would be helpful to know what liberals in general are doing about the increasingly popular conservative challenge.

A third reason for paying attention to liberal appeals—indeed, the appeals of any candidate—is that they bear on the educative value of campaigns themselves. We often assume that campaigns are educative; that the electorate learns something of consequence as a result of its exposure to and involvement in them. Yet it is not altogether clear that most election campaigns do extend the level of political awareness appreciably beyond what it is at the beginning of the campaign period. Horse-race journalism, ambiguous candidate rhetoric, and disinterested citizens all seem to work together to delimit considerably the typical campaign's educative effect.[8]

One especially important aspect of the educative value of campaigns concerns the ideological understandings of the American populace. Although there is some disagreement within the field, the general consensus is that most Americans' belief systems lack ideological constraint and sophistication.[9] Although some observers attribute this lack of sophistication to the political capabilities of the voting-age population, others believe that political elites should shoulder much of the blame for the situation.[10] Candidates, for example, may not take advantage of the opportunity presented by an election campaign to present sophisticated, articulate, and constrained belief systems to the electorate for their consideration. If political elites rely on rhetorical appeals that are nonprogrammatic, illogical, morselized, or changeable over time, it would be little wonder if the belief systems of the electorate exhibited these attributes well. Consequently it will be interesting to discover whether the rhetorical appeals of candidates—in this case, of liberals—in 1984 were such that they would add to the constraint and sophistication of the electorate's belief systems.

In comparison to presidential elections, campaigns for the U.S. House of Representatives are thought by many to have a modest educative value at best. Given the prevalence of incumbents seeking reelection and the perception that they are invulnerable to electoral challenge, the paucity of high-quality challengers with the resources to mount a robust campaign effort, and the apparent disinterest on the part of the electorate in the outcomes of congressional elections, it would surprising indeed if congressional campaigns had an educative effect.

Previous research has found that one consequence of the nature of congressional, especially U.S. House, campaigns is that voters have little sense of the ideology or policy preferences of the candidates in their districts. Although "traditional democratic theory" would seem to suggest that "voters need to know the candidates' stands on issues in order to choose who should represent them in the government,"[11] there is no assurance that congressional campaigns, as actually conducted, encourage the formation of such perceptions. In fact, the evidence suggests just the opposite. Hinckley estimates, for example, that at the congressional level, "information about issues drops sharply" and the "portion of citizens" who fulfill "the minimum conditions for issue voting" range around "10 or 30 percent."[12] Furthermore, when citizens are asked about the qualifications of candidates, "personal characteristics are by far the most frequently cited reason for liking or disliking House candidates—whether incumbents or challengers or candidates in open-seat races."[13] Jacobson concurs, noting "the relative paucity of information voters have about congressional candidates" and that the "positions taken by candidates on the issues of the day have little discernible impact on congressional voters."[14]

The systematic study of congressional campaign rhetoric may yield fresh insights into the reasons for the noneducative value of most congressional campaigns. If the appeals made on the campaign trail are similar to those developed by incumbents in the quest for a "Home Style," it would hardly be surprising if the congressional electorate learned little from its exposure to the biennial exercise.

A related question is whether the appeals of candidates ask voters to make their ballots a programmatic or a nonprogrammatic choice. Elsewhere I have argued that there are four general approaches to elections in the political science literature. These approaches may be referred to as *prospective policy choice*, *retrospective policy satisfaction*, *benevolent leader*, and *ritualistic*, to communicate the nature of the electoral choice and the meaning of the electoral outcome that each approach posits.[15]

The prospective policy choice approach views elections as a mechanism by which voters may choose between distinctive "bundles" of future-oriented policy promises and thereby influence the future course of American public policy. The retrospective policy satisfaction approach holds that voters mainly influence the future by evaluating the past and deciding whether or not the job performance of incumbents has been acceptable. In this view the main decision voters reach is whether the incumbents deserve to remain in office, or to be replaced. The benevolent leader approach focuses on elections as leadership selection processes in which the main consideration is the perceived fit between the role requirements of the office and the personal attributes of the candidates. The ritualistic approach tends to diminish the importance of the choices made by voters and to reflect, instead, on the consequences that participating in the electoral process has on the participants themselves. To the ritualist, elections do not allow citizens to influence public policy choices in any consequential way. They do, however, serve to reinforce in the electorate cultural values and a belief in the legitimacy of the political process.

Of these four approaches the first two are really the only ones that hold that elections fulfill the democratic ideal of permitting citizens to influence public policy choices. Even the retrospective approach does so mainly through the back door, by holding the citizens influence the future by evaluating the past, and that voters ponder social and political conditions instead of policy proposals and ideas. It is only the prospective approach, then, that thoroughly offers a view of elections in which competing, policy-oriented futures are at the center of electoral contests.

Despite the normative appeal of the prospective policy choice approach, the empirical evidence consistent with it is distressingly weak. At the presidential level neither candidate appeals, media coverage, nor voter behavior is especially consistent with the demanding conditions that the approach requires. At the congressional level it would be even more astounding if the conditions were ripe for prospective policy choices. The potential consequences are both theoretical and practical: theoretical, in that what we discover about congressional campaigns will help us refine our theoretical approach to elections generally; and practical, in that it will help us understand what meaning may be attached to congressional election outcomes.

In summary, then, the analysis that follows is about the electoral appeals made by liberal candidates for the U.S. Congress in 1984. The nature of these appeals, as I have argued earlier, should shed some light on such questions as:

1. What kind of public philosophy has New Deal Liberalism become?
2. Do the proponents of New Deal Liberalism continue to offer it as a legitimate and distinctive approach to politics and policy, or are they showing signs of a "realignment" in programmatic intentions and philosophical discourse?
3. To what extent could we expect the appeals of liberals to contribute to the electorate's ideological coherence, sophistication, and constraint?
4. To what degree did the appeals of liberals in 1984 encourage voters to make a prospective policy choice when casting their election-day ballots?

DATA AND METHODOLOGY

The analysis that follows is based on 131 television spot ads used by twenty-four U.S. House and Senate incumbents during the 1984 general election. The ads analyzed were selected in the following way.

First, to ensure that the ads represent the rhetoric of liberals, Americans for Democratic Action (ADA) scores were used to select those with liberal voting records over the preceeding three years. Although one might question the use of the ADA's definition of New Deal Liberalism, it seems to remain the best approximation of the conventional use of the term. In the years covered here, the ADA ratings were based on votes on a wide range of issues. On domestic issues the ADA supported such measures as extending fair housing laws, key enforcement provisions of the Voting Rights Act, targeting tax cuts to middle- and lower-income taxpayers, liberalized unemployment benefits, a public works job program, health care for the unemployed, increased funding for education, and the Equal Rights Amendment; and opposed spending cuts in a variety of social programs, limits on busing and abortion, cuts in the food stamp program, and the balanced budget amendment. On defense and foreign policy issues the ADA favored reduced funding for military programs and opposed the MX missile, the production of chemical weapons, the B-1 bomber, reduced payments to the United Nations, and funding for an anti-satellite missile. As *Congressional Quarterly* puts it, "since 1947, ADA ratings have been a standard, if sometimes disputed, measure of the term 'liberal.' Early ratings focused on lawmakers' support for New Deal-like programs and gradually grew to include support for a non-interventionist foreign policy.[16]

Of the U.S. House incumbents in the 1982-1983 term, 167 were judged to have voting records sufficiently liberal to be considered for possible inclusion in this study. Generally, this meant that their ADA scores averaged at least seventy-five over the preceding three years.

Second, those liberals who did not face a strenuous reelection campaign in 1984 were eliminated from the analysis. Some of the 167 liberal incumbents did not run for reelection in 1984 (9), some ran opposed (16), many faced challengers who spent less than $100,000 on their campaigns (73), some faced challengers who spent an unknown amount on their campaigns (21)—most of these challengers garnered less than 30 percent of the vote—and one faced a challenger who spent $111,000 but he only spent $30,000 on his own campaign. This left 47 incumbent liberals who faced vigorous opponents in the 1984 general election.

An attempt was then made to secure the television advertisements used by these forty-seven liberals. Two major collectors of campaign ads were contacted: Julian Kanter, a private collector located in Highland Park, Illinois, and the Democratic Congressional Campaign Committee.[17] A Philadelphia campaign consulting firm, The Campaign Group, was also instrumental in securing several 1984 ads.

The search yielded, finally, ads from twenty-two of the forty-seven targeted U.S. House liberals.[18] Although this is not as high a number as I had hoped, the sample does represent different sections of the country (except the South) and different levels of seniority. In other respects, of course, the sample is homogeneous. All of the candidates are Democrats and all but two continue to be U.S. congressmen.

Finally, the sample was augmented with eight ads used in 1984 by two liberal U.S. Senate incumbents—Joe Biden and Bill Bradley.[19] This was done primarily because the ads were available to me and because of the two candidates' impeccable liberal credentials. Had time and resources permitted, I would gladly have added the commercials of other liberal candidates to the sample.

The end result, then, is a sample of 131 ads from twenty-four candidates. Table 3.1 lists the candidates included in this analysis, with data on their ADA scores, campaign expenditures, and 1984 vote totals.

Once the sample of ads was acquired, the next step was to devise a content analysis scheme for coding the appeals used by the candidates. The one I devised was relatively simple and was basically an attempt to categorize each ad into one of five mutually exclusive categories, depending on the ideological nature of the appeal used. The possible categories are as follows:

Category I: Definite Liberal Content

This category consists of those ads in which the candidate either explicitly identifies himself or herself as a liberal *or* offers policy goals and issue positions that are so precise, clear, and extensive that a viewer might easily deduce his or her liberal philosophy.

In order to reach the latter determination, of course, the analyst must have a conceptualization of Liberalism in mind. I have taken as mine, for the purposes of this study, a fairly conventional view of what New Deal Liberalism is: a belief in positive government; a general preference for national policy-making institutions over those of the states and localities; the advancement of the interests of labor in their contests with management; the expansion of the welfare state to benefit the infirm, ill, unemployed, poor, ill-housed, ill-fed, and poorly educated; the redistribution of income from the haves to the have-nots; the special attentiveness for the problems and civil rights of minority groups; and the willingness to extract resources from the population to initiate governmental ventures in mass transit systems, retarding environmental degradation, rebuilding the nation's cities, and eliminating poverty.

Below are three examples of ads coded as falling into this category. In the first the candidate claims to oppose reductions in social security and Medicare benefits and to be concerned, in general, with the interests of the elderly. In the second the candidate favors governmental job creation and aid to the unemployed, and in the third Bill Bradley expresses his preference for increased federal aid to education. Each of these ads would seem likely to contribute to the audience's perception that the candidate possesses a liberal ideology.

Morrison: When Larry Denardis was in Congress, he voted to cut Social Security. I voted against a bill to cut social security benefits. He voted to cut

Table 3.1
Liberal Congressmen Included in Study

Name (state-district)		ADA Scores 83	82	81	'84 Exp[a] OWN	OPP	% Vote 84	N
Albosta	(MI-10)	90	75	40	449	705	49[b]	1
AuCoin	(OR-1)	70	85	70	797	640	54	3
Carr	(MI-6)	85	--	--	554	378	53	2
Evans	(IL-17)	95	--	--	438	421	57	6
McCloskey	(IN-8)	85	--	--	481	419	50	4
Lundine	(NY-34)	85	80	85	461	287	56	6
Morrison	(CT-3)	90	--	--	931	505	52	6
Wirth	(CO-2)	95	95	85	580	149	54	13
Kostmayer	(PA-8)	90	--	--	608	388	51	6
Kolter	(PA-4)	80	--	--	205	105	57	1
Kaptur	(OH-9)	90	--	--	326	417	56	10
Brown	(CA-36)	90	75	85	600	358	57	2
Durbin	(IL-20)	85	--	--	439	218	61	7
McNulty	(AZ-5)	75	--	--	715	732	48[b]	21
Panetta	(CA-16)	90	75	90	273	417	71	6
Penny	(MN-1)	75	--	--	419	333	57	3
Richardson	(NM-3)	95	--	--	268	201	62	2
Edgar	(PA-7)	85	100	100	592	432	50	3
Carper	(DE-AL)	80	--	--	345	669	59	1
Sharp	(IN-2)	80	80	65	405	361	54	3
Feighan	(OH-19)	90	--	--	530	564	56	8
Daschle	(SD-AL)	75	80	70	678	283	57	9
Biden	(DE-S)	85	80	80	1,429	818	60	2
Bradley	(NJ-S)	85	100	90	4,252	966	65	6

131

[a]In thousands of dollars

[b]Lost

Sources: ADA scores were taken from Congressional Quarterly Weekly Report, July 3, 1982, pp. 1614 and 1616-1617; Congressional Quarterly Weekly Report, May 9, 1983, pp. 905 and 906-907; and Congressional Quarterly Weekly Report, July 14, 1984, pp. 1695-1697. 1984 election returns may be found in Congressional Quarterly Weekly Report, November 10, 1984, pp. 2923-2930. Campaign expenditure data were taken from Common Cause News, March 14, 1985, and April 12, 1985.

Medicare; I voted to cut doctor bills. His votes made low cost generic drugs harder to get; I helped lead the fight to make them easier to get. The National Council of Senior Citizens gave his voting record 58%. They rated my record 100% and I'm gonna keep it that way.

*   *   *

Narrator: When Marcie Kaptur ran for Congress in 1982, she promised that "Jobs will be my first priority." In Washington, Kaptur led the fight for 3 1/2 billion dollars for job creation, over 4 1/2 billion in emergency aid to the unemployed, for aid to unemployed homeowners and farmers who face foreclosures. Unemployment in our area has dropped, but Kaptur says "W·· still have a long way to go." Marcie Kaptur has kept her promise. Let's keep Kaptur. Marcie Kaptur, Democrat, for Congress.

*   *   *

Narrator: When it comes to fighting for more ₋id to education, Bill Bradley deserves an A+.

Man: There he is.

Narrator: Senator Bradley realizes that our children must have a good education to compete in and to understand the future. That's why he fought so hard to restore over a billion dollars to the education budget, and why he pushed the Senate to agree to no more cuts in education. Bill Bradley believes there are better ways to cut the budget without cutting our link to the future.

Category II: Possible Liberal Content

The second category of ads also contains liberal policy content. In this case, however, the policy goals and programmatic preferences articulated are not as precise, clear, or extensive as they are in the first category. Consequently an attentive audience might properly infer the liberal ideology of the candidate, but doing so would involve more of an inferential leap. The following ads illustrate this distinction. In the first ad the candidate expresses an interest in reducing unemployment, as well as a nonprogrammatic concern for constituent service. In the second the candidate favors a "sound defense without the frills" and a preference for reducing the deficit. In the third ad Peter Kostmayer relies on an ability to secure grants for and create jobs in his district.

These policy goals and preferences are clearly a good deal less revealing than the ones in the first category. In fact, they border on the kind of consensual values about which there is likely to be little disagreement. Nonetheless, because the mere raising of the issue of unemployment and the criticism of defense spending might suggest Liberalism to some citizens, these ads were placed in a distinct category reflecting possible liberal content.

Kaptur: Part of my job as your Congresswoman is representing the people of the 9th district here in Washington. But my major responsibility is back home: listening to your concerns, helping find a lost social security or veteran's check, and, most important of all, working to get our people back to work. This is the toughest job I've ever had, but also the most rewarding. I ask for your vote of confidence on November 6th.

Narrator: Let's keep Kaptur. She's getting the job done. Marcie Kaptur, Democrat, for Congress.

* * *

Narrator: Why are Coloradans standing up for Tim Wirth?

First Woman: Tim, as a member of the budget committee, has been very much concerned that we not waste our money; that we look at a sound defense but without the frills.

First Man: He wants the President, and Congress, to get together and work this thing out.

Second Man: He's the only one back there who consistently tries to get the Republicans and the Democrats together to do something about reducing this deficit.

Narrator: Tim Wirth. Standing up for Colorado.

* * *

Kostmayer: Some good people used to work here, but not anymore. I'm Peter Kostmayer. In Congress I intend to stop this nonsense of losing jobs.

Narrator: They're working again at that very same Morrisville plant, thanks to Congressman Peter Kostmayer. The eighth district's first urban action grant ever, which Kostmayer gained, reopened those doors. Kostmayer got yet a second grant to create 1,400 new jobs in Falls Township. Peter Kostmayer kept his promise. He put us back to work.

Kostmayer: There's still a lot to do, but jobs will always be my top priority.

Category III: Conservative Content

Although all of the candidates included in this analysis have liberal voting records, it is possible that they would articulate conservative policy goals and preferences in their television ads. This might be done in order to disguise their true ideology or as a way of deceiving the electorate about their true location in ideological space. Liberals might also sound conservative out of sincerity; after all, even the most extreme ideologues may well hold a conservative position on some public policy

question. Although we will not be able to judge here the sincerity of
the conservative positions taken by liberal candidates, we will be able to
say something about how frequently liberals sounded conservative on
the campaign trail in 1984.

The two ads that follow are examples of those in which the candidates took conservative positions. In the first the candidate attempts to
portray himself as a fiscal conservative, and in the second the candidate
is depicted as pro-business, opposed to waste, and a believer in traditional family values.

Narrator: Budget discipline. Every year he's been in Congress, he's voted for
less spending than every President asked for. Less than President Ford,
President Carter, even President Reagan. In the last two years, he opposed
17 out of 30 congressional spending bills. Now he's fighting for an immediate, across-the-board freeze on federal spending. Budget discipline. Les
AuCoin. Let's keep him in Congress.

* * *

Man: I'm a registered Republican, but this year I'm not voting for a Republican
for Congress because Ken McMillan is a right-wing extremist. I'm voting
for the Congressman we've already got, Lane Evans. Lane Evans works
hard to help business and cut waste and Lane Evans believes in traditional
family values. He's no political extremist. So this year I'm going to vote for
Congressman Lane Evans, even if he is a Democrat.

Narrator: Congressman Lane Evans. For Illinois. For all of us.

Category IV: Mixed Ideological Content

The last category of ad that contains policy-oriented content consists
of those ads in which the candidate's message is either ambiguous, confusing, or mixed. In some portions of these ads the candidates sound
liberal, and in other portions they sound conservative, or they voice
policy preferences that do not readily fit on a liberal-conservative dimension. Consequently I suspect that these ads would not be particularly helpful to viewers in identifying the ideology of the candidates;
they would be more likely to cause confusion than anything else.

The following ads are examples of a mixed message regarding the
candidate's policy preferences. In the first ad a citizen claims that conservatives and Republicans feel that the candidate represents them (a
conservative appeal); but the candidate is also depicted as favoring the
interests of the elderly and workers (a liberal appeal). In the second ad
the candidate is portrayed as being in favor of the recommendations of
President Reagan's Grace Commission (conservative) but also especially
concerned about waste in the Pentagon budget (liberal). Neither ad would

be likely to help voters decide if the candidates were liberal or conservative.

Narrator: Why are Coloradans standing up for Tim Wirth?

First Man: First of all, he's accessible.

First Woman: And he knows the people in this district. He comes here, he visits us, he talks to us.

Second Man: People who are conservatives or Republicans; when they have a problem they call Tim Wirth and they don't think of Tim Wirth as a Democrat. They think of Tim Wirth as someone who represents them.

Senior Man: I like his voting record, particularly for the elderly and the working people. He has those people in mind and at heart.

Narrator: Tim Wirth. Standing up for Colorado.

* * *

Narrator: Congressman Frank McCloskey is working overtime. A member of the House Armed Services Committee, he wrote the McCloskey Amendment to put President Reagan's Grace Commission recommendations to work. It will save $20 billion in defense waste, and passed the House unanimously. Frank's 95% voting record is the best of any eighth district congressman in 25 years. Frank McCloskey, working hard for you.

Category V: Nonideological Content

The final category of ad includes those that give no hints about the programmatic preferences of the candidate. Instead, these ads focus on the personal attributes of the candidate and his or her opponent, the constituent service or casework of the candidate, the repetition of newspaper endorsements, and the credit-claiming appeals by incumbents who have garnered appreciable federal largesse for their districts. Many of the ads in this category also contain consensual policy goal appeals—referred to as "valence" issues—that reveal nothing about a candidate's preferences between live policy alternatives.

The following three ads illustrate the nonprogrammatic appeals present in the ads in this category. The first revolves around the vigor and integrity of the candidate and the citizen's distaste for negative campaigns. The second draws a favorable comparison between the attendance record of the candidate and his opponent, and the third concentrates on the personal qualities of the two candidates in the race. Given the nonprogrammatic nature of these ads, they would seem unlikely to help the electorate assess the ideology of either candidate or his or her opponent.

Man: I'm a small businessman from Mt. Pleasant and I can honestly say that I
live in the 10th congressional district. I've known Congressman Don Albosta for a long time. He's one of the hardest working people I know and
is totally honest and above board in everything he does. You know, I'm
sick and tired of out-state groups financing mudslinging campaigns in this
area. No amount of mudslinging in the last few weeks of the campaign is
gonna change my mind on how to vote. I voted for Don Albosta before;
I'm gonna do it again. I hope you do too.

*   *   *

Presiding Officer: Very well. The clerk of the House Ways and Means Committee
call the role.

Clerk: Representative Haynes.
Here.
Representative Jones.
Here.
Representative McIntyre. (Silence). Representative McIntyre (Si-
lence). Representative McIntyre (Silence).

Narrator: McIntyre missed 60% of the votes in the State House Ways and Means
Committee. But our Congressman, Frank McCloskey, has a 95% voting
record, the best of any 8th district Congressman in 25 years. Frank Mc-
Closkey, working hard for you in Congress.

*   *   *

Narrator: There's a clear choice in this year's race for Congress. One candidate,
Stan Lundine, takes clear stands on the issues and makes concrete proposals for solving our problems. The other candidate, Jill Emery, does not.
Stan Lundine has a proven record of being effective and responsive to our
needs. The other candidate has no public record. Stan Lundine is a lifelong
resident of our district; the other candidate doesn't live in our district. The
right choice is clear and we can't take a chance. We need Stan Lundine in
Congress.

RESULTS

The distribution of the advertisements across the five content categories is given in Table 3.2. Almost half of the ads contained no programmatic content whatsoever, while an almost equal number of ads
contained nonliberal as liberal appeals. Only 16 percent—or 30 percent
by a less stringent definition—of the ads would allow a voter to infer
that the candidate had a liberal voting record.

The twenty-one ads containing explicit liberal policy preferences touch
on a variety of policy areas. Nine of the ads deal with preserving social
security benefits, five with preserving Medicare benefits, four with op-

Table 3.2
Ideological Content of Televised Advertisements

Category I:	Definite Liberal Content	16%	(21)
Category II:	Possible Liberal Content	14%	(18)
Category III:	Conservative Content	8%	(10)
Category IV:	Mixed or Ambiguous Policy Content	15%	(20)
Category V:	Non-Ideological Content	47%	(62)
		100%	(131)

Source: Computed by author.

posing increased defense spending, three with favoring increased taxes on the wealthy and big corporations, and two with increasing federal aid to education. Single ads also favor increased aid to the unemployed, the nuclear freeze, protecting wilderness areas, cleaning up toxic wastes, and opposing utility rate increases.

The eighteen ads containing less definite liberal policy appeals touched on a similar array of issues, but with less precision and breadth. Five of the ads criticize wasteful defense spending, four focus on the plight of the elderly, five mention a commitment to reducing unemployment, three are attentive to the needs of cities, and two mention the importance of education. Single ads oppose utility rate increases, favor extending Medicare coverage, and applaud the protection of a wilderness area.

Although it seems quite likely that the ads in Category I would help the electorate perceive the ideology of the candidate, it is not clear whether the policy appeals in the Category II ads are apt to have a comparable educative effect. Whereas a Category I ad might contain an appeal that says the candidate opposes any reduction in social security benefits, a Category II ad would say that a candidate "has the interests of senior citizens at heart," or that the candidate favors "a dignified lifestyle for the elderly." Whether or not this type of appeal would perceived as liberal is not altogether clear.

In ten of the ads analyzed the candidates sound more like low- than high-ADA scorers. Most of these are attempts by nine of the candidates included here to portray themselves as fiscally conservative and to per-

suade the electorate that they are opposed to increased federal spending. More than one of these candidates enlisted Peter Grace and Ronald
Reagan in their cause, quoting from laudatory letters written by each
of them.

Twenty more of the ads contained policy appeals of a sort that would
be unlikely to lead to a perception that the candidate is liberal. Some of
these ads presented the electorate with a mixed message, as in the Tim
Wirth ad, that says his voting record favors the elderly and working
people at the same time that conservatives think of him as someone
who represents them. Other ads in this category are programmatic but
do not contain an ideological appeal. It is difficult to say whether a
candidate (McNulty) who "voted for major crime bills" and opposes loans
to foreign copper producers is a liberal, a conservative, or something
else. The same is true for the candidate (Feighan) who favored cutting
off foreign aid to any country participating in the shipment of illegal
narcotics.

Finally, the most prevalent ads are those that have no programmatic
content. These ads tend to focus on the incumbent's personal characteristics, such as experience and integrity, the incumbent's relationship
with his or her constituency, and the incumbent's ability to perform
case work and return a portion of federal largesse to the district. None
of these ads would be likely to aid a viewer in assessing the ideological
predispositions of the candidate.

DISCUSSION

The purpose of analyzing the appeals in this sample of ads was to
address a number of questions about the condition of New Deal Liberalism, and the educative impact of congressional elections. Given the
distribution of the 131 ads analyzed across the five content categories
used here, the following conclusions seem warranted.

First, if the appeals used by these candidates are any indication, New
Deal Liberalism has become an extraordinarily truncated political philosophy. Apart from the belief in preserving social security and Medicare benefits, and opposition to wasteful defense spending, Liberalism
offered little else to the 1984 congressional electorate. Absent are traditional liberal concerns with the regulation of unfair business practices, the protection of vulnerable wage earners, the assistance of workers in their struggles with management, the advancement of consumer
interests and civil liberties, the reversal of environmental degradation,
and the role of government in overcoming social and political inequal-
ities. Instead, New Deal Liberalism has become, at least on the campaign trail, Interest-Group Liberalism for the elderly and the poor. It
is little wonder that liberals have found it difficult to construct winning

coalitions out of such rhetorical appeals. Second, the appeals of these candidates show only a slight sign of the creativity and inventiveness that most theorists believe are necessary to forestall, or even benefit from, an ideological realignment. Most of the appeals used by liberals are either thoroughly conventional (preservation of social security and Medicare; opposition to reducing the tax bite on the wealthy) or obvious attempts to mimic conservatives (the concern with "budget discipline" and reducing the federal deficit). In the Category IV ads, the ones that are programmatic but neither clearly liberal nor conservative, the candidates stake out positions in favor of protecting our servicemen overseas, undefined major crime bills, compensation for Agent Orange victims, lower utility rates, and cutting off foreign aid to countries participating in illegal drug traffic. It is difficult to see how such appeals could engender popular support or serve as the basis for a revised and revitalized public philosophy. In fact, about the only policy goal articulated by our sample of liberals that might have broad implications and serve as the basis for policy innovation was the reference by some to so-called "industrial policy."

One gets the distinct impression, after viewing these ads, of an ideology struggling with the twin millstones of an increasingly unpopular philosophical tradition and an equally suspicious "me-tooism." If there are truly inventive and intelligent liberals capable of recasting their ideology for popular consumption, their appeals have not yet been adapted to the lexicon of the thirty-second television commercial.

Third, the dearth of programmatic appeals in most of these ads confirms our expectation that congressional campaigns are not terribly educative. At least 47 percent of the ads—those in Category V—contain no programmatic information and another 15 percent—those in Category IV—present the electorate with ambiguous or confusing policy-oriented messages. In addition, one could argue that the ads in Category III are deceptive, since they attempt to disguise the candidate's liberal voting record, and that those in Category II also lack clarity and breadth. In short, it is only the 16 percent of the ads in Category I that provide citizens with the kind of information that would encourage the accurate perception of the policy preferences of congressional candidates.

Finally, in terms of the four approaches to elections enumerated earlier, it seems quite clear that the appeals contained in these ads are most consistent with the benevolent leader and elections-as-ritual approaches. The policy appeals of the candidates are too sparse to support the prospective policy choice approach, and the policy performance appeals are too infrequent and district case work-oriented to support the retrospective *policy* satisfaction approach. In contrast, the ads contain abundant cases of the type of personal characteristics and consensual policy goal appeals that the other two approaches involve. Consequently the meaning of electoral outcomes is more apt to be found in the reaffirmation of cultural values and the fit between the role expectations for public offices and the personal attributes of candidates than in the electorate's preference for a particular programmatic alternative.

NOTES

I would like to thank Julian Kanter of *The Political Commercial Archives*, Melissa Maxman and Jim Francis of the Democratic Congressional Campaign Committee, and Doc Sweitzer of The Campaign Group in Philadelphia for helping me locate the ads used in this analysis. I am also indebted to Robbie Honig for her help in designing and conducting the content analysis discussed in this chapter.

1. Wilson Carey McWilliams, "The Meaning of the Election," in Gerald Pomper, ed., *The Election of 1984* (Chatham, N.J.: Chatham House, 1984), p. 161.

2. Linda J. Medcalf and Kenneth M. Dolbeare, *Neopolitics: American Political Ideas in the 1980s* (New York: Random House, 1985), p. 39.

3. McWilliams, "The Meaning of the Election," in Pomper, op. cit., pp. 160-61. Opinion is divided, however, about the extent to which the populace has embraced conservative causes and ideology. For an argument that the populace has *not* moved to the right, see Scott Keeter, "Public Opinion in 1984," in Pomper, op. cit., pp. 107-9. Gerald Pomper, on the other hand, cites polls showing "more people willing to call themselves conservatives, and fewer concerned with promoting social welfare and minority rights." "The Presidential Election," in Pomper, op. cit., p. 88. On the "collapse" of liberalism, and the various challenges to it, see Medcalf and Dolbeare, op. cit. They argue that "from the late 1960s on, many Americans began to display deeply negative reactions toward the changes that had occurred under liberal beliefs and government practices" (p. 53).

4. Pomper, op. cit., p. 88.

5. McWilliams, op. cit., p. 159.

6. Everett Carll Ladd, Jr., and Charles D. Hadley, *Transformations of the American Party Systems* (New York: W. W. Norton, 1975), p. 84.

7. Gerald Pomper has warned that "imitating Republican calls for fiscal restraint or rapid armament would make the (Democratic) party little more than a 'me too' party, a pale moon in the political solar system, reflecting the light of the opposition's dominant sun." In Pomper, op. cit., p. 88.

8. Richard Joslyn, *Mass Media and Elections* (Reading, Mass.: Addison-Wesley, 1984).

9. For an informative summary of this literature, see Philip E. Converse, "Public Opinion and Voting Behavior," in Fred I. Greenstein and Nelson W. Polsby, eds., *Handbook of Political Science: Nongovernmental Politics*, Vol. 4 (Reading, Mass.: Addison-Wesley, 1975).

10. W. Lance Bennett, *Public Opinion in American Politics* (New York: Harcourt Brace Jovanovich, 1980).

11. Barbara Hinckley, *Congressional Elections* (Washington, D.C.: Congressional Quarterly Press, 1981), p. 95.

12. Ibid., p. 109.

13. Ibid., p. 79.

14. Gary Jacobson, *Money in Congressional Elections* (New Haven, Conn.: Yale University Press, 1980), pp. 15, 28.

15. Joslyn, op. cit., chapter 9.

16. *Congressional Quarterly Weekly Report*: July 3, 1982, p. 1609; May 7, 1983, pp. 901-2; July 14, 1984, pp. 1691-92.

17. Mr. Kanter's collection has recently been donated to the University of Oklahoma.

18. Insiders' accounts of the campaigns involving three of the incumbents included in this study—Kostmayer, Brown, and Penny—indicate that the challengers made a concerted effort to depict the incumbents as "too liberal." See Stuart Rothenberg, ed., *Ousting the Ins* (Washington, D.C.: Free Congress Research and Education Foundation, 1985).

19. Both Bill Bradley and Joe Biden had ADA scores greater than or equal to eighty and CCUS (Chamber of Commerce of the U.S.) and ACARI (Americans for Constitutional Action Research Institute) scores of less than forty for the 1981-1983 period. Only a handful of senators had ADA scores greater than theirs over this time period.

4

Why Some Constituencies Are Better Informed Than Most About the Positions of House Incumbents

Robert O. Simmons, Jr.

This study concerns the extent to which mass media and House candidates effectively meet what Jennings (1987) calls their duty to inform constituents about House incumbents' issue positions. The study was inspired by the desire to test two competing explanations for a finding by Simmons (1984). In contrast to previous research (Hinckley, 1980a; Mann and Wolfinger, 1980), Simmons found that while incumbents were helped by constituents' knowledge of their general issue positions, incumbents were not helped by constituents' knowledge of their specific votes. Incumbents actually were seriously hurt by knowledge of their votes when it was widespread in the district.

The dangers of widespread information were anticipated from the following set of assumptions. Many scholars have noted that, unlike senators, who receive relatively heavy news coverage and often attract strong challengers, House incumbents tend to control the information that voters have about them.[1] Furthermore, negative opinions about incumbents tend to have stronger effects on voting behavior than do positive opinions (Kernell, 1977), and specific policies tend to generate more negative opinions than do general policy goals (Page, 1978). Because incumbents tend to be endangered by widespread information about their specific positions, one can assume that they usually try to publicize such positions only to narrow targeted audiences. Thus, people's propensity for negative voting based on knowledge of incumbents' specific positions normally is nullified because incumbents communicate mainly with those likely to agree with them.

However, sources of information other than incumbents usually will try to publicize incumbents' votes, not only directly, but also perhaps by pressing incumbents to discuss them (Goldenberg and Traugott, 1984, pp. 122-24). Therefore, it was also assumed that the abnormal situation of incumbents' votes being well known is usually a sign that the incumbent has lost his or her monopoly on information. Incumbents can lose control of information when they have *challengers* who run well-funded issue-oriented campaigns and/or when the *news media* give issue positions unusual publicity. This publicity usually occurs during the campaign when incumbents have strong issue-oriented challengers but can also occur before the campaign when incumbents sponsor a famous bill or plan to seek higher office.

In short, a previous study found that widespread information about specific issue positions hurt incumbents, while less widespread information did not; this difference was interpreted to mean that some incumbents were less able than most to be the only source of information about their positions.

AN ALTERNATIVE INTERPRETATION

There is, however, another possible interpretation of this difference: incumbents with the best-known issue positions may have taken positions that were less representative of their constituents than did other incumbents, unrepresentativeness being both necessary and sufficient to indirectly cause issue positions to be widely known to voters and harmful to incumbents.[2]

This alternative interpretation is based on findings about the 1958 congressional elections by Miller and Stokes (1963). The general picture drawn by Miller and Stokes was that of a Congress whose members' issue positions were almost completely unknown among the voters of 1958. However, Miller and Stokes also described an important exception to this general pattern: Representative Brooks Hays, whose unrepresentative civil rights position was evidently very well known in his Arkansas constituency and this was apparently why a write-in candidate defeated him. Miller and Stokes concluded that a major cause of voter ignorance was that most House incumbents took at least fairly representative positions on the issues most salient to their constituents.

Although the Hays case is the main empirical evidence about the relationship between the visibility and the representativeness of incumbents' positions, many authors have speculated about this alleged link. Most of these authors have supported the view that serious misrepresentation would lead to high visibility (e.g., Kingdon, 1973, pp. 40-41;

Mann and Wolfinger, 1980), but a few have dissented (e.g., Polsby, 1976, pp. 192-93).

POSSIBLE INFLUENCES ON THE PUBLIC'S INFORMATION

Regardless of what the relationship is between the visibility and the representativeness of issue positions, it is unclear what causes visibility directly. Three possible explanations for the extent of knowledge about an incumbent's issue positions are television advertising by the incumbent, television advertising by the challenger, and newspaper content.

Even if incumbents usually try to limit discussions of their specific positions to narrow audiences, they would still be expected to communicate more broadly those specific positions that are not controversial in the district.[3] Several studies indicate that incumbents occasionally do just that (Fenno, 1978; Goldenberg and Traugott, 1984; Joslyn, 1987).

However, various examples suggest that the effect of some incumbents' issue-oriented commercials may be less than educational. An incumbent studied by Joslyn (1987) used at least one 1984 spot to talk convincingly about his lifelong personal frugality, with obvious implications for his views on government spending. Likewise, the senator in Goldenberg and Traugott's (1987) study ran a commercial that started by lingering over a state map showing numerous military bases while the narration detailed his aid to these bases. As the voice-over continued in this promilitary vein, the senator was shown chatting amiably with a small group of officers, and the spot concluded with the incumbent climbing into a military plane.[4] This commercial could have made viewers doubt reports of his consistent votes against proposed weapons systems and his actual leadership in the fight against military spending; likewise, the House member's commercial could have inoculated viewers from messages about his vote against the president's omnibus budget cuts and his annual Americans for Constitutional Action ratings that were approaching single digits. It also was not unusual in the early and middle 1980s to observe the spectacle of Republicans voting for wide-ranging cuts in social spending and then advertising their deep empathy with the recipients of federal aid. If incumbent commercials are usually this "disinformative," then that might explain why Clarke and Fredin (1978) concluded that heavy television viewing actually suppressed the ability of viewers to develop reasons for liking or disliking Senate candidates.

Many challengers' campaigns can also be expected to address incumbents' positions (Raymond, 1983; Simmons, 1984). Indeed, challengers are accused more often than incumbents themselves of distorting incumbents' general records, and these accusations usually concern commercials that mention specific votes. Whether distorting a vote or not, such commercials potentially enable constituents to recall it.

Newspapers vary both in coverage of congressional candidates in general (Vermeer, 1987; Goldenberg and Traugott, 1987) and in coverage of their issue positions in particular (Tidmarch, 1985; Orman, 1985; Hale, 1987). The amount of issue coverage on average is lower than coverage of other aspects of congressional campaigns (Clarke and Evans, 1982), but issue coverage tends to be unusually high when the newspaper circulates largely within one district and the challenger is strong and emphasizes issues (Goldenberg and Traugott, 1984, chapter 8).

While mass media have the potential to cause incumbents' positions to be unusually well known, two things remain unclear: whether the media fulfill this potential, and whether the media are merely the means by which such knowledge inevitably follows from unrepresentativeness. In what follows I show the latter to be false: unrepresentative incumbents' positions are not always unusually well known. I then turn to the former question and find that mass media content does help to explain why the constituents of both unrepresentative and other incumbents may or may not be well informed.

DATA

The data described below allow a more systematic test than previously possible of the relationship between incumbent representativeness and voter information. These data also will be used to analyze the impacts of the information provided by television advertisements and by newspapers on the public's information. These data then will be used to go further back in the chain of causality to analyze the impacts on newspaper content of the issue emphasis of candidates, the closeness of the race, and the fit between the newspaper circulation area and the congressional district.

The findings reported below are based on five sets of data that were collected as parts of two separate but related studies. Two of these data sets are part of the American National Election Study, 1978, hereafter referred to as simply the "election study;" these data are based on interviews of approximately twenty-one adults in each of 108 systematically selected congressional districts and on campaign literature from the headquarters of candidates in the same districts. The other data sets are part of Goldenberg and Traugott's Congressional Campaign Study, 1978; these data are based on interviews with campaign managers of major party candidates in each of the eighty-six contested races that took place in the 108 election-study districts, on Federal Election Commission expenditure reports for the candidates in these eighty-six races, and on analyses of the content and circulation areas of the major newspapers covering forty-three of these eighty-six races.[5]

Sometimes testing hypotheses on these data requires dividing incumbents into two categories, one of which may have to be extremely small. For example, one hypothesis is that the most unrepresentative incumbents differ from others, and another is that the incumbents with issue positions of highest visibility differ from incumbents in the lower-visibility category. These hypotheses are based on the Brooks Hays example. It is evident from Miller and Stokes' (1963) use of Hays as a solitary exception, and from the views of scholars such as Kingdon (1973) and Mann and Wolfinger (1980), that the great majority of House incumbents evidently hold issue positions that are by and large both invisible and representative.[6] Indeed, a strict replication of Miller and Stokes' study would compare one incumbent with all others. However, while the 1978 election-study sampling procedure was uniquely suited to provide estimates of information held by people in *groups* of congressional districts,[7] we cannot use such district-level measures to talk about a single district (Miller, 1979). Therefore, the appropriate number of cases in the highest-visibility and most-unrepresentative categories is small, but greater than one.[8]

The following are descriptions of how visibility, representativeness, and other variables are measured.

Visibility (i.e., information or knowledge about incumbents' issue positions) is measured by the percentage of election-study respondents in a congressional district who said they could recall a particular vote cast by the incumbent in that district.[9]

The overall representativeness of a House incumbent is measured by an index based on the incumbent's campaign manager's placements of the incumbent and the district on four separate domestic issues.[10]

The amount of information in newspapers about an incumbent's issue positions was measured by calculating the average number of stories per newspaper that indicated these positions.[11]

Candidates were measured as being issue-oriented or having an issue emphasis in their campaigns if at least one issue was given more than a peripheral emphasis in their campaign-headquarters materials. The amount of information about incumbents' positions in the television advertisements of incumbents and of challengers was estimated as zero for the candidates who did not have an issue emphasis in their campaigns and by the amount spent on television in the last half of 1978 for those candidates who did have an issue emphasis in their campaigns.[12]

The closeness of the race in a district was measured by Goldenberg and Traugott's (1984, chapter 3) categorization of campaign managers' preelection assessments of their chances of winning the election. The closest races were those in which vulnerable incumbents faced hopeful challengers, and the most one-sided races were those in which sure winners faced sure losers.[13]

The fit between the newspaper circulation area and the congressional district—the newspaper's "efficiency"—was measured as the percentage of the circulation that fell within the district.[14]

FINDINGS

Starting here I will often refer to the House incumbents best known for their specific positions[15] as "Extreme Visibles." I will refer to the incumbents who were unrepresentative[16] as "Discrepants" and to the Discrepants who were most unrepresentative[17] as "Extreme Discrepants." Extreme Visibles and Extreme Discrepants are somewhat different groups of incumbents, contrary to the idea that visibility and unrepresentativeness are strongly related.

Information about specific votes cast by incumbents was volunteered by not quite 10 percent of the public near the climax of the election campaign in 1978. Although this figure is higher than studies such as Miller and Stokes (1963) would lead one to expect, it is undeniably low.

Nevertheless, this figure camouflages considerable variation. The minority in the public who actually voted was better informed than the majority. Districts with contested races (i.e., those analyzed below) were better informed than those without contests. In districts with contests the percentage of well informed adults ranged from 0 percent to 31 percent.

Causes of Issue Knowledge

What explains why some incumbents running for reelection are relatively well known for their issue positions while most incumbents are not? Possible explanations include variations in representativeness and differences in mass media content.

As noted earlier, Miller and Stokes (1963) found that the most visible incumbent in 1958 was unrepresentative of his constituents. In 1978 a similar phenomenon occurred: on average, Extreme Visibles were in fact 70 percent farther from their districts than were the less visible incumbents. This seems to support the idea that the representativeness of most incumbents leads their specific positions to be nearly invisible.

However, findings such as those reported here and by Miller and Stokes (1963) are inadequate to establish that incumbent unrepresentativeness will lead to voter awareness. What we really want to know is not whether Extreme Visibles are unusually unrepresentative, but whether Extreme Discrepants are unusually well known. It would be quite possible to have the former pattern without the latter.

As it happens, the latter pattern also occurs: the Extreme Discrepants were indeed better known for their issue positions than were the incumbents who were closer to their districts. More specifically, Extreme Discrepants were, on average, about twice as well known for their issue positions as other incumbents, a statistically significant[18] difference, despite the small number of cases in the former category. Thus we now have adequate support for the decades-old hypothesis that unrepresentativeness in House incumbents tends to become relatively well known to their constituents.

At the same time, however, the relationship between unrepresentativeness and visibility is nonlinear and far from perfect. Even within the naturally tiny subgroup defined as Extreme Discrepants there is variation in how well known the incumbents were. In addition, Discrepants as a whole were actually slightly less well known than were representative incumbents.[19] In short, there were many Discrepants whose positions were relatively or even completely unknown.

It remains to explain these findings: first, why the Extreme Discrepants generally were better known than other incumbents; second, why Discrepants as a whole were nevertheless not better known than other incumbents; and third, why all Discrepants were not equally well known for their issue positions. Surely the answers involve mass media, but what kinds? The analyses that follow look at three possible media explanations: issue information in newspapers, issue information in the television advertisements of incumbents, and issue information in the television advertisements of challengers. I will compare the races involving Extreme Discrepants with the races involving relatively representative incumbents to see whether the former races were richer in media content. I also will compare the races involving incumbents more broadly defined as "Discrepants" with other ("representative") incumbents to see whether the former races had media content that was not richer. I also will look at the impacts of the three media variables, while controlling for representativeness, to see whether media content explains why both Discrepants and representative incumbents usually were not as well known as the typical Extreme Discrepant.

Table 4.1(a) shows that the races with Extreme Discrepants did differ substantially and in the expected direction on two of the three media variables suspected of causing the positions of these incumbents to be comparatively well known. Although these differences are not statistically significant, and therefore should be viewed with caution, they do support the idea that newspaper content and the television advertising of incumbents were at least partially responsible for the statistically sig-

nificant difference between knowledge about Extreme Discrepants and
knowledge about those who were relatively representative.

In contrast, the difference in challenger advertising is not in the expected direction.[20] In fact, Extreme Discrepants typically faced challengers who did virtually no issue-oriented television advertising. Therefore, the commercials of challengers were not responsible for the relatively high knowledge about Extreme Discrepants.

The scarcity of issue-oriented commercials by challengers to Extreme Discrepants is surprising. According to conventional wisdom, such chal-

Table 4.1
Mean Amounts of Issue-Oriented Media by Level of Incumbent Representativeness[a]

(a)	Relatively Representative Incumbents	Extreme Discrepants
Mean Newspaper Content[b] (N = 27)	10.2	41.0
Mean Incumbent Advertising[c] (N = 59)	.38	1.23
Mean Challenger Advertising[c] (N = 57)	.57	.01

(b)	Representative Incumbents	Discrepants
Mean Newspaper Content (N = 27)	12.4	8.5
Mean Incumbent Advertising (N = 59)	.42	.43
Mean Challenger Advertising (N = 57)	.75	.27

[a]The index scores defining these groups are: Relatively Representative Incumbents, less than or equal to two on the index; Extreme Discrepants, greater than two; Representative Incumbents, less than or equal to one; Discrepants, greater than one.

[b]Measured as the number of articles per newspaper indicating the incumbent's issue positions.

[c]Measured in tens of thousands of dollars for those incumbents with issue-oriented campaigns; measured as zero otherwise.

Source: Computed by author.

lengers should attack their opponents' records and attract enough funding to televise these attacks. And, in fact, some of these challengers did attack and/or attract. Nevertheless, few issue-oriented commercials resulted. One such challenger did emphasize issues but did not attract money because the district was safe for the opposite party. Another such challenger attracted money but did not emphasize issues, perhaps because of the district's unusual concerns about candidates' personal characteristics. The third such challenger both attacked the incumbent's record and attracted money but spent mysteriously little on television, despite being in a television market that reached district voters fairly efficiently.

The expectation that Extreme Discrepants would have been in relatively information-rich campaigns was based on their relative visibility; based on the relative obscurity of Discrepants, we would conversely expect them to have been in campaigns of no better than average information output. This expectation is supported by Table 4.1(b). Underlying the averages for Discrepants is the fairly high proportion of their districts where there was little or no information about incumbent positions either from newspapers or from television advertising. Media information may lead to an informed electorate, but unrepresentativeness generally does not lead to media information.

Although Extreme Discrepants tended to be fairly well known, this group is emphatically not the same as the Extreme Visibles; therefore the patterns observed in Table 4.1(a) do not necessarily apply to a comparison of the races involving Extreme Visibles with the races involving incumbents whose positions were less known. Table 4.2 presents this comparison. As in the previous comparison, the amounts of newspaper content and incumbent television differ in the expected direction, but the amounts of challenger advertising differ in the expected direction as well. It is no surprise that a group whose very definition is a high level of information in the public is also characterized by high levels of similar information in the mass media; the high level of issue-oriented advertising by the challengers of Extreme Visibles may be an important characteristic of the races involving Extreme Visibles that is not shared by the races involving the Extreme Discrepants.

Whereas Table 4.1 shows that Extreme Discrepants virtually monopolized the discussion of issues on television,[21] Table 4.2 shows that Extreme Visibles tended to have the televised statements on issues dominated by their challengers. Table 4.2 also shows that the Extreme Visibles received more than twice as much issue-related newspaper coverage as did other incumbents. These tables support the idea that the reason widespread information about specific positions hurts incumbents is that the incumbent is not the only source of such information. This idea is different from the idea supported by the previously discussed finding

Table 4.2
Mean Amounts of Issue-Oriented Media by Level of Visibility of
Incumbent's Issue Positions[a]

	Less Visible Incumbents	Extreme Visibles
Mean Newspaper Content[b] (N = 35)	10.9	23.0
Mean Incumbent Advertising[c] (N = 71)	.50	1.17
Mean Challenger Advertising[c] (N = 72)	.40	1.99

[a]The percentages defining these categories are: Less Visible Incumbents, 0% up to but not including 23% of respondents in a district; Extreme Visibles, 23% or higher.

[b]Measured as the number of articles per newspaper indicating the incumbent's issue positions.

[c]Measured in tens of thousands of dollars for those with issue-oriented campaigns; measured as zero otherwise.

<u>Source:</u> Computed by author.

that the positions of Extreme Discrepants were unusually well known; this finding supported the alternative idea that widespread information hurts because this information concerns positions that are not representative of district opinion. Evidently, then, there is some truth to both of these interpretations of the finding that information about specific positions hurts incumbents when that information is widespread among constituents.

Tables 4.3 and 4.4 provide further information on the impacts of newspaper content and television advertising. Here knowledge is measured as an actual percentage of constituents holding this knowledge, affording a better test of the causes underlying the high visibility of some incumbents than does the meaningful but crude categorization of knowledge in Table 4.2.

Tables 4.3 and 4.4 also address the question of whether media content explains why all Discrepants (or all representative incumbents) were not equally well known. This question is answered by looking at Discrepants separately from representative incumbents.[22]

Table 4.3(a) shows that television advertising by Discrepants helps explain variation in knowledge about their issue positions. Only about

Table 4.3
Regression of Incumbent's Issue-Position Visibility[a] on Incumbent's Television Advertising[b] and Challenger's Television Advertising:[b] Results for Discrepants and Representative Incumbents[c]

	Standardized Coefficients	Unstandardized Coefficients
(a) Representative Incumbents		
Incumbent Advertising	.21	1.21
Challenger Advertising	.04	.13
Constant		9.84
(b) Discrepants		
Incumbent Advertising	.65**	5.85**
Challenger Advertising	-.07	-.08
Constant		7.02
(c) Discrepants and Representative Incumbents (Full Equation)		
Multiple R	.490	.490
R^2	.240	.240
Standard Error		7.25
N	57	57

**Statistically significant at the .05 level.

[a]Measured on a scale of 0 to 100 (percent).

[b]Measured in tens of thousands of dollars for those candidates with issue-oriented campaigns;   measured as zero otherwise.

[c]The index scores defining these levels are: Representative Incumbents, less than or equal to one; Discrepants, greater than one.

Source: Computed by author.

7 percent of constituents of a Discrepant who did no issue-oriented television advertising are expected to have been able to recall a specific vote cast by that incumbent. But for a Discrepant who spent $30,000 on television as part of an issue-oriented campaign, the expected percentage of well-informed constituents more than triples to about 25

percent. In addition, an analysis not shown finds that television advertising by Extreme Discrepants is even more strongly related to the extent of knowledge about their votes.

These findings thus reduce our doubts about the informativeness of
incumbent advertising. Recall that these doubts were based on examples of such advertising suggesting that Discrepants' commercials could
actually suppress information in the public. This possibility receives no
support from these data, although it is still possible that the information was given to constituents by Discrepants in a way that was highly
selective or even inaccurate.

Table 4.3 also *increases* our doubts that *challenger* advertising had any
direct effect on knowledge about incumbents' positions. Even though
some challengers to both Discrepants and representative incumbents
spent substantial sums on issue-oriented commercials, this is not associated with public knowledge once incumbent advertising is held constant. Recall that the doubts about challenger advertising were based on
the finding in Table 4.1 that issue-oriented television advertising by
challengers to Extreme Discrepants was unsubstantial; challenger advertising thus could not account for the unusually great public knowledge about these incumbents. Although it is still possible that a substantial amount of issue-oriented advertising by their challengers would have
made the positions of Extreme Discrepants still more widely known,
Table 4.3 suggests that this would have occurred only if the advertising
of these challengers had been different in content or credibility from
the advertising of most challengers.

Table 4.4 shows that newspaper content is a second explanation for
why some incumbents were not as well known as others. If a Discrepant
had received the amount of newspaper coverage shown in Table 4.1 to
be typical of Extreme Discrepants (i.e., forty-one issue-related items per
paper in three weeks), we estimate from Table 4.4(a) that this would
then result in an additional 12.3 percent of constituents being able to
recall at least one of the incumbent's votes. The importance of newspaper coverage is particularly clear, considering that we estimate that
less than 1 percent would have recalled this information in the absence
of both newspaper coverage and incumbent advertising. Table 4.4(b)
shows that newspaper content also may have a small impact on knowledge about incumbents who were representative.[23] Thus newspaper
content not only joins television advertising by incumbents[24] as a powerful explanation for variation in issue-position knowledge about Discrepants, but also seems unsurpassed as an influence on how much was
known about incumbents in general.

Causes of Newspaper Content

Newspaper content helps to determine whether the public knows the issue positions of incumbents, but what determines newspaper content? Obviously this content is determined by journalists, but what informal decision rules underlie their judgments?

Table 4.4
Regression of Incumbent's Issue-Position Visibility[a] on Newspaper Content, Controlling for Incumbent's Television Advertising:[b] Results for Discrepants and Representative Incumbents[c]

		Standardized Coefficients	Unstandardized Coefficients
(a)	Representative Incumbents		
	Newspaper Content	.33	.15
	Incumbent Advertising	.21	1.12
	Constant		9.58
(b)	Discrepants		
	Newspaper Content	.62**	.30**
	Incumbent Advertising	.64**	4.18**
	Constant		.76
(c)	Discrepants and Representative Incumbents (Full Equation)		
	Multiple R	.736	.736
	R^2	.541	.541
	Standard Error		5.46
	N	27	27

**Statistically significant at the .05 level.

[a]Measured on a scale of 0 to 100 (percent).

[b]Measured in tens of thousands of dollars for those incumbents with issue-oriented campaigns; measured as zero otherwise.

[c]The index scores defining these levels are: Representative Incumbents, less than or equal to one; Discrepants, greater than one.

Source: Computed by author.

Goldenberg and Traugott (1984, chapter 8) found in their data that the issue content of newspapers was largely a function of newspaper efficiency (the fit between the district and the newspaper circulation area) and the closeness of the race. In the similar data used here, these factors account for 44 percent of the variance in content about the issue positions of incumbents.

These data also replicate another Goldenberg-Traugott finding. The authors found that more than three times as much issue attention was given by newspapers to incumbents whose challengers emphasized issues in their literature than was given to incumbents whose opponents ignored issues. We find an even stronger relationship in these data, with an average of fourteen issue articles about incumbents with issue-oriented challengers, more than four times the number of issue stories about other incumbents.

Table 4.5 shows that candidates' issue emphasis seems to remain an influence on newspaper issue content even when efficiency of the newspaper and closeness of the race are held constant.[25] The emphasis variable in this table includes the incumbent's emphasis as well as the challenger's but gives more weight to the latter; this variable's construction is based on the Goldenberg-Traugott finding that it was the challenger who mattered and on analyses of the present data, which showed that challenger emphasis was more important but that incumbent emphasis seemed to make some contribution as well.

The relationships of newspaper content both to closeness and to issue emphasis imply that newspaper content may also be related to the television advertising variables discussed previously. These variables had two components—issue emphasis and amount of spending—and the latter is related to closeness. Even apart from this almost built-in correlation, one might suspect that as issue-oriented advertising increased on television the amount of issue-related content would also increase in newspapers as journalists commented on these commercials (Hale, 1987). In fact, this suspicion is confirmed, although not strongly and consistently. Issue-related newspaper content is quite strongly related to issue-oriented television advertising by both candidates when the incumbent is representative and also when the incumbent is among the more unrepresentative of the Discrepants. Surprisingly, though, newspaper content is related to these advertising variables neither among the Discrepants as a whole[26] nor among Extreme Discrepants, and for the sample as a whole the relationship is not strong. Also, a precise statement about the indirect effects of the television variables necessitates a more sophisticated statistical model than the ones tested here. Nevertheless, these results raise one particularly interesting possibility: that television advertising by challengers, which was found to have no direct effect on

Table 4.5
Regression of Incumbents Issue Coverage[a] on Race Closeness,[b] Newspaper Efficiency,[c] and Challenger and Incumbent Issue Emphasis[d]

	Standardized Coefficients	Unstandardized Coefficients
Race Closeness	.345**	4.59**
Newspaper Efficiency	.406**	14.51**
Issue Emphasis	.235*	3.07*
Constant		−12.40
Multiple R	.727	.727
R^2	.529	.529
Standard Error		10.02
N	37	37

*Statistically significant at the .10 level.

**Statistically significant at the .05 level.

[a]In contrast to previous tables, where the unit of analysis was the congressional district and the number of newspaper articles, if used, was averaged across papers, here each case is a newspaper-district combination.

[b]Measured on a scale from one (lopsided) to four (close).

[c]Measured on a scale from zero (no circulation in district) to one (all circulation in district).

[d]Measured on a scale where one equals issue emphasis by neither candidate, two equals issue emphasis by the incumbent but not the challenger, three equals issue emphasis by the challenger but not the incumbent, and four equals issue emphasis by both candidates.

Source: Computed by author.

information about the positions of incumbents, may instead have an indirect effect through newspaper content.

Any impact of unrepresentativeness on issue coverage is difficult to establish with these data. There is a tendency for issue attention to increase with unrepresentativeness, even when other factors are held constant, but this relationship is small and statistically insignificant.

The last possible cause I will consider is the journalists' values or interests. There were nine races covered by more than one newspaper in these data. Generally the amount of issue coverage was either similar in the two papers or greater in one paper than the other, owing to the better fit of its circulation area with the district and consequent greater coverage of all aspects of the campaign. Like the rather high R^2 in Table 4.5, these nine races show that most journalistic news judgments are strongly influenced by the closeness of the race, the fit between the district and the newspaper circulation area, and the issue emphases of the candidates. One race, however, shows that these unwritten rules that usually govern coverage of congressional campaigns can sometimes be ignored by a newspaper. The reelection campaign of a Republican incumbent in the Northeast was covered by two large papers in the same city. Both papers gave about the same amount of total coverage to the race, but one paper had only a single item with content about the incumbent's positions, whereas the other paper had such content in all thirteen of its items or stories. None of the items in either paper was a column, letter, or advertisement, so the source of the content was very much the newspapers themselves.

All in all, then, substantial newspaper coverage of the positions of incumbents, including Discrepants, is far from certain to exist. Rather, it is a function of the efficiency of the newspaper with respect to the district, the idiosyncrasies of the newspaper's staff, the closeness of the election, and the issue emphases of both the incumbent and, especially, the challenger.

FUTURE RESEARCH

Fruitful further avenues of exploration are suggested by the research findings reported here. For instance, hypotheses tested on the 1978 election should be tested on subsequent elections. It is quite possible that the congressional electorate of the 1980s is better informed about incumbents' issue positions because of the televising of House floor activities, the publicizing of Democrats' roll call votes by the national Republican party, and the increased advertising by independent political action committees (PACs).[27] Although the negative advertisements of groups such as the National Conservative Political Action Committee have been sharply criticized, they certainly seem as issue-oriented as most advertising by the candidates themselves.

Currently we know little about the information supplied either in 1978 or more recently by the television advertising of challengers. Two possible explanations for the finding in this study that even challengers' issue-oriented commercials had no apparent impact on information about the specific positions of incumbents could be investigated: that challengers' commercials simply did not address the specific positions held by incumbents, or that these advertisements did address these positions but lacked credibility.

The nature of incumbent advertising, already investigated by Joslyn (1987), deserves further attention from researchers. It is not yet firmly established whether most issue-oriented incumbent advertising, even in a given year, is as misleading as some parts of Joslyn's study imply or as informative as this study suggests. Two lines of research can investigate whether either of these implications is warranted. First, content analysis of the advertisements of all types of incumbents is advisable. The other line of research would be to compare the impacts of different types of advertisements, using experiments and/or panel surveys. Such research designs are well suited to test whether issue-oriented advertisements have the effect this study attributes to them.

Research also should be continued on other conditions that lead to different kinds—and amounts—of advertising. For instance, Raymond (1987) found that being in the party out of power was associated with emphasizing issues; it would be interesting to learn if the emphasis on specific bills was disproportionately negative (compared with the emphasis of the "ins"), which may be safer than being positive about something specific. Cook (1987) finds that incumbents being unrepresentative and appearing on the national news increases the PAC contributions of the challengers. This in turn presumably enables challengers to run vigorous advertising campaigns. It would now be interesting to know the extent to which unrepresentativeness encourages strong potential challengers to enter the race and encourages existing challengers to run issue-oriented campaigns.

Another area for continued research is the conditions leading to increased attention to issues by mass media. This study found little support for the hypothesis that incumbent unrepresentativeness led to emphasis on their issue positions by newspapers, but it did support Goldenberg and Traugott's (1984) conclusion that the amount of coverage of these positions was strongly related to the closeness of the race, the emphases of the candidates, and the fit between the district and the newspaper's circulation area. However, both studies found that these factors left some variance unexplained. What could explain the remaining variance? Goldenberg and Traugott (1984) suggested that it was the values of editors; Hale (1986, 1987) suggested that it was the values of reporters and the content of television advertisements; and Dewhirst (1986) suggested that it was the economic health of the newspaper (because weak newspapers may turn away from issues and toward sensationalism). All of these hypotheses are testable.

Another aspect of media coverage that has received some attention (e.g., Robinson, 1981; Goldenberg and Traugott, 1984, chapter 8; Clarke and Evans, 1983), and should receive more, is the degree to which, and the conditions under which, local media are biased toward incumbents. Particularly related to the current study would be focusing this research on coverage of issue positions. The press' options in covering the issue positions of incumbents range from passively reprinting their press releases to aggressively presenting opposing views. Where a newspaper falls on this continuum affects the degree of control an incumbent can be said to have over what the district knows, and this in turn affects the impact that this knowledge has on the incumbent's popularity. The findings presented here show that an incumbent's positions being well known was often a sign that the local newspaper provided information about these positions. But only to the extent that newspapers are independent of incumbents and attentive to their opposition can we say that issue information in the newspaper meaningfully breaks the effective monopoly that incumbents normally have over information about their issue positions. Further research should therefore discover the center of gravity of the continuum both for incumbents as a whole and for Discrepants in particular.

Finally, research should proceed not only on the direct and indirect causes of constituencies being well informed, but also on the effects of this information. Well-informed constituencies are less positive than others in their evaluations of incumbents (Simmons, 1984), but it is not yet known whether this translates into a greater likelihood of incumbent defeats. For example, it is possible that attacking an incumbent's record hurts not only the incumbent, but also the challenger, as Jim Hunt may have learned in his unsuccessful campaign to oust Jesse Helms from the Senate in 1984.

CONCLUSIONS

Someone has observed that answering research questions is like clearing a circle in a forest: as a bigger and bigger circle is cleared, more and more unfelled forest is visible. Now that we have looked at the unfelled forest, let us look back at the area we have cleared.

This study supports the frequently advanced but inadequately tested idea that House incumbents being unusually well known for issue positions may be a sign that these incumbents are seriously out of step with their districts; however, it also supports the idea that such knowledge may be a sign of other things instead. Being unrepresentative is not necessary for being visible. Nor is it sufficient. Unrepresentative incumbents (Discrepants) can hide their issue positions unless they encounter newspaper coverage of these positions or unless they themselves interpret their positions on paid television.

Challengers were found to contribute to knowledge about the positions of incumbents, but not through television advertising. In fact, the typical Extreme Discrepant achieved above-average visibility despite facing virtually no issue-oriented commercials by the challenger. This supports the idea that extreme unrepresentativeness leads to at least moderate visibility some other way, but it is crucial to realize that this other way did indirectly involve challengers. Rather than informing the public through commercials, challengers did it through their influence on newspaper content.[28] Both the challenger's ability to make the election close and the challenger's decision to emphasize issues were found to be among the important causes of newspapers presenting information about the incumbent's positions.

Above-average visibility of incumbents thus was largely dependent on actions and characteristics of challengers that were often absent even when the incumbent was unrepresentative. The frequent absence of strong issue-oriented challengers is apparently the main reason Discrepants as a group were not well known even though (a) the subgroup consisting of Extreme Discrepants was well known and (b) campaign communications, when present, appeared to have more impact on knowledge about Discrepants than on knowledge about representative incumbents.

The impact reported here of some incumbents' television advertising does not support Clarke and Fredin's (1978) negative view of television's ability to convey the policy positions of congressional candidates. Instead, these results are more supportive of Patterson and McClure's (1976) view that although television is generally uninformative about candidates' issue stands, television *can* inform viewers about these stands when it mentions them frequently and in a way that is simple and yet coordinated with the television visuals. Patterson and McClure said that these conditions occurred not in television news, but in television advertising during the presidential election of 1972. It appears that during the congressional elections of 1978 these conditions were met in the advertising of issue-oriented incumbents.

The amount of incumbent advertising of specific stands was modest but nevertheless surprising, especially for the Extreme Discrepants. Though it is likely that incumbents tended to ignore votes that were controversial, the assumption that incumbents avoid broadcasting all specifics is false. Yet the hypothesis that followed from this assumption was supported: widespread information about specific positions is a sign that newspapers had joined the incumbent as an information source.

Unfortunately the importance of incumbent advertising and newspaper reporting is in many districts more potential than actual, particularly in large urban areas where races are not close, newspapers are not efficient and commercials are not cheap. Discrepants cannot be relied on to publicize their positions, much less in a balanced and accurate way. Nor do these incumbents always give rise to issue-rich news reports and strong issue-oriented challengers. The analysis reported here is thus as much a description of how House incumbents avoid being known for their votes as it is a description of how incumbents sometimes are held accountable for these positions.

NOTES

The data used in this paper were made available in part by the Inter-university Consortium for Political and Social Research and in part by Edie Goldenberg and Michael Traugott. The data for the American National Election Study, 1978, were originally collected by the Center for Political Studies of the Institute for Social Research, The University of Michigan, under a grant from the National Science Foundation (NSF). Likewise, the Goldenberg-Traugott data were collected by them with a grant from NSF. I am grateful to Goldenberg and Traugott for making their data available to me and for advising me on how to use them. Others who generously shared their time and knowledge with me include Frank Baumgartner, Julio Borquez, Philip Converse, Timothy Cook, Fay Edwards, John Kingdon, Giovanna Morchio, Paul Raymond and Jan Vermeer. Whether any of these organizations or persons would approve of this particular synthesis, however, is a question on which further research is needed.

1. "Controlled" information means information coming directly or indirectly from one source (the incumbent). See similar usage in Abramowitz (1980) and Jacobson (1983, p. 95). However, "controlled" does not refer to the legal obstacles to having or disseminating this information that exist in some countries and that were common in the United States before the reforms of the 1970s put most congressional votes in the public domain.

2. This interpretation is not completely contrary to the first one: unrepresentativeness may well become known due to challengers and news media. However, this second interpretation suggests that unrepresentativeness makes information from these sources inevitable.

3. This expectation is based on Fiorina's (1974) assumption that incumbents would benefit from agreement with a homogeneous district, even though they would be hurt by any position in a closely divided district. This expectation also corresponds to Raymond's (1987) finding that when candidates discussed issues, they tended either to avoid specifics or to advocate specific but noncontroversial positions.

4. Neither this advertisement nor the one discussed earlier is explicitly described in either Joslyn (1987) or Goldenberg and Traugott (1987), but these investigators did facilitate my viewing tapes of these advertisements.

5. Certain races in these data sets were excluded from all or part of the analyses presented here. Races for open seats were excluded because the focus of this study is incumbents. Also, one race was excluded from the analyses predicting voter knowledge because the predictors used in these analyses concern the campaign period, and the incumbent in this race was probably well known for at least one specific position before the campaign period began. Some estimates were derived only for particular groups of incumbents, such as those who

were unrepresentative. Finally, the races for which newspaper content was unavailable were naturally excluded from the analyses of the effects or causes of this content. The forty-three races for which newspaper content was available were not a systematic subsample of the original set of races and so could not be relied on to be as nationally representative as the larger set. Moreover, after excluding races for open seats and subdividing the remaining races into groups, the number of races remaining in a single group became quite small for multivariate analysis. Therefore, the larger set of races was used to test hypotheses not involving newspaper content.

6. In addition, Mayhew (1974b) speculated that House incumbents may have become even more representative after the advent of district-level opinion polls. Also, Hale (1986) questioned whether there were any issues in 1978 that were similar to the issue of civil rights in 1958, implying that serious misrepresentation of most constituencies was no longer possible after the early 1970s since there was no issue about which they felt as strongly as they had about civil rights.

7. Studies that have exploited this characteristic of the 1978 election study include Erikson (1981) and Wattenberg (1982). In addition, the lack of systematic bias in estimates based on a group of district samples is suggested by the high correlation $(r-.89)$ between the estimated and the actual district-wide vote for Congress.

8. The inclusion of very few cases in certain categories is justified theoretically, but is it justified statistically? Since significance tests take into account whether the number of cases per category is large or small, the only problem that arises from a small number of cases in a key category is deciding on the proper test. When testing whether one category is different than another, the choice is between a difference-of-means test, such as a t-test, or a nonparametric alternative, such as the median test (Conover, 1971, chapter 4). Nonparametric tests can be useful in small samples that may not be drawn from normally distributed populations. In particular, the median test is insensitive to the value of an outlier, whereas a difference-of-means test may be unduly influenced by such a value. On the other hand, the t-test has its own virtues. Like other significance tests it does take the number of cases into account, so that different values of t are critical for different sized samples. As a result, for normal populations the t-test is as valid for samples of three as it is for samples of 3,000. Furthermore, the t-test takes more information into account than does the median test. The t-test may therefore actually be preferable in tiny samples because every piece of information is so precious that one should hesitate to discard any of it. In addition, for normal populations the t-test is more powerful than a nonparametric procedure and is therefore more likely to indicate statistical significance when warranted. Finally, the t-test is reasonably robust under many conditions, so that it is often considered advisable even when assumptions such as normality are not met (Blalock, 1972, chapters 5, 13, and 14).

The solution to this statistical problem, like the solution to many political problems, is a compromise. Neither the t-test nor the median test is indisputably preferable, although the t-test seems to have more advantages. Therefore, while the t-test will be our primary technique for evaluating regression coefficients and differences between the central tendencies of different categories, the median test will be reported as well when appropriate.

9. Respondents who had indicated that they had an opinion on the incumbent's general voting record were asked, "Was there any bill in particular that you remember how (he/she) voted on that bill?" Those answering "yes" to this question were measured as having such information. This question is valuable because it is the only one in the election study to request information this specific about incumbents' positions. Because this question is open-ended, and because those who were asked this question were members of the minority who had already passed a filter (the question about the general voting record) designed to eliminate those with nonattitudes, this question compares well with other ways of measuring whether respondents have issue information. Those answering this question "yes" were probably as well informed as those volunteering issue-based likes and dislikes of the incumbent and were probably much better informed than those who merely agreed to place the incumbent on an issue scale. Although none of these measures guarantees that the information held by respondents is correct, the validity of the measure used here is further supported by the overwhelming majority of those saying that they could remember a particular bill then going on to recall details of the bill: less than 5 percent answered "don't know" to any of a series of follow-up questions, including "What was the bill?" In comparison, 14 percent of the respondents in this survey misreported whether they voted in the 1978 general election, and other measures of participation commonly used in surveys contain 15 percent to 25 percent error (Katosh and Traugott, 1981).

10. The issue questions took the form of seven-point scales, as follows: "Some people feel that the government should solve inflation even if it means higher unemployment. Others feel that the government should solve unemployment even if it means higher inflation. Where would you place your candidate on this scale? . . . Where would you place most people in this district?" The other three domestic-issue questions posed the following three choices: (1) the government in Washington should make every possible effort to improve the social and economic position of blacks and other minority groups, or the government should not make any special effort to help minorities because they should help themselves; (2) government effort to see that everyone has a job and good standard of living, or government's letting every person get ahead on his or her own; and (3) preferential treatment for women and minorities, or a person's ability and experience should be the only consideration for hiring. The index is the average absolute value of the difference between incumbent and district on each issue. For example, differences of minus two, one, one, and one would yield an average of 1.25 (the result of five divided by four).

11. When the number of issue articles is an independent variable (as it is when the percentage recalling a vote is the dependent variable), the number of such articles was averaged across all available newspapers in a district; but when the number of issue articles is the dependent variable, this number was calculated for each newspaper-district combination. Newspaper content was coded for each major candidate according to five themes; political characteristics; personal (image) factors; campaign organization; party affiliation; and ideology, issue and group ties. Stories indicating the incumbent's issue positions were

those that had content about the incumbent's ideology, issue and group ties. The "stories" represent everything about the campaign (including news articles, opinion columns, editorials, letters and advertisements) that appeared in the selected newspapers during the weeks of October 3, October 17 and October 31, 1978. This content is equivalent to that in the 1978 Congressional Campaign Study available from the Inter-university Consortium for Political and Social Research. Evidently this content includes not only the stories from these periods used in Goldenberg and Traugott (1984) but also additional content not used in that analysis. This and the Goldenberg-Traugott content also overlap with but differ substantially from the Clarke-Evans (1982, 1983) content. For more information on these content data, see Goldenberg and Traugott (1984, especially pp. 124-33).

12. Even if candidates' emphases are not related to voters' perceptions generally (Raymond, 1983), their emphases still may be related to people's perceptions when these emphases appear not just in brochures, but also on television.

13. Managers were asked in September, "In this year's election, would you say that one candidate has a much better chance of winning, or would you say both candidates have a good chance of winning? If the election were held today, which candidate do you think would win? Would it be a close election or not close at all? On election day, do you think (same candidate) will win? Now let's think about your opponent. How much money will it cost (him/her) to run a winning campaign in this district? Do you think (he/she) will be able to raise it?" Those who anticipated that the outcome would change as a result of their campaign efforts, that the eventual outcome would be close, or that their opponent might raise enough money to win were labelled either "vulnerable" or "hopeful," depending on whether the candidate was an incumbent or a challenger. Those who indicated more certainty about the outcome were labeled either "sure winners" or "sure losers."

14. The fit between district and circulation area was calculated using county population. For more information see Goldenberg and Traugott (1984, p. 133).

15. This category consisted of two incumbents and was defined as those incumbents whose issue positions were known by at least 23 percent of the respondents in their districts.

16. An index score of greater than one defined these 25 incumbents as unrepresentative.

17. An index score of greater than two defined these three incumbents as most unrepresentative.

18. The difference between these categories is significant at the .05 level, according to a t-test. A nonparametric alternative to the t-test, the median test, characterizes this difference as not significant but does show that all three Extreme Discrepants were above the median in issue-position visibility, with an average rank of 45.2 out of 60 cases. This reassures us that there is no outlier in the Extreme Discrepant category that would have unduly influenced the t-test.

19. If one dispenses with categories altogether and calculates the correlation between knowledge and the raw representation scores, knowledge is correlated with lack of representation to a trivial degree ($r-.053$).

20. The amount of issue-oriented television advertising by the challengers

compared with relatively representative incumbents is high not only compared with the amount by other challengers, but also, surprisingly, with the amount of such advertising by these incumbents. There is both a substantive and a technical reason for this: challengers tended to emphasize issues more than did incumbents, and those few incumbents whose representativeness was not measured tended to spend more on issue-oriented commercials than did those incumbents represented in this table.

21. This refers only to television advertising. Although the amount of issue information in television news programs probably varies by area (Campbell, Alford and Henry, 1984; Goldenberg and Traugott, 1984, pp. 125-26) and has the potential to educate the electorate (Behr, 1983; Campbell et al., 1984), this amount seems to be quite small in general, even concerning the positions of senatorial candidates (Katz, 1985).

22. Although the category "Discrepants" is broader than the category "Extreme Discrepants," it still contains a fairly small number of incumbents; this plus the lack of newspaper content for half the incumbents necessitates analyzing the impacts of newspaper content separately from the impacts of incumbent and challenger commercials. Analyzing all three media variables together produced reliable estimates only when no distinction was made between representative incumbents and Discrepants. Reassuringly, these estimates (not shown) were affected very little by whether or not the newspaper and television variables were analyzed separately. In short, separation of variables was necessitated owing to separation by type of incumbent and evidently caused no problems of its own.

23. Although the estimated per-article impact for representative incumbents is only half as strong as it is for Discrepants, the difference between these estimates is not statistically significant. And although the newspaper coefficient in Table 4.4(b) is not significantly different from zero in a statistical sense, this is largely due to the fairly small number of representative incumbents for whom we have a measure of newspaper content.

24. The estimated impacts of incumbent advertising are slightly lower in Table 4.4 than in Table 4.3, but this is due only to the exclusion from Table 4.4 of those cases for which no measure of newspaper content was available. The difference is not due to controlling for the effects of newspaper content, since the estimated impact of incumbent advertising in the subset of cases in Table 4.4 is virtually the same whether or not newspaper content is controlled for.

25. Because newspaper content was shown in Table 4.4 to influence public knowledge primarily of Discrepants, the type of analysis done in Table 4.5 of influences on newspaper content was repeated after excluding those districts with incumbents who were representative. Candidates' issue emphasis remained an influence on newspaper content in the districts of Discrepants.

26. This lack of relationship has the statistical benefit that the television variables in Table 3(a) are not explaining any variance that should be explained by the omitted newspaper variable.

27. In addition to the phenomena that have definitely changed since 1978, it is also possible that issues have become more or less salient to the public. However, a change in salience may have no net impact on public information because, although it may have a positive direct impact it also may have a neg-

ative indirect impact: the public's information about incumbents' votes apparently is affected not only by the salience of the issues, but also by the unrepresentativeness of the votes, and Kingdon (1973) has shown that as the salience of an issue goes up, the likelihood of an unrepresentative vote goes down (and vice versa). This also has implications for Hale's (1986) suggestion, discussed in another footnote, that serious misrepresentation was possible in 1958 but not in 1978. Assume that civil rights in 1958 was in fact more salient than taxes, affirmative action or any other issue in 1978. As a result, no one vote would have the same impact in 1978 as did a vote on civil rights in 1958. But in addition, votes contrary to constituents' wishes may have been more common in 1978, and a string of such votes would be serious misrepresentation.

28. Although the existence of "reactive spending" (Jacobson, 1978) suggests that challenger advertising also influences incumbent advertising, challenger advertising apparently had no indirect effect on constituent information in this way. As suggested by the finding in Table 1(a) that Extreme Discrepants averaged a high amount of issue-oriented advertising despite a low amount of such advertising by their challengers, among incumbents in general there was no relationship either between incumbent and challenger advertising of this type or between incumbent and challenger commercials in general. For more on spending allocations and the limits of reactive spending, see Goldenberg and Traugott (1984, chapters 6 through 8) and Goldenberg, Traugott, and Baumgartner (1986).

5

Congressional Campaign Coverage in Rural Districts

Jan P. Vermeer

Warren Miller and Donald Stokes pointed out years ago that voters in elections for the House of Representatives responded to the candidates chiefly in terms of party identification (Stokes and Miller, 1962). In succeeding years that conclusion has been modified, with increasing attention paid, first, to the impact of incumbency on the outcome of congressional elections and, later, to other campaign-related variables that voters respond to in making their voting decisions. Whereas scholars once saw congressional elections based on factors unrelated to campaigns, they now recognize that election outcomes are also the result of factors under the control of the candidates.

Gary Jacobson has pointed out two major sets of these factors: the amount of money the challenger spends in his campaign for election and the background of the challenger (1980, 1983). The more a challenger spends, the better he does, and the more he spends, the more the incumbent must spend in order to keep his seat. And the more qualified the challenger is, the more likely it is that he can attract the substantial sums of campaign money needed to give the incumbent a close race. The money raised and spent and the strength of the candidate help account for the outcome of elections, notwithstanding the importance of incumbency and party identification.

Voters tend not to vote for congressional candidates with whose names they are unfamiliar (Mann, 1978; Hinckley, 1981). Building name recognition is therefore an important goal for candidates, a goal that a great deal of campaign money is spent to reach. One of the reasons an incumbent has such a great advantage clearly has to do with the edge in name recognition that incumbents enjoy among constituents. To overcome that edge, and therefore to have a chance to defeat an incumbent, challengers have to spend sizable sums to generate the public exposure necessary to make the electorate aware of their candidacies. Name recognition comes through effort; challengers cannot rely on party labels to see them to victory over incumbents, nor can they rely on party campaign efforts to marshal electoral support for their candidacy. They must go out to build name recognition themselves.

The preferred method for doing so is through the mass media, whether paid media (advertising) or free media (news). Challengers cannot hope, generally, to raise their name recognition high enough to overcome the advantage of incumbents merely through distributing pamphlets, canvassing neighborhoods, or putting up yard signs. All these help, but they are unlikely to be sufficient to raise name recognition to a level where a challenger is competitive with a well-entrenched incumbent. Reliance on media, then, is an imperative for challengers to congressional incumbents, just as it is an imperative for candidates for president and for governor.

CONGRESSIONAL NEWS COVERAGE

Congressional candidates generally have a difficult time with media as a means of reaching voters. The problem involves the disparity between media markets, the portion of the electorate reached by a particular media outlet, and congressional districts. Goldenberg and Traugott used the concept of "fit" in *Campaigning for Congress* to account for different strategies that candidates for Congress used in attempting to reach voters through the media: "If the fit is poor between a district's boundaries and the area served by local media outlets, then the news coverage of congressional races will be limited" (Goldenberg and Traugott, 1984, pp. 2–3). Campbell, Alford, and Henry refer to the problem as "incongruence between a media market and a congressional district" (Campbell, Alford, and Henry, 1982, p. 1). It may be worthwhile briefly to illustrate three kinds of media fit.

One is a relatively close congruence between a media market and a congressional district: the news outlets in the district reach a high proportion of the voters in the district and few voters outside it. Here media use can be efficient, since virtually everyone the candidates want to communicate with can be reached and few they do not wish to communicate with will be reached. In terms of advertising charges, the candidates do not pay for talking to voters who cannot vote for them. A second is a media market that encompasses several congressional districts at the same time. Congressional candidates in these situations can communicate with their entire potential electorate through the news outlets in that market, but they must also pay for access to a substantial number of voters who live outside their district. The third kind of media fit exists when a district contains several media markets. In order to reach all the voters, candidates must generate news coverage in two, three, or even more media markets throughout the district.

Attention in this chapter is focused on the third kind of media fit, primarily using rural districts. McNitt points out that "in larger rural districts candidates are more likely to favor media-centered campaign techniques" (McNitt, 1985, p. 268). I shall examine the news coverage generated by congressional candidates in newspapers in rural districts, for a couple of reasons. One is for convenience' sake: records of television news coverage are difficult to resurrect after the fact, but copies of newspapers can be retained and reexamined. A second concerns the fact that the newspaper is a major source of news and information for voters in rural areas for local developments (cf. research cited in Manheim [1974]).

Even though fewer congressional districts in the United States today are predominantly rural than in the past, the newspaper coverage that congressional candidates generate is still worth examining. It indicates, among other things, the publicity that can be generated in relatively favorable circumstances. Candidates for Congress in metropolitan areas cannot hope to receive extensive, daily coverage in the major urban press (and in fact many incumbents are glad of the fact). But neither is coverage in the rural press automatic. Congressional candidates will receive some ink, although not nearly the amount of space they desire. The campaign news generated in rural areas represents publicity almost impossible to generate through personal contacts, public appearances, and direct mail. Further, there is a modicum of respect accorded news coverage that advertising does not receive (Vermeer, 1982). Rural districts, then, give us an opportunity to gauge press coverage that campaigners in metropolitan districts can seldom hope to achieve.

THE DATA AND HYPOTHESES

The data come from an examination of thirty-three newspapers in small towns in rural districts in three midwestern states—Iowa, Kansas, and Nebraska. (One of these papers is published in a district that had a contest for an open seat in 1984; therefore, results comparing incumbents and challengers are based on data from thirty-two newspapers.) The newspapers were randomly selected from among the state's dailies, and news coverage in eleven congressional districts was monitored. The year selected was 1984, and all issues of the sampled newspapers from September 1 through November 6 were consulted. For several analyses of data, these papers were divided into circulation categories, using 15,000 and 10,000 as cut-off points. The picture that emerges can be expected to be different from that drawn by Clarke and Evans, who examir.ed only the largest circulation daily in each of the eighty-six districts (Clarke and Evans, 1983, p. 12).

The study addresses several main concerns. The first is simply descriptive. I shall attempt to characterize the amount of coverage (although not the content) received by candidates for the House of Representatives in rural districts. Both the frequency of news items dealing with the candidates and the space allocated them will be examined. Further, the trends over the course of the campaign in this coverage will be noted.

The second and third test hypotheses. The second concern deals with the prominence of the news coverage of incumbents and challengers. Three measures of prominence will be used. The hypothesis is that news coverage of campaigns for Congress in rural newspapers will feature incumbents more prominently than challengers.

The third concern deals with generating news coverage. Because incumbents are more newsworthy, given the office they hold, their activities are more likely to be covered. It is more difficult for challengers to generate news coverage. The hypothesis is that a lower percentage of news items dealing with incumbents are generated through a public appearance by the candidate in the circulation area of the newspaper than those dealing with challengers.

Prominence was measured in three ways. One measure was simply the page on which the item appeared. The further to the front of the newspaper, the greater prominence the item had. Because these newspapers were generally of comparable sizes (in terms of the number of pages per issue), it is unlikely that great variation in size of newspapers affected this measure. No news item was found on any page further back in a paper than page 36 (and only three items were as far back as page 30).

A second measure was the mention of the candidate's name in a headline. In effect, this measure was subdivided: On the one hand, I counted simply the number of mentions, treating all headline mentions separately. On the other hand, I measured the volume taken up by the headline, with the notion that headlines taking up greater space were more likely to be noticed by newspaper readers, even skimmers. The advantage of this measure over the ordinal method used by researchers such as Manheim (1974) is that it yields interval data. (See Vermeer and Mouer [1986] for an earlier use of this measure.)

A third variable measured how far into a news story a reader had to plunge before the candidate's name was mentioned. Under the assumption that newspapers generally used the inverted pyramid style of writing, it would be expected that the more important the candidate was to the story, the earlier he or she would be mentioned, and therefore the more prominently his or her name would appear in the story. Only the first mention of the candidate's name was coded.

For source of news stories, several categories were developed. If the story was explicitly based on a personal appearance by the candidate in the circulation area of the paper in question, or announced a forthcoming appearance, it was coded as a personal appearance story. If the story was picked up from the wire services, it was coded as a wire service story. If the story was written by a local reporter, it was called a local story. If the story was clearly based on a release issued by the candidate,[1] it was coded as a release story. Finally, editorials were coded as such.

FINDINGS

Generally, coverage of House races by rural newspapers is sparse, at best. The number of news stories about these races recalls the coverage Salmore and Salmore found in Wyoming:

In Wyoming in 1982 . . . there were races for governor, for senator, and for the one at-large (statewide) congressional seat. Both the senate and gubernatorial races received extensive front-page coverage in the three newspapers in Casper and Cheyenne. But the House race got exactly one front-page story late in the campaign, with a telling headline: "Who vs. What's His Name: Wyoming's Other Campaign." Asserting that the senatorial and gubernatorial races "are both household conversation topics and certainly issues for debate in social circles," the reporter went on to observe of the House race, "But what about Ted Hommel vs. Dick Cheney? Discussion about that contest is almost as hush-hush as hemorrhoids." (Salmore and Salmore, 1985, p. 62)

One would expect coverage in urban areas to be even lower. As early as 1974, Manheim reported that "the relative amount of congressional coverage [in newspapers] does indeed tend to increase as one moves from urbanized congressional districts to predominantly rural ones, though it remains remarkably low throughout. . . . [But] roughly twice as much newspaper coverage is devoted to the congressional campaign in rural areas as in more urbanized areas" (Manheim, 1974, p. 653).

Amount of Coverage

The sampled newspapers mentioned the local congressional candidates in a total of 475 news stories. The fourteen Kansas newspapers published 138 such stories, for an average of just under 10 stories per paper. The average for the nine Iowa papers was considerably higher: they ran 135 such items, for an average of 15 per paper. The total and the average per paper was the highest for the Nebraska press, the ten papers using a total of 202 articles, an average of just over 20 stories per paper.

No matter how one looks at these totals, it is not heavy coverage by any means. The Nebraska average of 20.2 stories means that a news item mentioning a congressional candidate appeared about twice a week during the fall months. The Kansas press ran such a story only once a week. The highest number of stories carried by any sampled paper in Kansas was eighteen (by the Dodge City *Daily Globe*), by an Iowa paper twenty-one (by the Atlantic *News Telegraph*), and by a Nebraska paper twenty-five (by the Beatrice *Sun*). The lowest numbers of items carried by papers in these states were five (the Norton, Kansas, *Daily Telegram*), eight (the Newton, Iowa, *Daily News*), and fourteen (the Columbus, Nebraska, *Telegram* and the Nebraska City *News-Press*).

The length of the stories did not make up for these scant totals. The measure I used was area, simply determined by width of the news columns multiplied by the length of the column in inches, to simplify adjustments between papers using nonstandard column widths. To convert to column inches, divide the results given here by two. The average news item mentioning a local congressional candidate was just barely more than twenty square inches in area, a mere ten column inches. The figures for Iowa and Nebraska news coverage were quite similar, both slightly under 20: 19.7 for Nebraska papers and 18.5 for Iowa papers. But the Kansas stories were strikingly longer, more than twenty-four square inches per story. For the Kansas press, length compensated somewhat for infrequent coverage, but not tremendously.

News stories mentioning incumbents substantially outnumbered items naming challengers, 380 to 280, not an unexpected margin, but certainly not an overwhelming one. Challengers managed to reap quite a bit of news coverage in the aggregate, although they still received significantly less coverage than did incumbents. Because all of the incumbents won reelection by margins of at least 60 percent, the results do not indicate that close races made these challengers more newsworthy than such challengers normally are.[2] Challengers were mentioned in the rural press in 1984. Differences between the states were minor.

More surprising is that the differences in length of the stories mentioning incumbents and those mentioning challengers were insignificant. For each group, the stories averaged approximately twenty-one square inches (21.6 for incumbents and 21.1 for challengers). In each of the three states the margin between challenger and incumbent in average space per story was small, and only in Kansas were the challengers' stories on average longer, but only 6 percent longer. Overall, this picture does not add up to an overwhelming incumbent advantage in news coverage.

If we divide the newspapers into three categories by circulation (over 15,000, between 10,000 and 15,000, and below 10,000), we find that the length of the stories mentioning local congressional candidates does not vary much among these categories, averaging 20 square inches for large, 22.5 for medium, and 19.3 for small papers. The larger the paper, however, the more stories it carried over the course of the campaign, ranging from 16.7 for the large papers through 15.5 for the medium dailies, down to 11.8 for the small papers. In all three categories, papers were more likely to carry stories mentioning the incumbent, but the difference was greatest for the small papers, which carried 66 percent more stories mentioning incumbents than challengers, compared with only 21 percent more such stories in the largest papers. The smaller the paper, the more difficult it was for challengers to get their names into print.

Coverage increased at a steady rate over the course of the campaign. For the purposes of this analysis, I divided the campaign into nine week-long periods (adding September 1 to the first week and adding the last two days of the campaign to the ninth week). The number of stories mentioning incumbents averaged 24.5 the first four weeks, increasing steadily from that point up to 74 the eighth week and 90 the last week. The number mentioning challengers was 17.5 the first four weeks, growing steadily to 54 the eighth week and 67 the ninth week. By the end of the campaign the press ran stories involving local congressional candidates four times more frequently than during September.

Stories mentioning incumbents were generally 50 percent more numerous each week than those mentioning challengers, a figure that remained remarkably constant. Increase in coverage, then, was equally distributed between incumbents and challengers. During September, a month of generally low coverage, incumbents reaped more coverage than did challengers, but although challengers got a great deal more coverage in October, they were unable to narrow the incumbents' advantage.

The same conclusions hold for the amount of space allocated to stories mentioning incumbents and challengers. Stories were generally somewhat shorter during the first six weeks of the campaign, averaging less than 18 square inches, but by the last two weeks the stories averaged approximately 24.75 square inches. The rural press saw local congressional candidates as more newsworthy toward the end of the campaign, then, as measured by frequency of news items and by the length of the stories.

Prominence

The matter of prominence is less straightforward. The first hypothesis to be tested is that stories mentioning local incumbent candidates for Congress are run on pages closer to the front of the newspaper than are stories mentioning challengers. (For two newspapers, two of the four smallest in the sample, all stories mentioning the candidates ran on the front page. There being no variation to account for, these papers are not considered in this part of the analysis.)

Overall, incumbents' news items received more prominent placement than stories mentioning challengers in sixteen of the thirty newspapers, with challengers' news articles more prominently placed in the remaining fourteen. This is an insignificant difference. The difference in placement between incumbents' and challengers' stories in each newspaper was generally rather small, with an advantage of even one page in only nine of these papers and an advantage of as much as two pages only three times.

These results, however, mask a little variation. For large papers, challengers were more likely to receive more prominent placement for their stories than were incumbents, winning in six papers and losing in four. In medium-size newspapers and in small papers incumbents received more prominent placement six out of ten times. Although, as a whole, these figures are not overwhelming, for small papers separately, the data indicate that incumbents have an opportunity to generate prominent news coverage that challengers do not share. In the small papers where challengers had the edge, the advantage averaged less than a quarter of a page, but in the small papers where incumbents had the advantage, the edge averaged more than a whole page. When we recognize that small papers tend to have fewer pages, such an advantage is sizable.

Incumbents were more frequently mentioned in the rural daily headlines. Their names appeared a total of 185 times during the campaign in the thirty-two papers included in the sample. Challengers, on the other hand, found their names in newspaper headlines only 137 times. Although this is a substantial margin for incumbents, their advantage in this measure is directly comparable to their overall advantage in the number of news stories using their names. There were approximately 57.6 percent more stories citing incumbents than there were citing challengers, and the edge here in headline mentions is 57.5 percent. A closer correspondence could not have been expected.

Two observations come to mind. The first is simply that decisions by editors to run stories and to use candidates' names in newspaper headlines are likely to be based on similar criteria. There is no reason to think, based on these results, that editors were more likely to use incumbents' names in the headlines because incumbents were more likely to be known to the readers or to be newsworthy. Rather, if the story was worth running, the name of the candidate involved, whether challenger or incumbent, was equally likely to be found in the headlines. The second is that this equal-handed treatment was no benefit to challengers. Challengers would have to outdistance incumbents tremendously in the number of headline name mentions in order to raise their name recognition factor among voters to the levels generally enjoyed by incumbents. (See Vermeer and Mouer [1986] for further discussion of this point.)

Overall, there was little difference in the prominence of the headline itself, as measured by the space it took up. For challengers and incumbents alike, the average headline mentioning their names occupied a little over three square inches of newspaper space, not a large headline by any means. If we break the newspapers down by circulation category, we find that challengers have a slight advantage in the medium-size papers, averaging three and a half square inches per headline, compared with three and a third square inches for incumbents. Again, it is a minor difference, the only interest lying in the fact that challengers were ahead. Incumbents had similar edges over challengers in large and in small daily papers. Again, the headlines mentioning challengers did not receive the prominence that would have been necessary to extensively increase their name recognition.

The final prominence measure used here was based on the inverted pyramid style of journalism. It was assumed that the more important a fact was to a news story, the more likely it would be that the reporter would refer to it early in the article. Therefore, if incumbents were more likely than challengers to be mentioned higher up in the news stories involving them, incumbents would be the beneficiaries of more prominent news coverage.

The results do not support this hypothesis. If we simply add the paragraph numbers in which the candidates' names are first mentioned, for stories citing both candidates (the lower the number, the greater the prominence), the totals are virtually identical, with challengers holding a slight edge, 890 to 910. The numbers themselves mean little; it is the margin between them that matters. And, contrary to expectations, challengers receive barely more prominent coverage.

This conclusion is buttressed by looking at the stories separately. Challengers were cited earlier in news stories fifty-three times, compared with forty-five times for incumbents. (In the other stories the candidates were first named in the same paragraph.) Again, the margin is not great, but it is in an unexpected direction. Examining large, medium-size, and small papers separately does not change the picture. Incumbents did not receive more prominent treatment within news stories than did challengers.

The reason for this nonobvious result is probably that reporters found some place in stories about challengers to mention the current office-holder. This background information would not necessarily be reported early in the story; its placement would not be important. However, stories about incumbents would be less likely to mention the challenger. A number of incumbents ignored (or tried to ignore) the challenger. Several news items were based simply on "official" congressional business. In those cases the challenger's name simply would not come up. If this interpretation is accurate, then the closeness of the scores by incumbents and challengers on this measure is in effect testimony to incumbents' strength.

Sources of News

Sources of news items mentioning local congressional candidates were divided into five categories: wire reports, locally written stories, items clearly based on news releases from the candidates, stories based on a local public appearance by the candidate, and miscellaneous items, chiefly editorials. Not all news stories could be accurately classified, but data could be gathered for 333 news items mentioning incumbents and 268 items mentioning challengers. Of course, quite a number of stories mentioned both candidates.

The hypothesis is that proportionally more stories mentioning challengers than those mentioning incumbents arise from public appearances by the candidates in the circulation area of the paper. The rationale is simply that editors tend to choose local news for their papers; when candidates come to town they are news, even though their identical comments made elsewhere would not be considered newsworthy by themselves. Incumbents, however, are more likely to be considered newsworthy whether they make public appearances in town or not.

The data support this hypothesis. More than 25 percent of news items mentioning challengers were based on their public appearances, whereas barely 20 percent of stories citing incumbents were based on such appearances. The absolute number of such news items, by the way, is slightly higher for incumbents, sixty-seven to sixty-five, no doubt reflecting an incumbent's greater ability to find appropriate forums for appearances. Incumbents' press releases resulted in a sizable news advantage, both proportionally (more than 10 percent of their coverage versus less than 6 percent for challengers) and in absolute numbers (thirty-five stories versus fifteen). But surprisingly, a larger proportion of challengers' news items came off the wires than did incumbents' articles. Perhaps this result reflects the ease with which a story citing challengers coming off the wires can be used, compared with allocating the newspaper's other resources to campaign coverage. Incumbents may be worth expending those resources—challengers can be left to the wires.

These conclusions hold for the data broken by newspaper circulation categories. For the smallest papers the proportion of stories based on candidates' public appearances yields challengers the smallest advantage, 27 percent to 25 percent, and the largest advantage for challengers comes in the largest dailies, 31 percent to 23 percent. Because none of the races in the districts covered here was close, challengers probably made most of their public appearances where more of the voters were, in the cities where the larger papers are published.

DISCUSSION AND CONCLUSION

The results found in this examination of the daily rural press in Nebraska, Iowa, and Kansas do not contradict the findings of others that incumbents benefit from news coverage patterns (Clarke and Evans, 1983; Goldenberg and Traugott, 1984). Incumbents fared well in the coverage they received in 1984. They were more frequently mentioned in headlines, they were more frequently mentioned in news stories, and they were generally more prominently featured than challengers. Further, they found it somewhat easier to generate news coverage in these dailies, being able to stimulate coverage more readily than challengers by methods other than public appearances. Campbell, Alford, and Henry's point that "it is to the incumbent's advantage to run in an incongruent district" (Campbell, Alford, and Henry, 1982, p. 7) clearly applies to these rural districts, none of which fits well with one media market.

That is, however, not to say that challengers were mistreated by the press. Challengers received substantial coverage, even though it was less than that received by incumbents. But in only a few cases was a paper's coverage almost entirely concerned with the incumbent and his campaign. Challengers managed to stimulate some press coverage of their campaigns, even though they were more likely to have to resort to making public appearances to do so. The treatment they received was not as prominent as the treatment accorded incumbents, but it was not disproportionately less prominent. They were virtually as likely to have their names in the headlines and their names mentioned high in news stories as were incumbents; the incumbents' edges in these regards generally reflected their greater ability to attract news coverage (an ability Clarke and Evans say reflects their "special access to the press" [1983, p. 70]).

But for challengers to have made a strong run at the incumbents in these races, they needed to do much better in attracting news coverage. It is not enough to come close to getting the ink the incumbents do—it is not enough to receive as prominent a play in the headlines and in the news stories themselves as incumbents do. To come out even with incumbents in these matters is enough only if it occurs at a much higher level. It is enough only if there is so much news coverage that the incumbents' edges in name recognition can begin to be overcome. The situation is parallel to Jacobson's (1978) argument about challenger spending in elections. It is not enough merely to spend at a level equal to the incumbent's, if the level generally is low. If the challenger is to overcome the incumbent's advantage, his spending must far exceed the incumbent's, or at least be so high that he can successfully make his name known throughout the district.

Here the level of news coverage for challengers to accomplish this goal was too low. When the coverage is at the level found here, it does not really matter whether incumbents or challengers received marginally better treatment at the hands of reporters, editors, or headline writers. The differences are not enough to make a dent in the advantage incumbents enjoy. Only at a higher level of coverage would challengers have had the chance to make an impact.

But challengers can do more to overcome their handicaps. In rural districts, it seems, challengers can generate news coverage through personal appearances. The rural press still seems to follow the pattern for country newspapers cited long ago by Charles Allen: "getting all the local news" (Allen, 1928, p. 17). And a local appearance is local news. There was no way to be sure, but I gather that virtually all the public appearances made by congressional candidates were covered by the local daily. Reaching out to voters, even in the media age, can lead to greater press coverage.

The coverage accorded these races does not correspond to the model of media politics Christopher Arterton describes in *Media Politics* (Arterton, 1984). There he argues that presidential campaigning, at least, is conducted through the media, and that the media are the means whereby the candidates communicate with each other, making accusations and answering charges. Raymond's study of candidates' campaign brochures also found "parallel campaigning."[3] There was little indication in the coverage reviewed for this analysis that the rural press in Nebraska, Kansas, and Iowa functioned in this manner. The press was very much an outside force in the campaigns, not an integral part of the process. And yet for an effective dialogue between incumbent and challenger to ensue, so that voters can choose reasonably well (according to the criteria that voters themselves have in mind), some intermediary must facilitate such interaction. The press can perform this function—they can do more than merely report what occurs when a candidate visits. By seeking out candidates and confronting each with the statements of the other, the press can make available to the voters the information they need to choose. The current pattern benefits incumbents needlessly. The onus for change does not fall only on politicians.

NOTES

1. The news stories in question did not explicitly cite a press release as the source for the item; however, the style of the articles is a strong indication that a release was the basis. Such stories frequently carry an out-of-town dateline, but no date, no reporter by-line, and no wire service designation. They typically report an announcement or development, quote the candidate in the second or third paragraph, and conclude with background facts. For a look at different kinds of uses newspapers make of campaign press releases, see Vermeer (1982).

2. The research on the invisibility of House challengers is extensive. For a representative reference, see Hinckley (1981).

3. See Paul Raymond's essay (1987).

6

The Scribes of Texas: Newspaper Coverage of the 1984 U.S. Senate Campaign

Jon F. Hale

MASS MEDIA AND SENATE ELECTIONS

In competitive campaigns for the U.S. Senate, particularly those in geographically large and heavily populated states, newspapers play a key role in providing the information necessary for citizens to make their voting decisions (see Westlye, 1983; Hibbing and Brandes, 1983; Dodd, 1981). Candidate advertising also plays a key role, but because it is so obviously biased and superficial, it cannot provide the quality information that an unbiased medium can (see Joslyn, 1980; 1984, p. 46; Elebash and Rosene, 1982; Patterson, 1980). In most states, daily newspapers are the only mass medium providing substantive and unbiased information on Senate campaigns. Local television news programs are heavy on soft news, while radio news comes in occasional bursts of brief headline reading (see Leary, 1977).

Certainly candidates believe that this type of coverage is important. In fact, competitive campaigns for the U.S. Senate are planned with an eye toward press coverage. Press secretaries for two of the candidates in the 1984 Texas Democratic senatorial primary wrote: "In Texas, perhaps more than any other state, political candidates rise and fall on their press coverage. . . . [E]ven well-heeled candidates must rely heavily on good press coverage—in addition to paid political ads—for exposure" (Vest and Paul, 1984, p. 18).

Candidates and their strategists know that, to a significant extent, most campaign events do not enter into voters' minds until those events have been mediated by the press (Denton and Woodward, 1985, pp. 151–59). For example, the two candidates in the 1984 Texas Senate race met in a debate televised on a statewide educational television network at the same time that *Dallas* was making its season premiere. Obviously only a fraction of voters saw the debate in person, and even the television audience was small. Yet neither campaign could discount the debate because it was sure to be well covered by the press.

To support their contention that they are unbiased, newspapers point to the journalist's professional norm of objectivity, which is said to ensure "fair" and "unbiased" coverage of campaigns. This research shall examine the extent to which this practice of objectivity provides substantive information to the citizen who seeks to make an informed choice at the ballot box.

What does "substantive information" mean? On the one hand, it may simply mean an accurate accounting of the facts, which in a campaign would include reporting on candidates' appearances, statements, and strategies. Citizens would then have "the facts" and would be left on their own to interpret and analyze them.

On the other hand, it may be that "substantive information" requires that reporting include explanation and analysis beyond the simple realm of facts. Today more than ever, campaigns are managed events—managed for the press. Thus simple reporting of the facts amounts to little more than the recitation of official statements made by the competing campaigns. Although the method of reporting these official positions may be unbiased, or objective, in the sense that reporters assiduously allow each camp a relatively equal share of coverage, the resulting news stories contain "facts" manufactured by the campaigns themselves and designed to favor their view of the world.

This research will examine press coverage of a Senate campaign by taking two paths. The first path assumes that the coverage is rooted in the objective method of reporting the facts as enunciated by the candidates. It then looks at what kinds of facts, or what types of subjects, are covered. In fact, most research on the content of press coverage does just that.

The major categories are coverage of the campaign as a contest, or "horserace," coverage of the candidates' personal and professional characteristics and qualifications for office, and coverage of public policy issues (Tidmarch and Karp, 1983; Tidmarch, Hyman and Sorkin, 1984; Tidmarch, 1985; Goldenberg and Traugott, 1985b). At the very least we would hope that coverage of public policy issues would be extensive and that coverage of candidate characteristics and qualifications would be adequate, particularly at a time when parties have less ability to vouch for their candidates. Unfortunately most previous research has found that reporting the "horserace" is the most prominent form of coverage.

The second path this research takes assesses the extent to which coverage goes beyond simple reporting of the facts as given by the candidates to a more detailed explanation of the issues in the campaign. This type of coverage need not carry the journalist away from the professional norm of objectivity. It may simply require finding an unbiased source or conducting background research, often in the public record, in order to provide readers with some sort of context for understanding the facts as given by the candidates. Further, it may not be too much to expect that, on occasion, a reporter who is knowledgeable about the campaign and the issues will step out of the realm of objectivity long enough to present an analysis of what is going on in the campaign.

In order to provide further insight into the role of the press in Senate campaigns, I have selected for a case study the press coverage of the 1984 Texas U.S. Senate campaign for the seat vacated by four-term Republican John Tower. This campaign fits the conditions under which press coverage is likely to be the most important: a hard-fought competitive race for an open seat in a geographically large and heavily populated state.

THE 1984 TEXAS U.S. SENATE RACE

The Texas Senate race pitted Republican U.S. representative Phil Gramm of College Station against Democratic state senator Lloyd Doggett of Austin. Gramm, a forty-two-year-old former Texas A&M economics professor, was a three-term congressman from the Sixth District, a sprawling rural district that stretches from the outskirts of Dallas to the outskirts of Houston. Gramm was a Democrat until he switched parties in 1983, after the House Democratic leadership stripped him of his seat on the Budget Committee for siding with, and providing confidential information to, House Republicans supporting President Reagan's first budget. Gramm, who co-sponsored the 1981 Reagan tax cut legislation, had an extremely conservative voting record in Congress. Gramm handily defeated three opponents for the Republican nomination. His dominant campaign themes emphasized his close ties to Reagan and his conservative views being similar to those of most Texans.

Doggett, a thirty-eight-year-old Austin attorney, was a five-term state senator with a reputation for being a progressive and a consumer watchdog in the cliquish Texas Senate. His path to the nomination was perilous. When he announced his candidacy, before Senator Tower had announced his retirement, Doggett was a decided underdog. The early front-runner for the Democratic nomination was the man Tower had narrowly defeated in 1978, Bob Krueger, a moderate-to-conservative former congressman and ambassador from New Braunfels. Also in the race was U.S. representative Kent Hance, a conservative from the small West Texas city of Lubbock. Hance has subsequently become a Republican. With Krueger and Hance to his right, Doggett became the "liberal" candidate in the primary. The primary was extremely close, with Doggett and Hance eliminating Krueger from contention. Only about 2,000 votes out of nearly 1.4 million cast separated the three candidates. With the man in the middle eliminated, Hance and Doggett fought it out in the run-off. When the dust had settled Doggett emerged the nominee by another razor-thin margin: 1,345 votes out of nearly a million cast.

Nicknamed "Landslide Lloyd," Doggett entered the general election campaign with several distinct disadvantages. First, the primary had positioned him as a liberal candidate in a predominantly conservative state. His nomination demonstrated only that the Texas Democratic party was nearly equally split among liberals, moderates, and conservatives. To win a general election, however, Doggett would have to deemphasize ideology. A second problem was Walter Mondale. The presence of an unpopular liberal heading the ticket would make it difficult for Doggett to shake his liberal image. Third, Phil Gramm proudly wore the conservative label and embraced the popular Ronald Reagan at every opportunity. Finally, aside from Jesse Helms, Gramm was the best-financed Senate candidate in the nation.

Doggett, nonetheless, gamely tried to turn these disadvantages to his favor by emphasizing that the race was between himself, "David," who represented the hardworking, self-reliant Texan, and "Goliath" Gramm, who represented the interests of the goliath corporations and privileged interests. Gramm would counter Doggett's "David and Goliath" routine by pointing out that "David" Doggett was himself a millionaire.

The general election campaign was nasty and hard fought. The level of discussion of public policy issues was not elevated by any stretch of the imagination. Much time and attention was focused on the candidates' television advertisements and various personal charges the candidates made against each other. Although most observers figured the race to be close, Gramm consistently led opinion polls and convincingly won the election, taking 59 percent of the vote.

THE DATA: A CONTENT ANALYSIS

The data for this study include newspaper articles appearing in six Texas dailies during the general election period, September 1, 1984, to November 6, 1984, and interviews with reporters who covered the campaign for four of these newspapers. The newspapers selected represent different geographical areas of the state, different size media markets and circulations. In all, 366 news stories, editorials, and commentaries were examined for this project. The analysis below is based on the 338 news stories about the campaign. A content analysis of these stories allows us to describe the nature of press coverage. The interviews with reporters will help us to explain the coverage.

OVERALL COVERAGE

The two largest circulation newspapers, the *Dallas Morning News* and the *Houston Post*, ran the most stories on the campaign, but the smallest paper, the *Amarillo Daily News* and Sunday *News-Globe*, ranked third of six in total coverage. The Amarillo, Austin, El Paso, and San Antonio papers ran similar amounts of stories, between forty-five and fifty. The *Dallas Morning News* displayed the campaign on the front page thirteen times—much more often than any of the other papers. In contrast, the campaign made the front page only once in the *El Paso Times* and the *San Antonio Express-News*.

COVERING THE CONTEST

In order to determine the primary thematic focus of coverage, articles were classified exclusively into one of the following four categories:

1. *Contest*: coverage of candidate public appearances, crowd size and response, polls, finances, advertising, endorsements (when not illuminated by issue content), voter mood and turnout predictions, general campaign strategy, "insider" analyses of campaign, and campaign issues (controversies devoid of issue content)
2. *Candidate Characteristics*: coverage of candidates' personality, family, background, qualification for office, and career
3. *Issues*: coverage of public policy issues
4. *Mixed*: coverage for which it was impossible to ascertain a single primary thematic focus. These articles were coded as "Contest/Candidate Characteristics," "Contest/Issues," "Candidate Characteristics/Issues," or "All."

More than 60 percent of the articles about the campaign in the six newspapers were focused on the contest (see Table 6.1). Contest coverage in four of the papers ranged between 64.4 and 71.9 percent but was much less frequent in two other papers. The smallest paper, the *Amarillo Daily News* and Sunday *News-Globe*, devoted barely more than one-third (34 percent) of its coverage to the campaign as contest, whereas the two largest circulation papers, Dallas and Houston, devoted at least 70 percent of their coverage to the campaign as contest.

Jon F. Hale

Table 6.1
Thematic Focus of Articles

Newspaper	Contest		Candidate Characteristics		Issues		Mixed		Total
	#	%	#	%	#	%	#	%	#
Amarillo Daily News	17	34.0	9	18.0	18	36.0	6	12.0	50
Austin American-Statesman	24	51.1	6	12.8	11	23.4	6	12.8	47
Dallas Morning News	59	70.2	4	4.8	15	17.9	6	7.1	84
El Paso Times	29	64.4	3	6.7	13	28.9	0		45
Houston Post	46	71.9	5	7.8	11	17.2	2	3.1	64
San Antonio Express-News	32	66.7	1	2.1	13	27.1	2	4.2	48
Total	207	61.2	28	8.3	81	24.0	22	6.5	338

Source: Computed by author.

Sixty-three percent of front-page coverage was focused on the campaign as a contest. In contrast, only 8.6 percent of front-page coverage focused on issues. Front-page play was generally reserved for features on how the campaign was progressing and for out-of-the-ordinary campaign events or controversies. For example, two newspapers gave front-page coverage to the mayor of Boston's response to a derisive remark made by candidate Gramm about Boston. Four of the six papers provided front-page coverage to the candidates' "negotiations" in late October for a truce on negative campaigning. At one point Doggett taped a phone conversation he had with Gramm that Gramm abruptly ended by hanging up. It all made for an exciting story—and front-page play.

As the example above demonstrates, one easy explanation for the frequency of contest coverage is simply that contest stories often contain the attributes of good news stories. "Horse-race" coverage highlights the intrigue of campaign strategy and the sport of winning and losing. And as campaigns have become more lengthy, more space has been created for contest coverage because the substance of political campaigns has remained about the same (Patterson, 1980, p. 30). The reporters, however, indicated that at least three areas of contest coverage are newsworthy because they contain information that informed voters ought to know about the campaign.

First, contest stories on campaign finances are important for citizens to learn the source of a candidate's funding. These sources clue voters in on what kinds of groups support the candidates. Whether or not a candidate is following Federal Election Commission reporting guidelines reflects on the candidate's character and qualification for office. Said one reporter: "Where [the candidates] are getting their money from is important. . . . I'm interested in looking at the campaign from different aspects, like the candidate's money and finances."

Second, contest stories that chronicle candidates' daily campaign activities without detailing issues are important because they convey a sense of what the candidate is like and how the campaign is progressing. "I try to convey the flavor of a candidate's character in my stories," said one reporter. "I want to know something about their character. Would I trust my life to this man?" said another.

Traveling with the candidates provides the opportunity for reporters to get a close-up view of what the candidates are like. Although such travel allows for contest stories that reflect on candidate character, it inhibits incisive issue coverage because of time limitations. The travel often provides "no new issues," but it gives reporters "a good chance to assess the character of the candidates—how they handle things like crowd response or being behind schedule." Travel gives reporters "a visceral feeling of what [candidates] are like."

Finally, much of the contest coverage centered on the candidates' advertising campaigns. All the reporters indicated that television was "the name of the game" in Texas statewide races. Paid media "sets the whole agenda" for the campaign, said one reporter. "TV is the biggest part of the campaign, especially in Texas," claimed another. Still another stated that a candidate with the resources to run an effective advertising campaign can "adjust the torque" of the campaign to his liking. "We wanted to cover the media advertising, to act a sort of a truth squad for what they were saying in their ad campaigns . . . because we're not what decides elections, TV does that." Thus coverage of what the candidates were doing and saying in their advertising campaigns was deemed extremely newsworthy by reporters. As the only substantive outlet for objective news on the campaign, it was the press' job to act as a "truth squad" for the claims made by candidates in their advertising.

COVERING THE ISSUES

Articles with public policy issues as their primary thematic focus constituted only 24 percent of total coverage. When we analyze the issue content in each article, regardless of its primary thematic focus, we find a great deal more issue coverage than the primary thematic focus categories divulge. In order to determine the extent of issue coverage, articles were placed exclusively into one of the following categories:

0. *None*: articles containing no mention of public policy issues.

1. *Peripheral*: articles containing passing mentions of issues or candidates' positions on issues without any extra information or explanation provided by the reporter

2. *Reportorial*: articles containing reporter's quotes or paraphrases of what a candidate or his supporters said about issues without any extra information or explanation of the issues provided by the reporter

3. *Explanatory*: articles containing extra information provided by the reporter that supplies context for understanding the issue, by explaining either the issues or the candidate's position on the issue

4. *Analytic*: articles containing analysis provided by the reporter on issues, either by discussing the implications of issue positions for public policy, for the voters, or for the campaign, or by comparing the positions of candidates in such a manner as to give a clear understanding of the similarities or differences in their positions

Some articles with issue content contained different treatments of different issues. When this occurred the article was coded into the more comprehensive category. For example, if an article contained a peripheral mention of one issue but an explanatory treatment of another issue, it was coded "Explanatory."

Analytic issue content is most likely to occur in commentaries and editorials. News stories present more problems as to the distinction between explanatory and analytic issue content. The critical distinction is whether a story goes beyond the simple inclusion of contextual information that helps the reader understand what is being discussed to the inclusion of information on the implications of what is being discussed on public policy, groups of voters, or the campaign itself.

As indicated in Table 6.2, two-thirds of the articles contained some mention of issues. Nineteen percent of the articles, however, mentioned issues only peripherally. Articles that either did not mention issues or mentioned issues only in passing accounted for 51.1 percent of the total. In all but the Amarillo paper, articles containing no mention or simply peripheral mentions of issues constituted at least 46 percent of total coverage. The largest and smallest circulation newspapers covered issues the most extensively, when actual number of articles is taken into account. Nonetheless, we see that the more frequent overall coverage of the *Dallas Morning News* was largely geared toward coverage of the campaign as "contest." Thirty-four more stories appeared in the *Dallas Morning News* than in the *Amarillo Daily News*, yet the number of articles

Table 6.2
Issue Content of Articles

Newspaper	None		Peripheral		Reportorial		Explanatory		Analytic		Total
	#	%	#	%	#	%	#	%	#	%	#
Amarillo Daily News	12	24.0	4	8.0	19	38.0	9	18.0	6	12.0	50
Austin American-Statesman	18	38.3	7	14.9	15	31.9	5	10.6	2	4.2	47
Dallas Morning News	28	33.3	21	25.0	20	23.8	13	15.5	2	2.4	84
El Paso Times	16	35.5	9	20.0	16	35.5	4	8.8	0		45
Houston Post	20	31.2	16	25.0	17	26.6	10	15.6	1	1.6	64
San Antonio Express-News	15	31.2	7	14.6	23	47.9	3	6.2	0		48
Total	109	32.2	64	18.9	110	32.5	44	13.0	11	3.2	338

Source: Computed by author.

containing reportorial, explanatory, or analytic treatments of issues in the two papers was similar: thirty-five and thirty-four stories, respectively. Although most of the substantive issue content in each newspaper was straight reporting, the *San Antonio Express-News* displayed the greatest affinity for that type of coverage. At least part of this was due to the *Express-News'* reliance on wire service stories in its coverage. Practically all wire service coverage that dealt at all with issues was peripheral or reportorial.

More than half (51.7 percent) of the articles focusing primarily on the contest contained some issue content, and 27.1 percent of contest articles contained more than simple passing mentions of issues. This evidence, presented in Table 6.3, suggests that even though the press emphasizes the contest rather than the issues, it is impossible to cover a campaign without touching on issues. The implication is that readers, at minimum, are kept aware of issues through press coverage of the campaign.

Obviously it is in articles that have issues as their primary thematic focus that we would expect to find at least some explanatory or analytic

Table 6.3
Issue Content in "Contest" Articles

Newspaper	None		Peripheral		Reportorial		Explanatory		Analytic		Total
	#	%	#	%	#	%	#	%	#	%	#
Amarillo Daily News	10	58.8	1	5.9	5	29.4	1	5.9	0		17
Austin American-Statesman	14	58.3	5	20.8	4	16.7	1	4.2	0		24
Dallas Morning News	27	45.8	18	30.5	8	13.6	5	8.5	1	1.7	59
El Paso Times	16	55.2	7	24.1	5	17.2	1	3.4	0		29
Houston Post	18	39.1	13	28.3	11	23.9	4	8.7	0		46
San Antonio Express-News	15	46.9	7	21.9	9	28.1	1	3.1	0		32
Total	100	48.3	51	24.6	42	20.3	13	6.3	1	0.5	207

Source: Computed by author.

treatments of issues. As Table 6.4 indicates, issue articles most often contained reportorial treatments of issues. The papers varied a great deal in their explanatory and analytic treatments of issues. In its articles focusing on issues, the *Houston Post* was more explanatory and analytic than reportorial. In contrast, nearly all of the articles focusing on issues in the El Paso and San Antonio papers were reportorial.

When treating issues in news stories, reporters tend to report what a candidate or his surrogate says about the issues. The reportorial mode, the most frequent type of issue coverage, allows the candidates to emphasize what they want about issues. It also puts the burden of refuting claims made about issues on the candidates. It requires the reporter only to be a "scribe," a chronicler of the day's events.

Explanatory and analytic treatments of issues require prior knowledge of the context surrounding an issue and often require research. Because reporters are limited by news space and deadline pressures, it is not surprising that only a small percentage of issue coverage provides analysis of issues. As we saw earlier, only 13 percent of the stories were explanatory and 3 percent were analytic.

Table 6.4
Issue Content in "Issue" Articles

Newspaper	None		Peripheral		Reportorial		Explanatory		Analytic		Total
	#	%	#	%	#	%	#	%	#	%	#
Amarillo Daily News	0		0		12	50.0	6	25.0	6	25.0	24
Austin American-Statesman	0		0		10	66.7	3	20.0	2	13.3	15
Dallas Morning News	0		1	5.0	11	55.0	7	35.0	1	5.0	20
El Paso Times	0		0		11	84.6	2	15.4	0		13
Houston Post	0		0		6	46.1	6	46.1	1	7.7	13
San Antonio Express-News	0		0		11	84.6	2	15.4	0		13
Total	0		1	1.0	61	62.2	26	26.5	10	10.2	98

Source: Computed by author.

Reporters provided several related explanations for why issue coverage was not incisive. First, although reporters would like to improve issue coverage, they remain, to a large extent, scribes. They are concerned with reporting the daily events of the campaign. Their stories provide the permanent, written record of the campaign. Although reporters believe that television advertising and, to a lesser extent, television news are more important to the general public than newspapers, they see their chronology as important in other ways. For example, according to one reporter, newspaper coverage of the campaign serves as an informational tool for opinion leaders and as a daily "assignment sheet" for television stations.

Second, reporters remain a competitive lot. Their competitiveness is largely based on the fear of being "scooped." They generally thought traveling with the candidates was necessary because "everybody else was doing it, and if we weren't there, we wouldn't get those stories." Within the time and space constraints, most stories must consist of describing the day's events, complete with candidate quotes on issues, if there happened to be any that day.

Third, it is extremely difficult for reporters to get candidates to stray from their well-rehearsed statements on issues. "Candidates have their pat answers that it's hard to shake them out of," explained one reporter. This being the case, reporters who continue to report candidate issue positions run the risk of being used. In a paid advertisement a candidate can repeat over and over simple statements on issues, but should a candidate be able to accomplish the same thing in the news? Clearly reporters think not. Said one reporter, "The first time through, I let them basically say what they wanted, so as to eliminate any question of bias. But when an issue got repetitious, I dropped it. We didn't want to be used as a sounding board."

Candidates often try to keep "old" issues in the news by coming up with gimmicks or symbols to dramatize their positions. This leads reporters to use their space to report on the gimmickery rather than on the substance of the issue, which is often mentioned peripherally. A candidate may also keep an issue in the news by hurling charges at his opponent over issue positions. This spawns as "action-reaction" situation whereby the reporter is, more or less, obligated to write a story that merely quotes what each side says about an issue. Explained one reporter: "Issue coverage had a lot of action-reaction because much of what candidates said on issues was based on charges of the opponent."

Perhaps the biggest problem for reporters covering issues is the difficulty of doing effective research. One reporter explained the problem this way: "We could spend days going over candidates' records but there is a lot of ambiguity and newspapers just don't have time to do it." Another said, "We'll often ask our Washington bureau to check something out for us but with all the votes and votes on amendments and everything, it's hard to figure out exactly what's going on. The other guy always has an explanation." And when "the other guy" has an explanation, reporters are obligated to report it, regardless of its truth value.

Thus reporters have little time or space in their coverage of issues to provide much information other than what the candidates say. One implication, generally agreed on by the reporters, is that candidates are allowed to control the agenda of issues discussed in the campaign. They also agreed that the "general tone and content" of candidate appeals are communicated by means of media advertising. The nature of these appeals is determined by the candidate's private polling operations, not on some set issue agenda. What is left for reporting is often "action-reaction" stories consisting of candidates trading barbs over something said in an ad.

STATEWIDE VERSUS LOCAL MEDIA

Texas has its own "prestige" media. Newspapers from Dallas–Fort Worth, Houston, and Austin generally constitute the "statewide" press, and papers in other cities and towns constitute the "local" press. The Dallas, Houston, and Austin papers in this study covered the campaign from a general, statewide perspective, and the other three covered the campaign from a decidedly local angle.

Reporters for the statewide press thought it was their job to report on the entire campaign because the local press covered the race from a limited perspective and tended to be less critical of the candidates. Not surprisingly, candidates spent much of their time outside the state's largest media markets and inside the state's secondary media markets. By doing this, candidates can be sure to get local coverage and, at least in the final weeks when the statewide press goes "on the bus" with the candidates, statewide coverage as well.

Statewide candidates avoid the big cities because it's difficult to get in the paper and almost impossible to get on local TV unless you're caught doing something illegal.
So they go to secondary markets where the local press is flattered. They get on local TV news, which is the main thing, and they get a spot in the local paper, which is a bonus. Candidates show up, say what they want, get on TV and in the paper. The statewide reporters ask more astute questions.

The Austin, Dallas, and Houston papers each sent reporters out on the campaign trail to cover the final weeks of the campaign, while the Amarillo, El Paso, and San Antonio papers relied on wire services, mostly Associated Press, to provide nonlocal coverage of the race. Because wire service stories tend to steer clear of explanatory or analytic treatments of issues in order to live up to standards of objectivity, and because much of the total coverage in the local papers is made up of wire copy, we would not expect coverage to be as incisive in the local papers as in the statewide papers. Reporters for local papers, whether they are in large or secondary media markets, are not involved in the campaign on a daily basis and may lack the ability to offer explanatory or analytic insights on the campaign. This appears to be the case for the El Paso and San Antonio papers, which ran only seven explanatory and no analytic stories between them—6 percent of their combined coverage. In contrast, 17 percent of articles appearing in statewide papers were explanatory or analytic. Only four wire service articles, 3 percent, were explanatory and none analytic.

In contrast, we have the case of the *Amarillo Daily News*, the smallest circulation paper in the sample. Although smaller papers were proba-

Table 6.5
Wire Service Coverage

Newspaper	Number of Wire Service Articles	Percentage of Total Coverage
"Statewide" Press		
Austin <u>American–Statesman</u>	4.5*	9.6
Dallas <u>Morning News</u>	5.5	6.5
Houston <u>Post</u>	4	6.3
Total "Statewide"	14	7.2
"Local" Press		
Amarillo <u>Daily News</u>	27	54.0
El Paso <u>Times</u>	19	42.2
San Antonio <u>Express–News</u>	15.5	32.3
Total "Local"	61.5	43.0

* Articles in which some wire copy was included along with staff-written copy were classified as half wire service articles and half staff-written articles.

<u>Source:</u> Computed by author.

bly less likely to cover the campaign comprehensively, their "smallness" gives them an opportunity to cover local issues in some detail. The *Amarillo Daily News* is a good example. The Amarillo coverage was found to be more issue-oriented than any other paper's coverage. This is not because the paper, which is an example of "local" press in a "secondary" market, covered all issues extensively, but because the paper covered two issues extensively that were of particular importance to the area: agriculture and the siting of a nuclear waste repository.

Whereas economic, social security, and defense/foreign policy issues were the issues covered most frequently by the five other papers, the Amarillo focus was on the two local issues, even though it provided coverage of the others as well. Seven articles appeared in the *Amarillo Daily News* that were explanatory or analytic on the nuclear waste repository siting issue and another four appeared on agriculture-related issues.

The paper used the Associated Press wire for general statewide campaign stories, which freed its own reporters to cover the race in West Texas. Explained the reporter who wrote most of the stories on the campaign for the Amarillo paper: "My strategy was to cover the candidates like a blanket when they were in West Texas. My primary goal was to focus on issues of importance to the Panhandle, mainly agriculture issues. I know the copy editors would pick up stories of what was going on elsewhere in the state."

This reporter found himself setting the agenda for the candidates, or reminding them of the agenda, when they would visit West Texas. The candidates would try to focus on regional interests during their visits but, according to the reporter, neither was comfortable with agriculture issues. "I had to pin them down on agriculture," he said. "Both were more than happy to talk about nuclear waste policy though." Clearly this reporter took advantage of his position as a local reporter covering the campaign. The coverage in the Amarillo paper was certainly not "easy" on the candidates; rather, it was quite informative on the issue of particular importance to the region, while wire service stories kept readers apprised of what was going on elsewhere in the state.

CONCLUSIONS

Aside from variation in the amount and quality of information on the campaign available to citizens in different newspaper circulation areas, this research reveals that the amount of issue coverage is low relative to total coverage and that reporters, most of the time, report "just the facts" as provided by the competing campaigns. Although the amount of issue content found in press coverage is about what previous research would lead us to expect, most of it was reportorial quotes of candidates' pat issue positions, with little explanation or analysis to illuminate the issues. Thus we find that the most traveled path to providing substantive information to readers is the well-worn path of the scribe, dutifully reporting the facts as given to him by the campaigners. There were, however, some detours taken to the path of explanation and analysis. It is difficult to say whether the amount of issue coverage and of explanatory and analytic treatments of issues was enough. Indeed, it may not take many such articles to adequately put the campaign into perspective for readers. But few, including the reporters interviewed for this research, would deny that there is room for improvement.

The "Amarillo difference" found in this study suggests that, in some respects, smaller papers may have an advantage covering issues in campaigns. The Amarillo paper took advantage of its limited resources by relying on wire service copy for general statewide coverage in order to free its reporters to focus on issues of importance to the people of West Texas. The result was in-depth coverage of two key issues for the area.

Although we should not expect every small paper to follow this pattern, neither should we automatically assume that coverage in smaller papers is inferior to coverage in larger papers. Rather, smaller papers have perhaps more of an opportunity to follow the Amarillo pattern than do larger papers. This is because larger papers often circulate among a heterogeneous population for which it may be difficult to discern and focus on a few key issues.

The barrier to improving issue coverage consists of a mixture of institutional, professional, and candidate constraints. News organizations do not spend the time and money necessary for detailed research on issues for campaigns. Campaign reporters face strenuous deadline and news space pressures that mitigate against more detailed coverage. Because journalists are expected to play the role of the scribe, much coverage is focused on chronicling the campaign's daily events. This leads to superficial issue coverage as reporters simply chronicle candidates' quotes. Candidates seldom stray from their long-memorized scripts of issue positions, which often serves to obfuscate issues rather than illuminate them. Of course, this is the goal of most candidates—to avoid offending groups of voters by taking vague issue positions in order to appeal to the greatest number.

Because candidates take vague issue positions from which reporters cannot shake them, and because reporters do not have the resources necessary to do detailed research on issues, journalists look for other clues that may illuminate the campaign. This often leads to "contest" coverage, as reporters look at a candidate's finances, endorsements, and advertising ethics. This type of coverage gives voters useful cues about candidates but does little to illuminate public policy issues.

One implication of this type of coverage is that the press focus is on "politics" rather than on "policy" (cf. Hart et al., 1984; Carey, 1976). The political reality created from this type of political coverage is that to really understand public policy issues, one must know the political reasons that politicians have for their issue positions rather than the substantive merits of competing policy choices. To really understand a political campaign, one must know about campaign strategy and tactics, about finances and polls, rather than which candidate is being misleading on an issue or, perhaps most important, whether any significant differences exist between the candidates on their issue positions.

Another implication of this type of coverage is that the press generally does not set a campaign agenda that differs markedly from the candidates' agendas. Although we would have to examine campaign literature and interview candidates or their strategists to be sure, it is apparent from the content analysis and the interviews with reporters that the issues on which the press focused were the issues on which the candidates focused—and on which the candidates chose to focus. For the most part, candidates not only set the agenda, but the press allowed candidates' television advertising campaigns to set the agenda of much of its coverage. Thus two issues mentioned often in the press coverage were gay rights and social security, two issues featured in the candidates' advertising campaigns. Most coverage of these issues was peripheral.

The reporters interviewed indicated that they would like to cover issues more effectively but had few definite ideas about how they could do it. One suggested, somewhat halfheartedly, that the best way to improve issue coverage would be for a newspaper to focus on ten issues or so and provide plenty of space in which to explain the issue and present candidate positions. But within current institutional and professional constraints, journalists can do little to improve issue coverage. Any initiative must come from news organizations, to appropriate more resources to the task of explaining and analyzing policy issues in a campaign, or from candidates, to elevate the level of public policy discussion in their campaigns. This is not an encouraging prospect.

NOTE

This chapter is a revised version of a paper prepared for delivery at the Dwight P. Griswold–E. C. Ames Conference on Mass Media and Congressional Elections, Nebraska Wesleyan University, March 7–9, 1986, Lincoln, Nebraska. I would like to thank G. Cleveland Wilhoit, Linda C. Thomas, Carolyn L. Cooke, and participants in the Griswold–Ames Conference for their helpful suggestions and assistance on this project.

7

Mass Media Effects on Recognizing and Rating Candidates in U.S. Senate Elections

Edie N. Goldenberg and Michael W. Traugott

Models of congressional voting behavior are largely based on studies of elections to the U.S. House of Representatives. Our understanding of Senate elections is much less developed, largely because of a scarcity of appropriate data for studying them. One source of information on voters' knowledge and evaluations of Senate candidates is the 1978 American National Election Study, which included a series of questions about voting for Senate as well as House candidates. Those data have stimulated comparisons of House and Senate elections (Abramowitz, 1980; Mann and Wolfinger, 1980; Hinckley, 1980b; Parker, 1981; Ragsdale, 1981), and criticism of that work based on an analysis of state survey data (Westlye, 1983). Another source of data on voting in U.S. Senate elections is the CBS News/New York Times Congressional Poll and exit polls, which have been used in an analysis of policy voting in 1984 (Wright and Berkman, 1985).

All of these analyses are limited in that they primarily rely on cross-sectional survey data, collected late in the campaign (or even after the election), to study what is clearly a dynamic process. Most are additionally limited because they focus solely on voters, lacking information on the campaign context and how it varies across and within constituencies.[1] For example, campaign coverage in the mass media is widely assumed to be important in congressional races, although few analyses take that coverage into account. Yet the amount and type of media content varies from place to place, partly as a consequence of campaign targeting and partly as a result of media markets and the standard operating procedures of journalists. Moreover, different voters pay more or less attention to the information available to them.

Voters' information environments consists of information about the candidates or the campaign available from television (news and advertisements), newspapers (news and advertisements), other campaign-generated materials (billboards, posters, letters, pamphlets, and flyers distributed through door-to-door canvassing), and experience voters or their acquaintances may have had with either candidate. The research reported here presents the preliminary findings from a case study that analyzes the impact of media content on voter response to the candidates and their campaigns over the course of the 1984 Michigan race for the U.S. Senate.[2]

THE MICHIGAN RACE

In many ways the Michigan race was similar to other U.S. Senate races in 1984, and in some important ways it was different. Carl Levin, a first-term Democratic incumbent, was targeted as vulnerable by the National Republican Senatorial Committee and many political action committees, including the National Conservative Political Action Committee (NCPAC). He prepared for his campaign by raising large sums of money before January 1984, and was able to raise additional funds as well.

His Republican opponent, Jack Lousma, a former astronaut, won a contested primary. Although Lousma was reared in Michigan and attended school there, he spent his military career outside the state. In the primary he was opposed by Jim Dunn, a former one-term U.S. representative and owner of a small business, who attempted to label Lousma a carpetbagger. While Lousma handily defeated Dunn in the primary, the campaign was heavily targeted toward likely Republican voters. Lousma began the general election campaign with relatively low name recognition, especially among Independents and Democrats. For reasons that remain unclear and may never become fully public, the Lousma general election campaign also began with a substantial primary debt and a turnover in top campaign staff, complicating organized efforts to overcome Lousma's recognition disadvantage.

In Hibbing and Brandes' (1983) terms, Michigan is a heavily populated state with typically hard-fought Senate elections. The 1984 race was no exception. Candidates in Michigan cannot meet personally with a high proportion of the voting-age population in the course of a campaign, and the mass media inevitably become the major means of communicating campaign messages. Together, the two general election candidates spent more than five million dollars on their campaigns. Both were media-oriented in their spending and their campaign appearances. Both issued professional press releases at frequent intervals during the race. Both spent a great deal of money on television advertisements, allocating one-half (Lousma) to three-quarters (Levin) of their money to the production and placement of ads in eight television markets that cover portions of the state.[3] The cost of political advertising on a particular station is a function of the size of the audience for that station's programming. The candidates allocated their advertising dollars differently, each spending more money in some areas of the state than in others.

From a voter's perspective, the amount of advertising time purchased and the content of the messages are more significant than the dollars spent. Messages in political ads are controlled by the candidate, and the amount of advertising broadcast in a market reflects one important dimension of the information environment for potential voters who live in that market area. At the same time, the amount of news coverage of each candidate represents a measure of the uncontrolled messages in the environment. In the analysis that follows, media content, in conjunction with patterns of the electorate's exposure to that content, is related to the voters' recognition and evaluation of candidates.

MEDIA EXPOSURE AND THE ABILITY TO RECOGNIZE AND RATE CANDIDATES

Public recognition is usually a prerequisite for a candidate's electoral success. Although incumbents enjoy a considerable advantage over their challengers in House races (Goldenberg and Traugott, 1984), Senate challengers frequently have more resources to use in developing recognition and competing with incumbents on more even footing (Ragsdale, 1981). The recognition levels of Senate incumbents can be relatively low long before the general election period, but once they raise and spend large amounts of money and receive coverage in the local media, their recognition can become widespread by the start of the general election campaign, even if there is no primary challenge (Goldenberg and Traugott, 1985a; and 1985b). Senate challengers may be notables in their own right, and thereby begin the race with substantial recognition in at least part of the state. If they run hard in the primary and are able to wage a vigorous general election challenge, they can raise their recognition levels substantially over the course of the campaign.

Unlike House races, in which the correspondence between congressional district boundaries and media markets may be quite poor, Senate races involve statewide constituencies in which candidates can more efficiently organize and allocate advertising resources. These races tend to attract more news attention than the typical House race. As a consequence, potential voters typically see and hear more information about Senate than House races.

The patterns of newspaper readership in Michigan are relatively complex because of the presence of two large-circulation Detroit papers that are distributed across the state. Overall, in a statewide sample of Michigan adults in August 1984, 78 percent indicated that they read a daily paper.[4] Sixty percent said that they read about state and local politics with some frequency (at least once or twice a week), and 18 percent said that they read about it less frequently.[5] In the total sample of 1,094 preelection respondents, 41 percent indicated that they read one daily newspaper, 30 percent indicated that they read two, and almost 2 percent indicated that they read three daily newspapers. Of the one-newspaper readers, 18 percent said that they read the *Detroit Free Press* and 13 percent said that they read *The Detroit News*. Almost all of the two-newspaper readers indicated that they read either the *Detroit Free Press* or *The Detroit News* as their second paper, and 60 percent of them said that they read both papers. Every one of the three-newspaper readers included one or both of these Detroit papers among those they read. In combination, then, more than half (56 percent) of the respondents said that they read either the *Detroit Free Press* or *The Detroit News* on a daily basis.

As for television viewing, virtually all respondents indicated that they watched local evening news broadcasts. A total of 62 percent said that they watched frequently (at least a few times a week), and the remainder indicated that they watched less frequently. By October, 61 percent of those surveyed said that they had seen a senatorial candidate's television commercials. Almost half (44 percent) had seen ads for both candidates, while 13 percent said that they had seen only Levin's commercials and 4 percent said that they had seen only Lousma's commercials.

In combination, almost half of the respondents (44 percent) were heavy consumers of news about state and local politics, defined as being frequently exposed to both newspapers and television. Almost equal numbers of respondents (17 percent each) relied on one medium more than the other, while 21 percent described themselves as having little exposure to state and local news.

Media exposure is related to recognition of the candidates in the Michigan senatorial race, as shown in Table 7.1. Early in the campaign, frequent newspaper and television exposure to news about state and local politics resulted in greater recognition of both candidates. The relationship between exposure and candidate recognition in Table 7.1 is stronger for the challenger than for the incumbent, who was already widely recognized by the August interview. Those with low levels of

Table 7.1

The Relationship between Media Exposure and Candidate Recognition in the 1984 Senatorial Campaign in Michigan

	Recognize Levin (Incumbent)		Recognize Lousma (Challenger)	
	August RDD§ Sample	October RDD Sample	August RDD Sample	October RDD Sample
Newspaper Readership for Local Politics*				
Frequent	96% (1685)	96% (673)	78% (1685)	89% (673)
Infrequent	91% (515)	96% (227)	64% (515)	88% (227)
Nonreaders	89% (616)	91% (369)	58% (616)	63% (369)
TV Viewing for Local Politics**				
Frequent	94% (1170)	95% (888)	79% (1170)	86% (888)
Infrequent	93% (731)	93% (386)	59% (731)	71% (386)
Combined Media Exposure**				
Heavy	96% (845)	95% (547)	84% (845)	89% (547)
Primarily Newspapers	99% (328)	100% (127)	63% (328)	87% (127)
Primarily TV	97% (324)	95% (338)	64% (324)	80% (338)
Low	88% (403)	89% (258)	55% (403)	62% (258)

§Random Digit Dialing

*Frequent readers responded to a question about exposure to stories about state and local politics that they read them "almost every day" or "a few times a week." Infrequent readers described their exposure as a "few times a month" or "less frequently."

**Frequent viewers responded to a question about exposure to local TV broadcasts in the evening that they saw them "every evening" or "three or four times a week." Infrequent viewers described their exposure as "once or twice a week" or "less often." This question was asked in September and October but not in August, therefore, the August categorization is for responders interviewed then and in September.

***The Combined Media Exposure index distinguishes between who are frequent readers and viewers, frequent readers and infrequent viewers, frequent viewers and infrequent readers, and infrequent readers or nonreaders and infrequent viewers.

Source: Computed by authors.

exposure were much more likely to recognize Carl Levin than Jack Lousma. In combination, exposure to news resulted in recognition levels of the challenger that were twenty-nine percentage points higher for those with "heavy" exposure as opposed to "low" exposure.

Because of the residue from past campaigns, from mailings to constituents, and from constituent service during the preceding six-year term, incumbent senators may be recognized by constituents regardless of their media exposure habits. On the other hand, had recognition been measured earlier in the year, the relationship between media exposure and candidate recognition might have been stronger for the incumbent. Incumbents tend to increase activities in their constituencies as the reelection campaign begins, and recognition levels may increase as a result. If such an increase occurred in Michigan during the 1984 campaign, it happened before the August interviews.

In most cases at the start of the campaign the challenger is clearly disadvantaged in terms of recognition. The data show that early in the campaign, newspaper and television each made an independent contribution to challenger recognition; by October exposure to either media outlet was sufficient to raise recognition levels to 80 percent. Or, put another way, as the campaign progressed and information about the candidates became more plentiful, even those who paid attention to the mass media only occasionally had sufficient information to recognize the Senate candidates. For many respondents, media exposure made it possible to recognize both candidates, thereby providing rudimentary information helpful for comparative assessments leading to candidate choice. Although better-educated respondents tended to expose themselves to more news information (Goldenberg and Traugott, 1985a), these exposure relationships with recognition hold even when education is controlled.[6]

Developing recognition is not the only purpose of campaign strategy or the only result of exposure to news coverage of the campaign. Candidates also want to be judged positively. A candidate's positive image is widespread recognition coupled with positive evaluations. But not all potential voters who recognize a candidate's name are able to rate that candidate positively or negatively. Data presented in Table 7.2 show that the higher levels of exposure to news coverage are associated with an ability to rate Senate candidates. Those with little or no exposure are less likely than respondents with greater exposure to be able to supply a rating.

This relationship differs for the incumbent and the challenger in two ways. At the outset of the campaign the challenger is less familiar than the incumbent in terms of the public's ability to recognize and evaluate him, so the proportionate gains in recognition are potentially much larger. Nevertheless, Lousma failed to match Levin's level of familiarity in the electorate by Election Day. Almost nine in ten of the respondents could recognize and rate Levin by the end of the campaign. For Lousma, the proportion who could recognize and rate him varied with exposure to the news media. The movement among those with low media exposure from August to October was from 35 to 53 percent. Among those with heavy levels of exposure, the ability to rate the challenger rose

Table 7.2
**The Relationship between Media Exposure and Ability to Recognize and
Rate Candidates in the 1984 Senatorial Campaign in Michigan**

	August RDD Sample			October RDD Sample		
	Recognize and rate	Recognize Only	Doesn't Recognize	Recognize and Rate	Recognize Only	Doesn't Recognize
Levin (Incumbent)						
Newspaper Readership for Local Politics						
Frequent	88%	7	4 (1685)	93%	4	4 (673)
Infrequent	80%	11	9 (515)	91%	5	4 (227)
Nonreaders	73%	17	11 (616)	84%	7	9 (369)
TV Viewing for Local Politics						
Frequent	90%	4	6 (1170)	90%	5	5 (888)
Infrequent	81%	13	7 (731)	89%	3	7 (386)
Combined Media Exposure						
Heavy	93%	3	4 (845)	92%	3	5 (547)
Primarily Newspapers	89%	10	9 (328)	94%	6	0 (338)
Primarily TV	83%	8	1 (324)	86%	10	5 (127)
Low	73%	15	12 (403)	87%	2	11 (258)
Lousma (Challenger)						
Newspaper Readership for Local Politics						
Frequent	61%	17	22 (1685)	82%	6	11 (673)
Infrequent	42%	23	36 (515)	62%	25	13 (227)
Nonreaders	37%	20	42 (616)	54%	9	37 (369)
TV Viewing for Local Politics						
Frequent	57%	21	21 (1170)	75%	20	15 (888)
Infrequent	41%	18	41 (731)	60%	11	29 (386)
Combined Media Exposure						
Heavy	63%	21	16 (845)	84%	5	11 (547)
Primarily Newspapers	48%	15	37 (328)	75%	12	13 (338)
Primarily TV	41%	23	36 (324)	61%	19	20 (127)
Low	35%	20	45 (403)	53%	10	38 (258)

Source: Computed by authors.

from 63 to 84 percent across this same period, almost to the level of
the incumbent.

Levin's campaign improved his name familiarity among infrequent
readers and viewers more than among heavy media users, most of whom
knew he was at the outset. In contrast, Lousma was still benefiting from
improved familiarity even among heavy media users right up to the
end of the campaign, an indication that he might have benefited fur-

ther from additional news coverage and advertising exposure. An ability to rate a candidate appears to require more information than is required for simple recognition. By October those respondents who paid only modest amounts of attention to the media could recognize the challenger about as well as could heavy media users, but the low-exposure people were still less likely to be able to rate him.

Respondents must be able to recall a candidate's name in order to report whose commercials they have seen.[7] What is more interesting is the effect of exposure to political commercials on the respondents' ability to evaluate candidates and their opponents. Data presented in Table 7.3 show that those who reported seeing each candidate's ads by late in the campaign were more likely to recognize and rate the candidates than those who did not. The findings in Tables 7.2 and 7.3 show that exposure to TV ads, which contain a candidate's controlled messages, is a much more powerful predictor of the electorate's ability to recognize and rate the challenger than exposure to the news. By Election Day those who had seen Levin's ads were somewhat more likely to recognize and rate him (95 percent) than those who had not seen his ads (83 percent). Regardless of whether they saw Levin's ads, however, most people knew who he was and were willing to judge him. In contrast, seeing Lousma's ads made a substantial difference to whether respondents could recognize and rate him. Those who had seen Lousma's ads by Election Day were as likely to assess him as they were to assess the incumbent (94 and 95 percent). In contrast, only 49 percent of those who had not seen Lousma's ads felt able to judge him. Exposure to campaign coverage enhances the information that readers and viewers have about the candidates for public office. Controlled coverage through

Table 7.3
The Relationship between Exposure to Ads and Ability to Recognize and Rate Candidates in the 1984 Senatorial Campaign in Michigan

| | October RDD Sample | | |
	Recognize and Rate	Recognize Only	Doesn't Recognize
Levin (Incumbent)			
Saw Commercials	95%	2	3 (754)
Didn't See Commercials	83%	10	7 (557)
Lousma (Challenger)			
Saw Commercials	94%	2	5 (508)
Didn't See Commercials	49%	35	16 (684)

Source: Computed by authors.

advertisements appears to be more effective for the challenger than uncontrolled news in improving his recognition level and the ability of voters to evaluate him. This effect is even stronger in multivariate analyses, and holds for both candidates, when their advertising efforts are taken into account by constructing an interaction term consisting of self-reported exposure to the ads and the amount of advertising purchased by each campaign.

INFORMATION ENVIRONMENTS AND CANDIDATE VISIBILITY

Self-reported levels of exposure to the mass media tell part of the candidate visibility story; but the quantity and quality of the content to which potential voters are exposed are also important. This content consists of advertising placed by the candidates primarily on television as well as the news about the candidates and their campaign activities that appears mainly in newspapers.

In order to study the information environment of the campaign, two data-collection activities were undertaken. In the first the content of the news in all twenty-nine daily newspapers in Michigan with circulations over 10,000 was examined for coverage of the Senate race; stories from June 15, 1984, through the Sunday after the election were coded. The newspapers varied in size from *The Detroit News*, with a reported state-wide daily circulation over 600,000 (more than 800,000 on Sunday), to the *Petoskey News Review*, with a circulation barely exceeding the 10,000 threshold. Every story, letter, advertisement, column, and editorial that mentioned the name of any candidate for the U.S. Senate seat in Michigan anywhere in these twenty-nine newspapers was coded, for a total of 2,348 Senate stories. The second data-collection activity gathered information from individual television stations on the amount of advertising purchased by each candidate during the campaign. The analysis that follows relies on both sets of data.

Some general descriptive information about newspaper coverage of the Michigan Senate race is a useful place to start. The data presented in Table 7.4 show that, on average, there were .38 stories per paper per day up to the primary on August 6. The number increased to .56 after the primary but before the traditional Labor Day campaign kick-off, and to .62 stories per paper per day in the post–Labor Day period. Not surprisingly, coverage became even heavier just before Election Day. During the week before the November 6 election there was an average of 1.52 stories in the newspaper each day.

What follows is a comparison of the newspaper information that was available about the 1984 U.S. Senate race in Michigan with the newspaper information that was available for forty-three House races in 1978.

Table 7.4
Coverage of the 1984 Michigan Campaign for U.S. Senate in Twenty-Nine Newspapers

	Pre–Primary Coverage	General Election Coverage	
	June 15 – August 6	Post Primary to Labor Day	Labor Day to Election Day
Total Stories	591	439	1164
Average Stories per Newspaper per Day	.38	.56	.62
Papers Endorsing			
Levin	--	19	
Lousma	7	7	
Dunn	5	--	
Average Name Mentions per Newspaper			
Levin	43	242	
Lousma	101	248	
Dunn	93	--	
% of Stories with Names In Headlines			
Levin	18.2%	33.6%	
Lousma	36.6%	37.1%	
Dunn	32.0%	--	

Source: Computed by authors.

In drawing such comparisons we should remember that House and Senate information environments differ in at least one significant way. In the typical House constituency, voters read about the race in only one or possibly two newspapers. Therefore, there is little variation, if any, in relevant newspaper coverage within a House constituency. As we have shown elsewhere, there is substantial variation in information environments across House campaigns (Goldenberg and Traugott, 1984), and a cross-sectional analysis of voters in different House districts can be informative. The constituency for a Senate race is the entire state, however. There is substantial variation within the state in the amount and quality of the newspaper coverage of a given race, although most constituents are still exposed to only a small portion of the coverage that appears in their own locale. With data from only one state, analysis across states in not possible, but the variation across information environments within the state does permit useful cross-sectional analysis. In both House and Senate contests, however, analyzing data collected over the course of the campaign can be even more informative. Although we had no such over-time data in our study of the House, such data were collected and are reported in this study of the Senate.

As expected, news coverage of the Michigan Senate race was heavier than coverage of an average U.S. House race. Coverage was 50 percent greater for this Senate race in the last few weeks before Election Day; because the coverage of the Senate race began earlier than for most House races, the total accumulation of news about the Senate candidates in Michigan far exceeded what was typically available about candidates for the House.[8]

The study of the 1978 races also showed that incumbent House candidates were advantaged over their challengers in name mentions in daily newspapers during the campaign, but this incumbent advantage was not apparent in the Michigan Senate race. Because Jack Lousma faced a contested primary, he captured considerably more attention during the primary than Carl Levin, who ran unopposed. On average, Lousma was mentioned 101 times and Dunn 93 times per newspaper in the pre-primary period as compared with 43 name mentions for Levin. Average coverage in the post-primary period was almost identical for the two candidates, with Lousma enjoying a slight edge over Levin. Of the twenty-nine daily papers, nineteen mentioned the two candidates nearly equally after the primary, and both candidates had roughly equal numbers of mentions in headlines. Lousma had the name mention advantage in five of the remaining ten newspapers; Levin was advantaged in the other five.

Beyond the sheer amount of attention, newspaper coverage of House races and this Senate race differed in other ways as well. The typical House incumbent's news advantage was not enjoyed to the same degree by Michigan's Senate incumbent. For example, in the House, when an editorial endorsement is made, it nearly always supports the incumbent. Clarke and Evans (1983, p. 74) reported that in 1978, when incumbents ran against challengers for House seats, 30 percent of the large-circulation dailies did not endorse either candidate; if an endorsement was made, nine out of ten went to the incumbents. In his study of statewide races in 1972 and 1974, Coombs (1981) also found Senate incumbents to be favored in editorial endorsements by large-circulation dailies.[9] Incumbent senator Carl Levin was advantaged in Michigan in 1984, but by fewer than nine in ten newspapers. Twenty-six of the twenty-nine daily newspapers endorsed one of the candidates, and Levin was favored in nineteen of them. The two large papers with statewide circulation split their endorsements. This means that although an overwhelming proportion of daily newspaper readers in 1978 read papers that endorsed the incumbent representative, a substantial number of

Michigan readers were exposed to endorsements of the Senate challenger.

Attention to the Senate race varied considerably across daily papers.
During the primary campaign, coverage was as heavy as 1.04 stories
per day in the *Detroit Free Press* and as light as .15 stories per day in the
Macomb Daily. In the period after Labor Day, coverage did not increase
much on average in the most attentive papers (1.18 per day), but the
least attentive newspapers doubled the frequency of coverage to .31
stories per paper per day. Consequently, as Election Day neared, the
coverage gap narrowed; but even so, some dailies reported on the Senate race four times as often as others during the general election campaign.

Moreover, some papers mentioned one candidate substantially more
often than the other. During the primary the ratio of Lousma-to-Dunn
mentions varied from .74 in the *Houghton Daily Mining Gazette* to 3.22
in the *Royal Oak Daily Tribune*. The ratio of Levin-to-Lousma mentions
during the general election campaign varied from .74 in the *Alpena
News* to 1.31 in the *Bay City Times*.

The pace and amount of coverage, the balance of the candidates'
coverage, endorsements, and other types of content varied from place
to place. Where potential voters live affects how early they learn about
Senate candidates, as well as the amount of news and the type of information available about each candidate from the daily press. All of the
papers in Michigan have a circulation area that fits within the state's
borders better than most newspaper markets fit within congressional
district boundaries. Even if a newspaper's market takes in more than
one Senate race, the newspaper can cover each contest more easily than
big-city dailies can cover the many races in separate House districts in
which their readers reside. Although newspapers with the lightest coverage of the House run virtually no stories, those with the lightest coverage of the Michigan Senate race still run more than a dozen stories
in a comparable period late in the campaign. Moreover, Senate campaign coverage might have been depressed by poll results that made
the race appear to be quite lopsided in favor of Levin. Had the polls
indicated a closer contest, news coverage might have been even heavier.

Of equal interest is the similarity in amounts of coverage of House
and Senate campaigns for those newspapers highly attentive to electoral politics. In information-rich environments, citizens could have
learned as much about candidates for competitive House races in good-
fitting newspaper markets as they did about the 1984 candidates for the
U.S. Senate in Michigan. Westlye (1983) pointed out that some Senate
races are as lacking in vitality as noncompetitive House races, and some
House races are as hard fought as competitive Senate races. Our data
suggest further that a Senate race is more or less vital in different parts

of a state and that the richness of information environments varies accordingly. Given this variability, knowing a respondent's media exposure habits tells only part of the story. The amount of information available to readers with roughly equivalent reading habits varies considerably, depending on the content of their newspapers, providing one important contextual explanation for voters' reactions to the candidates.

Overall, the heavier the coverage of the Senate race in a person's newspaper, the more likely that person was to recognize and rate a candidate, especially the challenger. The data in Table 7.5 show this relationship, controlling for news reading habits. By August the unopposed incumbent had received less coverage than the challenger, but Levin was widely recognized and rated regardless of the amount of newspaper attention. For the challenger, more respondents were exposed to newspapers in the high-coverage category that reported on Lousma's active primary contest. Readers of more attentive newspapers were more likely than readers of less attentive papers to recognize and rate him. By October, coverage of both candidates had grown, and the total number of name mentions between mid-June and October was relatively large; therefore, the range for each of the categories is shifted upward.

For the incumbent, newspaper content contributed little beyond readership habits to an ability to rate him; levels already were quite high in August, with more than 80 percent of the readers able to recognize and rate Levin, regardless of the number of name mentions to which they were exposed. For the challenger, the most dramatic difference is shown for infrequent readers. They were much more likely to recognize and rate Lousma if their newspapers contained a lot of Senate coverage than if there was relatively little coverage across the 145-day period. The frequent readers apparently learned enough from their newspapers to recognize and rate the challenger, regardless of the amount of coverage of the campaigns in their newspapers.

Another important contextual factor is the amount of advertising purchased by the senatorial candidates in the various Michigan media markets. In the second contextual data-collection activity the public files maintained by each of the twenty-five largest commercial television stations in the state were examined. Information on the number of minutes of commercials placed on each station by week was coded and aggregated to the market and ADI level. An ADI, or Area of Dominant Influence, designates the geographical area of each television market. Each ADI consists of counties whose home market stations receive the majority of viewing, with each county being assigned to only one ADI. The coverage of Michigan ADIs ranges from 7,400 Michigan households in the Duluth, Minneota, ADI, to 15,300 households in the small-

Table 7.5
The Relationship between Media Content and Ability to Recognize and Rate Candidates, Controlling on Media Exposure, 1984 Michigan Senate Campaign

| | AUGUST RDD SAMPLE | | |
| | Respondent Can | | |
	Recognize and rate	Recognize only	Doesn't Recognize
Levin (Incumbent)			
FREQUENT Newspaper			
Readership for			
Local Politics			
Number of Name Mentions			
Low (less than 100)	86%	10	4 (316)
High (100 or more)	90%	7	3 (1240)
INFREQUENT Newspaper			
Readership for			
Local Politics			
Number of Name Mentions			
Low (less than 100)	82%	6	12 (110)
High (100 or more)	81%	15	5 (349)
NONREADERS	73%	11	11 (616)
Lousma (Challenger)			
FREQUENT Newspaper			
Readership for			
Local Politics			
Number of Name Mentions			
Low (less than 100)	53%	28	19 (126)
High (100 or more)	61%	17	21 (1431)
INFREQUENT Newspaper			
Readership for			
Local Politics			
Number of Name Mentions			
Low (less than 100)	31%	28	41 (62)
High (100 or more)	40%	25	35 (397)
NONREADERS	37%	20	42 (616)

Table 7.5 (Continued)

	Recognize and rate	Recognize only	Doesn't Recognize	
Levin (Incumbent)				
FREQUENT Newspaper				
Readership for				
Local Politics				
Number of Name Mentions				
Low (less than 700)	90%	5	5	(489)
High (700 or more)	98%	2	0	(117)
INFREQUENT Newspaper				
Readership for				
Local Politics				
Number of Name Mentions				
Low (less than 700)	88%	7	6	(169)
High (700 or more)	–	–	–	(123)
NONREADERS	84%	7	9	(369)
Lousma (Challenger)				
FREQUENT Newspaper				
Readership for				
Local Politics				
Number of Name Mentions				
Low (less than 700)	82%	4	14	(291)
High (700 or more)	83%	9	7	(315)
INFREQUENT Newspaper				
Readership for				
Local Politics				
Number of Name Mentions				
Low (less than 700)	50%	31	19	(112)
High (700 or more)	92%	4	4	(57)
NONREADERS	54%	9	37	(369)

Source: Computed by authors.

est intrastate ADI in Alpena, to 1,644,000 households in the Detroit ADI, the largest in the state. There are forty-seven commercial television stations in the eleven ADIs that cover the state of Michigan. Intrastate, they range from the largest market in Detroit in the southeastern corner of the state, where there are eight commercial stations, to small stations in the northern part of the state that carry the same broadcast signal as somewhat larger "sister" stations in Traverse City or Marquette.

Decisions about placing TV advertisements are a function of a number of factors. In strategic terms, they are related to the characteristics of the audience covered by the broadcast signal and targeted by the campaign. In resource allocation terms, placement decisions are related to how much money the campaign has available and the rates that the station charges. These rates are in turn a function of the market's potential audience and the station's share of that market during specific segments of its schedule.

For the purpose of the research reported here, the total number of minutes broadcast in the market by each candidate between June 15, 1984, and the respective interviewing dates of the surveys was used as a measure of a candidate's televised commercial effort. This was calculated by aggregating the number of ten-, thirty- and 60-second spots and five-minute ads. Through the October survey the range of placements extended from zero minutes in some of the markets where signals originated outside the state's border to 684.0 minutes in the Tra-

Table 7.6

Television Advertising Placements in Minutes by Candidates in the 1984 Michigan Campaign for U.S. Senate in Eight Markets

| | Through Mid–October | | |
	Levin	Lousma	Total
Green Bay, WI	75.0	0.0	75.0
Alpena, MI	237.0	83.5	320.5
Grand Rapids–Kalamazoo, MI	220.5	102.5	323.0
Marquette, MI	361.0	74.0	435.0
Flint–Saginaw–Bay City, MI	347.0	138.0	485.0
Detroit, MI	248.0	241.0	489.0
Lansing, MI	275.0	220.5	495.5
Traverse City–Cadillac, MI	473.0	211.0	684.0
	2,236.5	1,070.5	3,307.0

Source: Computed by authors.

verse City–Cadillac, Michigan, market. By the end of the campaign, almost
two weeks after interviewing was completed, Levin had placed a total
473.0 minutes of ads in the Traverse City–Cadillac market, whereas
Lousma had placed 241.0 minutes in the Detroit market and more than
200 minutes in both the Traverse City–Cadillac market and the Lansing market. The full range of placements in the eight ADIs for which
data are available is shown in Table 7.6.

The data by market illustrate not only the variation in individual candidate placements, but also the candidates' relative allocations and
priorities with respect to different markets. In every market Levin bought
more time than Lousma. By the end of the campaign the difference in
Detroit was relatively small; but in some markets Levin had a greater
than two-to-one advantage, and in Marquette his advantage was almost
five to one.

Members of the electorate are exposed to political advertising as a
combined function of their TV-viewing habits and the level of effort by
each candidate to advertise in his or her market. Using attention to
local evening news broadcasts as an indicator of general viewing habits,
data presented in Table 7.7 show that exposure to television in general
is related to exposure to the candidates' ads.

These data portray both the richness and the variety of information
environments in which the electorate was immersed during the 1984
campaign. Depending on where one lived, the news media carried vary-
ing levels of advertising by the candidates. In some of the media markets there are more than ten hours of commercials aired jointly by the
candidates. The survey respondents were somewhat more likely to report seeing Levin's ads than Lousma's, but virtually every one who saw
Lousma's also saw Levin's.

Beyond the observed effects of exposure to political ads on the view-

Table 7.7
**Exposure to Candidates' Television Advertising as a Function of TV
Viewing Habits, October, 1984**

	Saw Levin's Commercials	Saw Lousma's Commercials	Saw Both Candidates' Commercials	Saw Neither Candidates' Commercials
Television News Exposure				
Frequent Viewers	62% (909)	53% (909)	48%	33% (909)
Infrequent Viewers	50% (372)	37% (372)	35%	49% (372)

Source: Computed by authors.

ers' ability to recognize and rate the candidates, there remains the issue of the impact of advertising exposure on candidate evaluations. Data presented in Table 7.8 show that among all the respondents, those who saw the ads offered fewer neutral thermometer ratings than those who did not. The content of the ads themselves may also have affected the direction of the evaluations. To investigate this possibility empirically would require linking information gained by content analyzing the various ads with the particular respondents exposed to each ad. Unfortunately standard survey techniques and other available procedures cannot reliably be used to ascertain which ads particular respondents saw, so this analysis could not be done.

MULTIVARIATE MODELS OF RECOGNIZING AND RATING CANDIDATES

Data describing the information environment of the campaign were combined with relevant characteristics of the respondents in four dichotomous regressions to predict recognition of Levin (the incumbent) and

Table 7.8
The Relationship between Exposure to Candidates' Television Advertising and Candidate Evaluations, 1984 Senatorial Campaign in Michigan

Rating*	REPUBLICANS				DEMOCRATS			
	−	0	+		−	0	+	
Levin Evaluations (Incumbent)								
R Saw								
Levin's Commercials	43%	25	32	(283)	6%	28	66	(320)
Lousma's Commercials	42%	24	34	(245)	8%	24	67	(257)
Levin's & Lousma's								
Commercials	44%	23	33	(231)	6%	26	68	(234)
No Commercials	14%	47	39	(142)	22%	35	43	(231)
Lousma Evaluations (Challenger)								
R Saw								
Lousma's Commercials	10%	13	76	(245)	51%	31	19	(254)
Levin's Commercials	13%	20	67	(262)	42%	38	20	(297)
Levin's & Lousma's								
Commercials	11%	14	75	(231)	52%	30	18	(231)
No Commercials	6%	48	46	(100)	30%	46	24	(170)

*Negative ratings are the equivalent of 0- to 49-degree ratings on the feeling thermometer, neutral ratings of 50 degrees, and positive ratings of 51 to 100 degrees. Recognizing a candidate but not being able to rate him is categorized as a neutral rating. Those who could not recognize a candidate are excluded from this table.

Source: Computed by authors.

of Lousma (the challenger) as well as the respondents' ability to evaluate each candidate. The results are presented in Table 7.9. For recognition, the most important predictors are education and exposure to television ads. For Lousma, exposure to news coverage was also important, for both television viewers and newspaper readers. Party identification has no independent role to play in this process. Overall, the recognition levels for Levin were very high by the end of the campaign, and the additional predictive power of the campaign factors in the equation is relatively low for the incumbent compared with the challenger.

For evaluation, exposure to television advertising remains important, especially for the challenger. And education is significant as well. Party identification is significant in predicting the respondents' ability to rate the candidates. The role of party identification as a perceptual screen becomes clearer in additional analyses looking at *positive* evaluations of each candidate. But the effects of the media on the direction of candidate evaluations are more difficult to ascertain because measures of the tone and substance of the news coverage and the ads were not included in the analysis and because the respondents were not asked to recall specifically which ads they had seen.

CONCLUSIONS

This analysis shows that both news coverage and the candidates' use of television for advertising had important effects during the 1984 U.S. Senate race in Michigan. It expands our knowledge of the role of the media in congressional elections by exploring the relationship between the information environment in a Senate race and the voters' recognition of and ability to rate the contestants. This analysis of a Senate race also provides an interesting comparison with an earlier analysis of the role of the media in House elections.

In Senate races in populous states, where direct contact cannot reach many potential voters, the mass media consume a substantial portion of campaign resources and energy. Because there are alternative means of reaching the voters through personal contact in many House races, and because media markets are often inefficient for congressional district appeals, the mass media typically capture a smaller portion of campaign resources for House than for Senate contests. Moreover, the absolute size of the budget for most Senate races is substantially greater than the budget for a typical House race. Taken together, more money devoted more exclusively to mass media appeals means considerably more advertising information in the media about Senate than House candidates.

Relative market efficiencies also lead to greater news attention to the

Table 7.9

Dichotomous Regressions of Candidate Recognition and Evaluation on Media Exposure and Party Identification, October, 1984

	Recognize Levin	Recognize Lousma	Rate Levin	Rate Lousma
Proportion in the Sample	.957 (N=231)	.904 (N=231)	.913 (N=231)	.790 (N=231)
Predictive Power of the Mean	.836	.727	.742	.597
Predictive Power Due to Campaign Factors	.010 (X^2=9.95, 6 d.f.)	.041 (X^2=17.64, 6 d.f.)	.042 (X^2=17.53, 6 d.f.)	.067 (X^2=44.41, 6 d.f.)
Residual Predictive Error	.134	.232	.216	.336
	1.000	1.000	1.000	1.000

Predictors

	Recognize Levin	Recognize Lousma	Rate Levin	Rate Lousma
Constant	b=0.035	b=3.497	b=1.726	b=1.004
Exposure to Ads	b=0.006 (b/s.e.=1.82)*	b=0.009 (b/s.e.-2.55)**	b=0.009 (b/s.e.=3.39)***	b=0.014 (b/s.e.=4.85)***
Education	b=1.896 (b/s.e.=1.72)*	b=1.734 (b/s.e.=2.66)**	b=1.293 (b/s.e.=1.85)*	b=0.842 (b/s.e.=2.03)**
Newspaper Coverage	b=0.002 (b/s.e.=0.47)	b=0.003 (b/s.e.=1.14)	b=0.006 (b/s.e.=1.49)	b=0.001 (b/s.e.=0.37)
Party Identification	b=-0.024 (b/s.e.=0.06)	b=-0.375 (b/s.e.=-1.27)	b=0.247 (b/s.e.=0.86)	b=-0.103 (b/s.e.=-0.49)
TV News Exposure	b=0.076 (b/s.e.=0.09)	b=1.126 (b/s.e.=2.09)**	b=-0.157 (b/s.e.=-0.25)	b=0.768 (b/s.e.=1.79)*
Newspaper Exposure	b=-0.030 (b/s.e.=-0.04)	b=0.968 (b/s.e.=1.85)*	b=-0.109 (b/s.e.=0.19)	b=0.529 (b/s.e.=1.27)

$X = x$

*Significant at the .10 level
**Significant at the .05 level
***Significant at the .01 level

Source: Computed by authors.

Senate than to House races. As a result the impact of issues or personal traits may be more important in Senate than in House races simply because more information is available to voters about candidates for the Senate and their stands. News coverage appears to be more balanced overall in terms of allocations to the competing senatorial candidates, and that translates into considerably more news attention to challengers in Senate than in House races. Senate challengers often begin their campaigns with some reputation in their states, and media coverage enhances their recognition levels over the course of the campaign.

Nevertheless, there are substantial variations within a senatorial constituency. Reading habits vary in the electorate and result in individual differences in the degree to which potential voters are exposed to media coverage. Moreover, the amount of effort that newspapers devote to a Senate race and the quality of that coverage also vary from place to place. As a consequence the problem facing candidates as they try to develop a positive image is greater for some parts of the electorate than for others.

Two types of news media effects have significance for the campaign. First, general media exposure habits are related to the electorate's ability to recognize the candidates and rate them. Second, the candidates' advertising placements are also important. Across the wide-ranging set of differences in the amount of advertising by each candidate, exposure to commercials was related to an ability to recognize and rate the candidates. Advertising exposure was much more important for the challenger than for the incumbent.

This analysis reinforces the idea that the mass media are significant actors in political campaigns. It also underscores the need to account for the information environment when analyzing the strategic behavior of candidates and the electorate's response to their campaigns. Where you live makes a difference in what you know about politics, candidates, and issues; and it affects how attitudes and levels of information change across the campaign.

At the same time, this study highlights some of the difficulties of conducting systematic studies of campaign effects. The consequences of media attention in vital Senate contests may be more visible early in the campaign, requiring the monitoring of information levels and candidate assessments across a longer period of time than is customary for survey research. Longitudinal designs are necessary to understand the dynamics of the campaign. Because of the difficulty of assembling appropriate media data over a sufficient period of time for interstate comparisons, survey-based studies of how and why media effects vary across Senate races are unlikely to be mounted.

Moreover, linking specific campaign content either from ads or from news coverage with voter assessments of the candidates is a critical element of this form of contextual analysis, but one that is usually omitted because of problems in measuring exposure to specific ads or news stories. Complex research designs that combine experimental tests of voter reactions to specified media content with standard survey techniques hold promise for future efforts to illuminate the importance of mediated information for the direction and intensity of voters' evaluations of candidates.

NOTES

This chapter is a revised version of a paper prepared for delivery at the Dwight P. Griswold–E. C. Ames Conference on Mass Media and Congressional Elections, Nebraska Wesleyan University, March 7–9, 1986, Lincoln, Nebraska.

The paper is an extension of work presented at the 1985 Annual Meetings of the American Political Science Association in New Orleans, August 1985. It is based on data collections supported by a contract with *The Detroit News* and by the Center for Political Studies and the Horace Rackham School of Graduate Studies at the University of Michigan. The data were analyzed with computing funds provided through the Department of Political Science. The research assistance of Paula Drury and the clerical assistance of Anne O'Hagan are gratefully acknowledged.

The paper was completed while Goldenberg was a Fellow at the Center for Advanced Study in the Behavioral Sciences. She is grateful for financial support provided by the National Science Foundation under grant BNS-8011494.

1. Wright and Berkman are an exception in that they do consider the ideological/issue positions of pairs of Senate candidates and how those positions affect electoral support in the states.

2. Although advertising money went disproportionately to television, preliminary analysis of local news shows in two television markets indicates that relatively little campaign coverage appeared on the local television news (Katz, 1985). Most of the news about the Senate race came to potential voters through daily newspapers.

3. Eleven media markets, or Areas of Dominant Influence (ADIs), cover the state of Michigan. A few of the counties in Michigan fall within television markets that originate outside the state. Green Bay, Wisconsin, television, especially WFRV-TV, reaches households in the Upper Peninsula; South Bend–Elkhart, Indiana, stations reach households in the southwestern corner of Michigan; Toledo, Ohio, television is received in the southeastern corner of the state; and the Duluth, Minnesota–Superior, Wisconsin, market penetrates the far western corner of the Upper Peninsula. Incumbent Carl Levin did buy small amounts of time on the Green Bay station before the general election campaign began, but we could find no record of advertising purchases on stations in any of the other non-Michigan ADIs. These stations' signals generally cover sparsely populated areas of the state, and consequently few survey respondents had to be eliminated from the analysis because data are unavailable on ad buys in their TV markets. The largest penetration could have come from viewers of Toledo

stations because the signal overlaps with large portions of the Detroit ADI. But that fact, in and of itself, explains why time was purchased on the Detroit rather than the Toledo stations.

4. The analysis is based on data obtained from four surveys conducted by Traugott for *The Detroit News* in fall 1984. In August a statewide sample of 745 respondents was interviewed. In September 489 of the respondents were recontacted for interviews. In October 401 of these September respondents were recontacted and a new sample of 349 respondents was interviewed. In total, 1,094 respondents were interviewed before the election. An attempt was made to recontact all of these respondents after the election, and interviews were obtained from 838 of them. These data were weighted to account for stratification in the design of the sample and the combination of recontact respondents and the fresh sample in the last two surveys. The data presented in the tables are based on weighted N's, which are reported in parentheses. The average weight is approximately 4, and this number can be used to estimate the actual number of respondents on which the estimates are based.

5. In the smaller October cross section 71 percent of the respondents indicated that they read a daily newspaper; 53 percent said that they read about state and local politics frequently and 18 percent, infrequently.

6. The September recontact interviews in the Michigan survey data suggest an effect of panel participation on recognition of the candidates' names; therefore, a panel design presents a problem for assessing shifts in recognition. Repeated cross sections serve this purpose better. For measuring changes in evaluation, however, panel data are essential, and panel effects are much less troublesome.

7. Surprisingly, a few respondents who indicated at one point in the interview that they had seen a candidate's commercial could not indicate at another that they recognized the candidate's name. The most obvious explanation for this is that the recognition question came first and was followed near the end of the interview by the question about commercials. The context of the interview itself, then, may have stimulated a response to the self-reported exposure and/or served as a prompt to the respondents in recalling the candidates and their commercials.

8. In our 1978 study, newspaper coverage of forty-three House races was analyzed for three of the last six weeks (every other week) before Election Day. The same periods before Election Day in 1984 were examined for coverage of the Michigan Senate race to permit comparisons between coverage in the two electoral situations.

9. Coombs' newspaper sample was chosen to maximize the likelihood of including papers read by respondents in the National Election Study. This meant that large-circulation dailies were overrepresented in his study. This presented little difficulty for Coombs, given the purpose of his analysis, but further examination of endorsement patterns showed that by focusing only on the largest-circulation papers, Coombs underestimated the number of Republicans endorsed by daily newspapers. See Coombs, 1981, pp. 171–72.

8

Exploiting Televised Coverage of National Party Conventions on Behalf of Congressional Candidates: The Case of 1984

Dan Nimmo and Larry Smith

Before 1952 the International Amphitheater at Chicago's Union Stockyards, located at 43rd and Halsted streets on the city's South Side, had already achieved a modicum of fame. It was home to what was billed as the "Supreme Court of Live Stock Shows," the annual International Live Stock Exposition. But for two separate weeks in July of that year, one commencing on the seventh of the month, the other on the twenty-first, the bleating and bawling of show animals would forever become gentle whispers in comparison with the noise and color of two key events: the respective meetings of the National Conventions of the Republican and Democratic parties to select their nominee for president and vice-president in 1952.

As it turned out, the two party gatherings were to be historic in ways that even transcended their chosen nominees, the Republican ticket of Dwight Eisenhower and Richard Nixon and the Democratic pairing of Adlai Stevenson and John Sparkman. The Republicans in 1952, despite a close and bitter fight between supporters of rivals Eisenhower and Ohio senator Robert Taft, reached a first-ballot decision in less than an hour. It began a string of largely foregone first-ballot conclusions that extended through the renomination of Ronald Reagan in 1984. The Democrats in 1952 were more contentious, more time-consuming; it took four hours and three ballots to select Governor Stevenson of Illinois, who told supporters outside his home, "I did not seek it. I did not want it. But I am persuaded to shirk it would be to repay honor with dishonor." For Democrats, too, however, there would follow at ensuing conventions a string of unbroken first-ballot selections. Hence, after 1952, the quadrennial party gatherings took on a different flavor, still gatherings of fellow partisans disagreeing over how best to reach common goals but no longer rival, autonomous brokers making or breaking nominees.

Another trend began in Chicago's International Amphitheater in 1952. Radio broadcasts of the nominating conventions of the two major parties had begun in 1924 with coverage of Calvin Coolidge's first-ballot victory at the Republican assemblage in Cleveland and the seventeen-day marathon that produced the nomination of Democrat John W. Davis on the 103rd ballot in New York. Such coverage posed the same question for both parties, how broadcasts of the conventions could be used most effectively to party advantage.[1] Convention organizers were no sooner beginning to deal with that problem in the years that followed when television became a factor, first in 1940 in a small way, but by 1952 as a major force. As early as May 1951, broadcast network personnel urged party organizers to hold both party conventions in the same city, preferably in the central time zone, in a facility that could accommodate the technical requirements of television. In early 1952 both Republican and Democratic National Committees issued convention calls for Chicago, with an eye toward both saving money and meeting the needs of the four existing TV networks—CBS, NBC, ABC, and Dumont.[2]

If, after 1952, the national party conventions ceased to be the arenas for selecting presidential nominees that they had been in earlier eras of party history, so, too, did they cease to be the same undisciplined convocations of freewheeling delegates and spectators that Denis Brogan described as taking part in a "ritual of conversion by noise."[3] In fact, it was in 1952 that Democratic leaders at least took the magic eye of television into account in their proceedings, something the GOP had largely failed to do two weeks earlier, and admonished delegates to keep balloons from obstructing TV cameras, to watch TV monitors to note anything "going wrong," and to behave with decorum for they might be on the candid camera at any time.[4] Moreover, the 1952 Democratic conclave had no sooner ended than a story moved on the Associated Press wire that DNC chairman Frank E. McKinney would order a sweeping study of convention procedure to achieve a broadscale "streamlining." (This was not to be the last such "sweeping study" ordered by the Democratic party leadership.) A top priority, ran the account, was to establish rigid rules governing the polling of state delegations. Too many convention hours, noted Mrs. Margaret O'Riordian—a party leader from Massachusetts—were consumed in nose-by-nose checkups resulting from the desires of "crackpots who just like to get their voice on television."

The national party conventions in 1952 were watersheds in many respects, but we call attention to these two, the last of the multiballot nominations and efforts to adapt to television coverage, for they exemplify a shift away from the functions traditionally associated with the party gatherings. That tradition identifies four principal functions: nominating candidates for national office, drafting a party platform, mobilizing and rallying support for party candidates, and serving as governing assemblies for each major party.[5] Moreover, James Davis has suggested that there are "latent" functions that national conventions also perform that contribute to the maintenance of the two-party system: legitimizing the candidacy of a candidate hitherto outside the established party order (for example, Jimmy Carter in 1976); building a general consensus, or aura of unity, among diverse, conflicting interests; and providing ritualistic expression of compromise and accommodation. As the national conventions of both parties have evolved, the relative emphases on these manifest and latent functions have changed. Since 1952 the nominating function has become less emphasized, the platform-drafting function varies in emphasis from convention to convention, and the party-governing function has remained important, albeit not key. The remaining manifest function, one to which all of Davis' latent functions are linked, is that of mobilizing and rallying support for candidates.[6] These candidates need not be, and in many cases are not, limited to those for national office—president and vice-president. In an age of television, parties seeking to rally support behind their candidates seek to exploit convention coverage to showcase and publicize contenders for statewide, congressional, and local offices as well. How the two major parties attempted such exploitation, and their relative success in doing so on behalf of candidates for the House of Representatives and Senate in 1984, is the focal point of this analysis.

Although that focus differs from the emphases of other chapters in this book, it nonetheless complements them well. Whereas the concerns of chapters by Jon Hale, Jan Vermeer, and Edie Goldenberg and Michael Traugott center on media coverage of congressional and senatorial campaigns at the local level, our focus joins that of Timothy Cook in raising questions about the amount of national media visibility available to candidates, in this case visibility derived from national nominating conventions. Moreover, because our interest is on television coverage of congressional and senatorial candidates at national conventions, we supplement Richard Joslyn's interest in paid TV advertising with our findings regarding the relative success of candidates in garnering free televised publicity.

COMPARING TELEVISED COVERAGE OF NATIONAL PARTY CONVENTIONS IN 1984

In examining the conduct and televised coverage of national party conventions it is necessary to make distinctions. Each political party prepares in advance of its gatherings a detailed session-by-session program of scheduled events, including opening and closing ceremonies, forthcoming floor business, speakers, films, votes, demonstrations, light and sound shows, balloon drops, fireworks, and so on. The point at which each event is to occur and the elapsed time scheduled for each is specified in each session's printed instructions, along with other procedural details. However, convention organizers' desires to have proceedings unfold on schedule are not always successful. Hence a comparison of what a particular party schedules to occur with what television networks actually report is not useful in matching party intentions with mediated realities. More satisfactory is a comparison of what events actually occur on the convention podium and floor with what television networks report. This is possible if investigators have access to a record of floor proceedings as well as network presentations.

In 1984 such data set was available. First, C-SPAN, the Cable Satellite Public Affairs Network, provided televised gavel-to-gavel coverage of all podium and floor events for each of the key sessions of both Democratic (July 16–19) and Republican (August 20–23) national conventions. For purposes of this investigation, all such coverage was videotaped and content analyzed. Second, to explore which of these events were actually covered by the three commercial networks, all televised coverage of each session by each TV network was also videotaped and content analyzed. Through such analysis it is possible to compare what events occurred on the podium and floor with network coverage, to contrast similarities and differences in coverage between the three commercial networks and C-SPAN and to compare and contrast coverage of the two national party conventions.

For purposes of content analysis, the selected recording unit is the event. An event consists of any activity taking place on the convention podium or floor or in the environs of convention hall, the hotel headquarters of the candidates, or other locations for which either C-SPAN, ABC, CBS, or NBC provided visual coverage. Four such categories of events are included in this analysis, along with the following recorded subcategories:

1. Podium Events
    a. An officer of the convention (e.g., chair, co-chair, etc.) conducting business on the podium—speaking, introducing speakers and items, calling for

motions and votes, etc.

   b. A delegate speaking or presenting business from the podium

   c. A presidential or vice-presidential candidate at the podium—speaking, waving, acknowledging applause, etc.

   d. A member of Congress (other than a presidential/vice-presidential candidate) or candidate for House of Representatives at the podium—speaking, waving, etc.

   e. A U.S. senator (other than a presidential or vice-presidential candidate) at the podium—speaking, waving, etc.

   f. Any other person at the podium (e.g., singing the national anthem, giving the invocation or benediction, etc.)

2. Anchor-Controlled Events

   a. A TV network anchor on or off camera reporting events or with running commentary (i.e., a "talking head" or "voice over")

   b. A TV network anchor engaged in discussion with a network news correspondent or analyst (i.e., "cross talk")

   c. A TV network anchor interviewing a presidential or vice-presidential candidate on camera

   d. A TV network anchor interviewing a member of Congress (other than candidate for president or vice-president) or candidate for House of Representatives

   e. A TV network anchor interviewing a U.S. senator (other than candidate for president or vice-president) or candidate for the Senate

3. Floor Correspondent-Controlled Events

   a. TV network floor correspondent with "stand up" report

   b. TV network floor correspondent interviewing a delegate (other than congressional or senatorial member or candidate)

   c. TV network floor correspondent interviewing a member of Congress (other than presidential or vice-presidential candidate) or candidate for the House of Representatives

   d. TV network floor correspondent interviewing U.S. senator (other than presidential or vice-presidential candidate) or candidate for the U.S. Senate

   e. TV network floor correspondent interviewing other persons (celebrities, nondelegates, etc.)

4. Miscellaneous Events

   a. Films shown on or behind the podium

   b. Floor demonstrations

   c. Advertising and station breaks (on commercial networks)

For each session of each convention the number of events in each category was recorded, along with the elapsed time of coverage devoted to the event. The tabular presentations to be found in the Appendix to this chapter provide the number of coded events, elapsed time, and proportions of elapsed time (as a percentage of total coverage time for each network) recorded for each.

TALE OF TWO CONVENTIONS: THE GAVEL-TO-GAVEL STORY

With the exceptions of occasional video pans of the convention hall, shots of floor demonstrations, and airing of films prepared by convention organizers as portions of proceedings, C-SPAN's televised coverage of both Democratic and Republican national conventions centered on podium events (consult Table 8.1 in the Appendix). It is apparent in C-SPAN's combined coverage of both conventions that members of the U.S. House of Representatives and Senate figured prominently in podium events. Almost seven hours of the network's gavel-to-gavel coverage featured congressional personnel at the podium, not including the acceptance speech of Congresswoman Geraldine Ferraro or Senator Gary Hart's address to the Democratic convention or his concession remarks. In all, congressional personnel made ninety appearances at the podium, accounting for one-quarter of the time devoted to the combined party gatherings.

The showcasing of congressional partisans, however, stemmed from a variety of reasons—featuring congressmen and congresswomen in various roles and differing in elapsed time across conventions and days when proceedings were held. It is possible to distinguish the following roles among the ninety appearances by congressional members. First are congressional personnel who acted as *party officers*, that is, in an official convention capacity. For example, Congressman Robert Michel of Illinois and Senator Nancy Kassebaum of Kansas served as permanent co-chairs for the Republicans, Senator Howard Baker of Tennessee acted as temporary chair of that gathering, Representative Trent Lott of Mississippi was featured through his presentation of the Republican platform as chair of his party's platform committee, and Representative Tim Foley was parliamentarian of the Democratic convention. Republicans placed the spotlight on their congressional officials in this role more than did Democrats, whether rewarding party members for loyal service and stature in the Congress (as in Michel's case) or to publicize a coterie of young congressional talent (as with Lott). Second were the *partisan orators* placed on the program to whip up delegates with old-time appeals to party loyalty and a lambasting of the opposition; for example, Senator Edward Kennedy of Massachusetts, who introduced Walter Mondale's acceptance speech at the Democratic convention; Representative Morris Udall of Arizona, who introduced former president Jimmy Carter, Speaker of the House Tip O'Neill, Republican Senator Richard Lugar of Indiana, and, again, Senator Howard Baker of Tennessee (placed on the Republican program to provide a stem-winding warmup to balance the more low-keyed keynote address of Kathryn Ortega). Third were the *factional speakers*, congressional personnel addressing the convention on behalf of a particular candidate, platform plan, rules change, etc. Representative George Miller, Democrat of California (speaking on behalf of the Republican party platform), Representative Lynn Martin of Illinois seconding the vice-presidential nomination of George Bush, and Senator Daniel Inouye of Hawaii as a member of the Rainbow Coalition introducing Jesse Jackson exemplify this convention role. Fourth were a host of congressional speakers showcased as *campaigners* for the party or on their own behalf, be it in a current congressional contest or some future bid for higher office. Examples include Republican Phil Gramm of Texas, seeking a senatorial seat from that state; Congressman Jack Kemp, Republican of New York; and Richard Gephardt, Democrat of Missouri.

The two parties differed in the amount of attention they gave to appearances by congressional personnel in the conduct of their respective 1984 conventions. For Republicans, fifty-six of the total convention events, or 40 percent of coded convention events, consisted of appearances by members of the House or Senate in contrast with thirty-four by the Democrats, or one-fifth of events. Elapsed podium time for appearances by congressional members, however, was approximately the same for both parties, amounting to three hours each. A slightly higher proportion of total Republican convention time (29 percent) showcased congressional members than was the case for Democrats (24 percent). The greater Republican emphasis on congressional appearances is largely explained by the Baker–Michel–Kassebaum presiding triumvirate, whereas the Democratic convention, from gavel to gavel, was primarily under the control of Governor Martha Layne Collins of Kentucky.

The opportunities for exploiting gavel-to-gavel convention coverage to publicize congressional members and/or candidacies vary from one evening's prime-time programming to another. The tradition since 1952 has become firm regarding what parties feature on any given evening. For both parties, Monday serves as the keynote evening, Tuesday is platform night, Wednesday is nominating night, and Thursday is set aside for acceptance speeches and unity celebrations. Given that the keynote address for neither party was delivered by a congressional member, the opportunities for advancing congressional candidacies on the first evening of each convention were thereby diminished. Only three Democratic members of Congress appeared at the podium on the convention's opening night—Mo Udall's introduction of Jimmy Carter's address (rescheduled for prime time by the Democratic leadership), remarks by Representative Bill Alexander of Arkansas (who was unopposed for reelection), and a brief address by Senator Frank Lautenberg of New Jersey. Contrast this with the much more carefully orchestrated effort of Republicans to make pleas for the election of a party majority in both House and Senate by associating the party with praiseworthy causes. In addition to addresses by Phil Gramm and Howard Baker (and Baker's ensuing appearances as temporary chair), Senator Thad Cochran presided over a tribute to American Olympic athletes and Representative Guy Vander Jagt of Michigan, chair of the National Republican Campaign committee, addressed the convention, calling for Republican congressional majorities, and then introduced a five-minute film featuring the candidacies of six Republican House challengers to incumbents. The result was that Republicans featured members of Congress on keynote night by two-to-one ratio over Democrats.

If any convention evening is congressional in tone, it is platform night. Both parties devoted almost one-half of their time for proceedings to congressional personnel on their respective platform nights. Both parties, as part of the ritual of presenting their platforms to convention delegates, gave ample time for members of Congress to have their moment in the limelight. Of the two hours of speeches delivered by House members at the Democratic convention's second evening session, all but Tip O'Neill's addressed a host of platform-related policy issues. Republicans also used the platform presentation as an opportunity to showcase members of Congress (Trent Lott, Jack Kemp, Marjorie Holt of Pennsylvania) but found other rationales for doing so as well—Robert Michel's call for a Republican Congress in his address, Richard Lugar's plea to keep the party's majority in the Senate, and Senator Robert Dole's low-keyed convention presentation.

Both parties involved members of Congress in their nominating night's proceedings. The parties differed, however, in how that involvement came about. In the case of Democrats, congressional personnel were featured by the contending presidential candidates as speakers placing the candidates' names in nomination or as seconders. Thus, for example, Senator Christopher Dodd of Connecticut placed Gary Hart's name in nomination, and Representative Robert Garcia of New York seconded Walter Mondale's nomination. At the Republican convention in Dallas, Nevada senator Paul Laxalt's twenty-six minute address nominating Ronald Reagan and seconding speeches by Bobbi Fiedler (California) and Lynn Martin (for George Bush) accounted for more than one-third of the time at the podium spent by congressional members. Yet Michel's appearances as presiding officer and separate addresses by senators John Tower (Texas) and Barry Goldwater (Arizona) provided their own congressional focus, even though the evening's emphasis was clearly elsewhere.

For both parties, the final evening of their respective conventions were relatively brief sessions, approximately three hours for each. The acceptance speeches of presidential and vice-presidential nominees and the floor demonstrations surrounding them, as expected, dominated the evening's events and their coverage. The only congressional appearances for Democrats came from those placing Geraldine Ferraro's name in nomination (Representative Barbara Kennelly of Connecticut) or introducing the party nominees (Senator Kennedy introducing Mondale, Representative Jim Wright of Texas introducing Ferraro). Except for co-chairs Michel and Kassebaum, no congressional personnel appeared at the podium for the closing night of the Republican convention (although one of Michel's appearances, a duet rendering of "God Bless America" with Vikki Carr, drew applause!).

In sum, as represented in gavel-to-gavel coverage by C-SPAN, both political parties provided ample opportunities for members of Congress to exhibit their talents for one purpose or another at the 1984 party conventions. Republicans, perhaps wishing to leave the message with party members and with television viewers that the country would be in good hands if their party held a congressional majority, devoted more time to showcasing congressional members and to doing so in different convention roles. The Democratic congressional story was more muted, eliminating congressional personnel from official convention roles and exploiting their appearances in roles of party exhortation or as platform spokespersons. But whether these two tales reached the largest viewing audience for the national conventions depended not on what the parties proposed, but on what the commercial networks disposed.

NETWORK COVERAGE OF THE DEMOCRATS
IN SAN FRANCISCO

The bulk of coverage by the commercial television networks of the Democratic National Convention was focused away from the podium. (Consult Table 8.2 in the Appendix to this chapter.) Podium events occupied 41 percent of convention coverage by ABC and by NBC and 38 percent of the coverage provided by CBS. Network podium coverage centered on the addresses of the principal candidates for the Democratic presidential nomination and on the keynote address of New York governor Mario Cuomo. Whereas C-SPAN coverage of appearances by members of the House and the Senate on the podium constituted almost one-fourth of that network's air time, podium events revolving about congressional personnel contributed only 6 percent of the respective coverage of ABC and NBC and a mere 3 percent of the coverage of CBS. And whereas C-SPAN coverage publicized members of Congress in all of the four roles described earlier, the party orator role was that featured by the commercial networks. Congressional officials acting in the capacities of convention officials, factional spokespersons, or campaigners were largely ignored.

This is not to say that the three news networks failed to cover congressional members or candidates for the House and Senate. Rather than focus on podium activities, the networks devoted their time to interviews with members of Congress either by network anchors or by correspondents on the floor of the convention. With the exception of two interviews in the CBS anchor booth of House Speaker Tip O'Neill conducted by Dan Rather (one before Geraldine Ferraro's acceptance address and one after her speech) in which the Speaker essentially played the partisan orator role, such interviews were the province of network floor correspondents. But even then the twenty-eight interviews conducted by all three networks scarcely replaced the amount of publicity members of Congress were able to achieve in podium appearances pictured on C-SPAN. For each network, only 3 percent or less of total coverage time featured Democratic members of Congress or candidates for membership in any way. On any given evening the proportion of each network's time devoted to congressional members varied but never moved out of the range of 2 to 4 percent for any of the networks. Moreover, of congressional members or candidates available for network interviews, only one challenger to a sitting member of that body made it on to the TV camera for an opportunity to promote a candidacy, Governor James Hunt of North Carolina, who opined that Ferraro's candidacy would aid his bid to unseat Senator Jesse Helms (Helms proved victorious). The only other outright campaign-oriented interview with a member of Congress came with California representative Tony Coelho, chair of the House Democratic Campaign Committee, who viewed the brief controversy over the appointment of Bert Lance as campaign coordinator as no hindrance to House candidacies.

As NBC podium and floor correspondent Roger Mudd was to note at the Republican National Convention in August, one minor purpose of the roll call vote for selecting candidates for president and vice-president is to assist the candidacies of those in state delegations running for congressional office. The "roll call helps promote" them, said Mudd. The extended roll call vote at the Democratic conclave (lasting just short of one hour) gave ample opportunity for cameo appearances by congressional candidates on the news networks. Network bumpers (the printed material appearing at the bottom of the video picture) identified eleven such congressional members or candidates. Of those, the most notable were Tom Harkin of Iowa, Albert Gore of Tennessee, and Jay Rockefeller of West Virginia (all winners in their races) and November losers Judith Pratt of New Mexico and James Hunt of North Carolina.

Obviously, the commercial networks gave little emphasis to coverage of members of Congress or aspirants to that body in broadcasts of proceedings of the Democratic National Convention. Nor did delegates receive lengthy attention in anchor or floor interviews. Of what, then, did the three networks' coverage primarily consist? Aside from candidate speeches from the podium and the running of commercial advertising (which, combined, amounted to 35 to 40 percent of coverage), the focal point of network coverage was on their luminaries, the anchors. Consider CBS. Either alone as a talking head or off camera with voice over floor proceedings, or in discussion with floor correspondents or network analysts (Bill Moyers, Kevin Phillips, Mark Shields, and Walter Cronkite), Dan Rather was featured in 120 appearances of CBS coverage, 37 percent of all coverage time (i.e., more than four hours). No network's coverage was so consistently dominated by the anchor as was that of CBS. In air time he outshone all Democratic presidential and vice-presidential candidates at the podium combined. Introducing the nominating evening of Wednesday, July 18, as "Walter Mondale's Night," Rather then proceeded to be on camera more than two hours and twenty minutes, 50 percent of all coverage time. If anything, it was Dan Rather's night, not Walter Mondale's. Co-anchors Peter Jennings and David Brinkley of ABC and NBC anchor Tom Brokaw also captured the bulk of their network's camera time, but not to the degree as did Rather on CBS. In sum, from the network's point of view, the Democratic National Convention was not so much to be reported as to be commented on and discussed by anchors and analysts in the absence of hard news.

NETWORK COVERAGE OF THE REPUBLICANS IN DALLAS

Anchors, floor correspondents, and analysts from all three commercial networks frequently commented on the precise organization and orchestration of events at the Dallas meeting of the Republican party. This derived in part from the tendency of Democrats in San Francisco to make last-minute schedule changes, to let floor demonstrations extend longer than planned, to fail to have Walter Mondale nominated in prime time, and generally to run over the commercial networks' allotted program time. But network personnel were also making reference to the problems of finding hard news in the tightly controlled Republican proceedings. Indeed, on some evenings the networks were as hard pressed to get scheduled commercial breaks in as they were to air newsworthy events. For example, on the closing night of the Dallas convention, so rapidly did Republican proceedings move along that CBS and NBC managed only seven commercial breaks between them. (ABC, however, had no hesitation at breaking from convention events and thus managed as many commercial breaks as the other two networks combined and almost as much advertising time as the total for CBS and NBC.)

Perhaps owing in part to planning, the GOP in Dallas fared better in showcasing their congressional personnel, relative to other convention persona the networks might have covered, than had the Democrats in San Francisco. (Consult Table 8.3 in the Appendix to this chapter.) Consider the coverage of podium events by the networks. NBC, ABC, and CBS, respectively, devoted 37 percent, 39 percent, and 41 percent of their coverage time in Dallas to podium activities. Unlike the Democrats, however, the Republicans had but two candidates, hence far fewer speeches from the podium by contenders. Partly because of scheduling and partly because of the members of Congress given oratorical opportunities in Dallas, the networks focused on selected speeches by Republican House and Senate members. All three networks carried Congressman Jack Kemp's address on foreign policy, which put Kemp as much in a campaigner role as presentor of the party platform, and called to viewers' attention Kemp's likely race for the presidency in 1988. All networks carried the remarks of Senator Robert Dole, again calling attention to his membership in the nominal "Class of '88." CBS and NBC featured the partisan oratory of Senator Howard Baker, all three networks that of Senator Barry Goldwater and the nominating address of Senator Paul Laxalt. Overall, therefore, twice the proportion of network coverage at Dallas was devoted to members of Congress at the podium as had been the case in San Francisco.

Republicans were also more successful at showcasing senators than had been Democrats. For one thing, convention managers made a point, as NBC Tom Brokaw reported, of scheduling selected persons to "make the rounds" of network anchor booths. All three networks had a crack at Senator Robert Dole; in each case the interview focused in part on his plans for 1988. ABC's Jennings and Brinkley collared Senator John Tower as well and NBC's Brokaw added senators Howard Baker, Lowell Weicker, and Paul Laxalt. House members such as Newt Gingrich of Georgia and Trent Lott of Mississippi, House challengers including Ray Garland of Virginia and Peggy Miller of West Virginia, senators with nothing to fear in 1984 (Jeremiah Denton of Alabama and Strom Thurmond of South Carolina), incumbent senators up for reelection with much to fear (Jesse Helms of North Carolina, Charles Percy of Illinois), and senatorial challengers (Raymond Shamie and Eliot Richardson, contending for the party nomination in Massachusetts) had opportunities to promote themselves in interviews with floor correspondents. And, during what NBC anchor Tom Brokaw called the "anticlimax" and "routine" of the roll call, there were again brief but notable attempts at promoting senatorial candidacies, including those of winners Ted Stevens of Alaska and Jesse Helms and of loser Mary Mochary of New Jersey.

That the GOP showcased House members, senators, and challengers more successfully with the networks than had the Democrats a month earlier did not change the overriding fact of network coverage at both conventions. Once again anchors, alone or in discussion, dominated proceedings. In anchor candidacies Rather again won the most air time votes, more than three hours, over the twin ticket of Jennings and Brinkley and the single challenge of Brokaw. No presidential, vice-presidential, or congressional figure or candidate steals the limelight from the chief political actors at the networks' version of national party conventions, the anchors.

NATIONAL IMPLICATIONS OF CONGRESSIONAL ELECTIONS: THE UNCOVERED STORY

Political scientist Michael Robinson has remarked on the first and second laws of "videopolitics," to wit: "Television alters the behavior of institutions in direct proportion to the amount of coverage provided or allowed" and "the more coverage an institution secures, the greater its public stature and the more significant its role."[7] Whether they are laws is, at best, problematical. Be that as it may, there is no question that since the full rush to televised coverage of national party conventions in 1952, convention organizers have altered the behavior of their institutions, first to put the best foot forward in the face of networks' full coverage in the early years, now to streamline conventions to maximize favorable publicity in networks' shortened hours of prime time coverage. The focus of such streamlining has, of course, been on presenting each party's presidential ticket in the light of party unity and harmony. But the tasks of promoting the election of presidential tickets are not the sole campaign functions of the national conventions. Conventions can be used to promote an image of party coherence that extends to the election of sympathetic partisans in both houses of Congress as well. The preceding analysis suggests that at least in 1984, the Republicans may have been slightly more attuned to such promotional possibilities than were the Democrats, both from the standpoint of scheduling congressional leaders for appearances on prime time gavel-to-gavel coverage (on C-SPAN and on the GOP's own Republican National Convention Network Service, which provided coverage for 1,000 cable broadcast stations) and in exploiting coverage by commercial networks on behalf of congressional figures.

What is clearer, however, is that congressional candidacies—and the consequences for presidential politics of the outcomes of congressional elections—constitute largely uncovered stories insofar as the commercial networks are concerned. In this respect the national implications of congressional races provide but an added example of what Adams, in his analysis of coverage of the 1984 party conventions, labels as "missing interviews," "missing questions," "missing analysis," and "missing issues."[8] And, to the degree that the relationship of congressional to presidential candidacies goes uncovered, there is but another instance of what Ornstein and Robinson refer to as "our disappearing congress" in news coverage.[9] Surely the converse of Robinson's "second law" may well hold. If, as he suggests, "the more coverage an institution secures, the greater its public stature and the more significant its role," then the less the coverage, the less its public esteem, appreciated role, and even accountability. It remains to be seen whether future national party conventions are cut-and-dried formalities that but go through the motions of selecting presidential nominees and framing platforms. Even should that be the case, the national news networks might yet consider the possibility that a refocusing on the other major institution of government that plays a major role in party conventions (i.e., the Congress) will produce precisely the hard news they now find so lacking in the party conclaves. To paraphrase the closing of one of television's more popular entertainment programs of years gone by, the *Naked City*, there are eight million stories in the naked city. The TV networks might well start telling more than merely one of them.

NOTES

1. Samuel L. Becker and Elmer L. Lower, "Broadcasting in Presidential Campaigns," in Sidney Kraus, ed., *The Great Debates* (Bloomington: Indiana University Press, 1962), pp. 22–55.

2. Charles A. H. Thomson, *Television and Presidential Politics: The Experience of 1952 and the Problems Ahead* (Washington, D.C.: The Brookings Institute, 1956).

3. Denis Brogan, *Politics in America* (New York: Harper and Brothers, 1954).

4. Thomson, op. cit.

5. Paul T. David, Ralph M. Goldman, and Richard C. Bain, *The Politics of National Party Conventions* (Washington, D.C.: The Brookings Institute, 1960); T. R. Marshall, *Presidential Nominations in a Reform Age* (New York: Praeger, 1981).

6. James W. Davis, *National Conventions in the Age of Reform* (Westport, Conn.: Greenwood Press, 1983).

7. Michael J. Robinson, "A Twentieth Century Medium in a Nineteenth Century Legislature: The Effects of Television on the American Congress," in N.J. Ornstein, ed., *Congress in Change: Evolution and Reform* (New York: Praeger Books, 1975), pp. 241, 256.

8. William Adams, "Convention Coverage," *Public Opinion* 7 (December/January 1985): 43–48.

9. N. Ornstein and M. Robinson, "The Case of Our Disappearing Congress," *TV Guide* 34 (January 11, 1986): 4–10.

Table 8.1
C-SPAN Coverage of Democratic and Republican National Conventions

Coverage	Combined Coverage			DNC			RNC		
	N	Length	%	N	Length	%	N	Length	%
				4–DAY TOTAL					
Podium									
Official	43	2:44:40	10%	30	1:34:20	10%	13	1:10:20	11%
Delegate	38	3:25:40	13%	33	2:55:10	18%	5	0:30:30	5%
Candidate	10	4:16:40	16%	8	3:05:10	19%	2	1:11:30	11%
Congressman	61	4:06:40	15%	25	2:46:20	17%	36	1:20:20	13%
Senator	29	2:49:20	10%	9	1:08:30	7%	20	1:40:50	16%
Other	47	4:37:10	17%	13	1:55:40	12%	34	2:41:30	26%
Demonstration	59	3:31:50	13%	38	2:14:50	14%	21	1:17:00	12%
Film	17	1:24:10	5%	5	0:43:40	4%	12	0:40:30	6%
				MONDAY					
Podium									
Official	21	0:30:50	10%	11	0:20:30	11%	10	0:10:20	8%
Delegate	5	0:28:30	9%	5	0:28:30	15%	–	–	–
Candidate	–	–	–	–	–	–	–	–	–
Congressman	5	0:22:50	7%	2	0:12:30	7%	3	0:10:20	8%
Senator	7	0:23:40	8%	1	0:05:20	3%	6	0:18:20	15%
Other	16	2:40:50	51%	6	1:28:00	46%	10	1:12:50	57%
Demonstration	16	0:23:20	7%	10	0:12:30	7%	6	0:10:50	9%
Film	6	0:26:30	8%	3	0:22:40	12%	3	0:03:50	3%

Table 8.1 (Continued)

Coverage	Combined Coverage N	Length	%	DNC N	Length	%	RNC N	Length	%
				TUESDAY					
Podium									
Official	6	0:08:00	2%	6	0:08:00	3%	-	-	-
Delegate	18	1:24:20	20%	15	1:10:10	24%	3	0:14:10	11%
Candidate	1	0:54:00	13%	1	0:54:00	19%	-	-	-
Congressman	29	2:34:20	12%	18	1:59:30	41%	11	0:34:50	27%
Senator	13	0:50:30	12%	4	0:22:30	8%	9	0:28:00	22%
Other	8	0:39:30	9%	1	0:02:10	1%	7	0:37:20	29%
Demonstration	10	0:24:00	5%	1	0:02:10	1%	5	0:08:10	6%
Film	5	0:05:40	1%	-	-	-	5	0:05:40	4%
				WEDNESDAY					
Podium									
Official	12	2:03:10	22%	9	1:03:10	20%	3	1:00:00	25%
Delegate	13	1:22:50	15%	11	1:06:30	21%	2	0:16:20	7%
Candidate	5	1:10:10	13%	5	1:10:10	22%	-	-	-
Congressman	21	0:44:50	8%	3	0:12:40	4%	18	0:32:10	13%
Senator	6	1:10:20	13%	2	0:16:50	5%	4	0:53:30	22%
Other	12	0:37:30	7%	2	0:05:20	2%	10	0:32:10	13%
Demonstration	22	1:45:50	19%	16	1:09:40	22%	6	0:36:10	15%
Film	3	0:19:30	3%	1	0:10:10	3%	2	0:09:20	4%

Table 8.1 (Continued)

THURSDAY

Coverage	Combined Coverage			DNC			RNC		
	N	Length	%	N	Length	%	N	Length	%
Podium									
Official	4	0:02:40	1%	4	0:02:40	1%	–	–	–
Delegate	2	0:10:00	3%	2	0:10:00	5%	–	–	–
Candidate	4	2:12:30	41%	2	1:01:00	32%	2	1:11:30	52%
Congressman	6	0:24:40	8%	1	0:21:40	11%	4	0:03:00	2%
Senator	3	0:24:30	7%	2	0:24:00	13%	1	0:00:30	<1%
Other	11	0:39:20	12%	4	0:20:10	11%	7	0:19:10	14%
Demonstration	11	1:00:40	19%	7	0:38:50	21%	4	0:21:50	16%
Film	3	0:32:40	10%	1	0:11:00	6%	2	0:21:40	16%

Source: Computed by authors.

Table 8.2
Network Coverage of the Democratic National Convention

4–DAY TOTAL

Coverage	ABC N	ABC Length	ABC %	CBS N	CBS Length	CBS %	NBC N	NBC Length	NBC %
Anchor									
Alone	61	0:47:30	7%	88	1:30:00	13%	81	2:43:40	25%
Discussion	45	2:27:50	23%	32	2:49:00	24%	5	0:12:10	2%
Candidate	4	0:10:30	2%	2	0:08:30	1%	1	0:04:30	<1%
Congressman	–	–	–	2	0:10:00	1%	–	–	–
Senator	–	–	–	–	–	–	–	–	–
Floor Correspondent									
Alone	21	0:29:30	5%	16	0:17:20	2%	16	0:17:20	3%
Delegate	17	0:25:50	4%	22	0:41:00	6%	26	0:42:00	6%
Congressman	6	0:11:00	2%	4	0:08:00	1%	9	0:14:20	2%
Senator	2	0:02:50	<1%	4	0:09:30	1%	3	0:03:30	<1%
Other	6	0:14:00	2%	5	0:09:40	1%	13	0:24:20	4%
Podium									
Official	–	–	–	–	–	–	–	–	–
Delegate	3	0:09:30	1%	4	0:18:30	3%	5	0:26:00	4%
Candidate	8	2:48:20	26%	8	2:46:30	24%	8	3:04:00	28%
Congressman	2	0:18:50	3%	–	–	–	3	0:20:40	3%
Senator	2	0:20:50	3%	2	0:23:50	3%	1	0:20:00	3%
Other	2	0:54:00	8%	4	0:58:20	8%	2	0:54:00	8%
Advertisements	34	1:26:50	14%	31	1:16:10	11%	25	1:01:30	9%
Films	–	–	–	–	–	–	–	–	–

Table 8.2 (Continued)

MONDAY

Coverage	ABC N	ABC Length	ABC %	CBS N	CBS Length	CBS %	NBC N	NBC Length	NBC %
Anchor									
Alone	17	0:13:20	11%	18	0:17:10	13%	17	0:19:30	17%
Discussion	6	0:10:50	9%	5	0:19:30	15%	1	0:01:40	1%
Candidate	–	–	–	1	0:01:50	1%	–	–	–
Congressman	–	–	–	–	–	–	–	–	–
Senator	–	–	–	–	–	–	–	–	–
Floor Correspondent									
Alone	6	0:09:20	8%	8	0:08:00	6%	2	0:02:30	2%
Delegate	1	0:01:50	2%	4	0:07:30	6%	8	0:11:50	10%
Congressman	1	0:01:40	1%	–	–	–	2	0:02:30	2%
Senator	–	–	–	–	–	–	1	0:01:40	1%
Other	2	0:03:10	3%	3	0:05:30	4%	3	0:06:50	6%
Podium									
Official	–	–	–	–	–	–	–	–	–
Delegate	–	–	–	–	–	–	–	–	–
Candidate	–	–	–	–	–	–	–	–	–
Congressman	1	0:06:50	6%	–	–	–	1	0:07:00	6%
Senator	–	–	–	–	–	–	–	–	–
Other	2	0:54:00	45%	2	0:53:50	42%	2	0:54:00	46%
Advertisements	8	0:18:30	15%	5	0:14:20	11%	5	0:10:20	9%
Film	–	–	–	–	–	–	–	–	–

Table 8.2 (Continued)

	ABC			CBS			NBC		
Coverage	N	Length	%	N	Length	%	N	Length	%
				TUESDAY					
Anchor									
Alone	14	0:14:00	12%	25	0:16:20	11%	20	0:18:20	13%
Discussion	3	0:04:20	4%	9	0:33:40	23%	2	0:07:10	5%
Candidate	–	–	–	–	–	–	–	–	–
Congressman	–	–	–	–	–	–	–	–	–
Senator	–	–	–	–	–	–	–	–	–
Floor Correspondent									
Alone	2	0:06:00	5%	1	0:02:00	1%	4	0:06:10	5%
Delegate	5	0:06:50	6%	7	0:12:40	9%	5	0:10:20	8%
Congressman	3	0:03:50	3%	2	0:04:30	3%	2	0:04:10	3%
Senator	–	–	–	2	0:04:30	3%	–	–	–
Other	1	0:03:30	3%	–	–	–	3	0:05:30	4%
Podium									
Official	–	–	–	–	–	–	–	–	–
Delegate	1	0:01:00	1%	2	0:03:00	2%	2	0:02:40	2%
Candidate	1	0:54:00	46%	1	0:53:00	36%	1	0:53:00	39%
Congressman	1	0:12:00	10%	–	–	–	2	0:13:40	10%
Senator	–	–	–	–	–	–	–	–	–
Other	–	–	–	1	0:04:00	3%	–	–	–
Advertisements	6	0:12:50	11%	6	0:12:30	8%	7	0:16:10	12%
Film	–	–	–	–	–	–	–	–	–

Table 8.2 (Continued)

WEDNESDAY

Coverage	ABC N	ABC Length	ABC %	CBS N	CBS Length	CBS %	NBC N	NBC Length	NBC %
Anchor									
Alone	24	0:16:00	6%	33	0:38:40	14%	26	1:31:00	37%
Discussion	21	1:40:40	40%	14	1:42:00	36%	–	–	–
Candidate	3	0:09:30	4%	1	0:06:40	2%	1	0:04:30	2%
Congressman	–	–	–	–	–	–	–	–	–
Senator	–	–	–	–	–	–	–	–	–
Floor Correspondent									
Alone	10	0:11:30	5%	4	0:04:30	2%	5	0:06:20	3%
Delegate	7	0:11:30	5%	9	0:18:20	6%	10	0:16:50	7%
Congressman	2	0:05:30	2%	2	0:03:30	1%	2	0:01:50	1%
Senator	2	0:01:50	1%	1	0:01:50	1%	1	0:01:20	1%
Other	3	0:07:20	3%	1	0:02:30	1%	5	0:09:40	4%
Podium									
Official	–	–	–	–	–	–	–	–	–
Delegate	2	0:08:30	3%	2	0:15:30	5%	3	0:23:20	9%
Candidate	5	0:53:20	21%	5	0:52:30	18%	5	1:10:00	28%
Congressman	–	–	–	–	–	–	–	–	–
Senator	1	0:00:50	<1%	1	0:03:50	1%	–	–	–
Other	–	–	–	–	–	–	–	–	–
Advertisements	11	0:26:30	10%	14	0:34:10	12%	8	0:21:10	9%
Film	–	–	–	–	–	–	–	–	–

Table 8.2 (Continued)

THURSDAY

Coverage	ABC			CBS			NBC		
	N	Length	%	N	Length	%	N	Length	%
Anchor.									
Alone	6	0:04:10	3%	12	0:17:50	12%	17	0:34:50	24%
Discussion	15	0:32:00	22%	4	0:13:50	9%	2	0:03:20	2%
Candidate	1	0:01:00	1%	–	–	–	–	–	–
Congressman	–	–	–	2	0:06:00	7%	–	–	–
Senator	–	–	–	–	–	–	–	–	–
Floor Correspondent									
Alone	3	0:02:40	2%	3	0:02:50	2%	5	0:02:20	2%
Delegate	4	0:05:40	4%	2	0:02:30	2%	3	0:03:00	2%
Congressman	–	–	–	–	–	–	3	0:05:50	4%
Senator	–	–	–	1	0:01:40	1%	1	0:00:30	<1%
Other	–	–	–	1	0:01:40	1%	2	0:02:20	2%
Podium									
Official	–	–	–	–	–	–	–	–	–
Delegate	–	–	–	–	–	–	–	–	–
Candidate	2	1:01:00	42%	2	1:01:00	42%	2	1:01:00	42%
Congressman	–	–	–	–	–	–	–	–	–
Senator	1	0:20:00	14%	1	0:20:00	14%	1	0:20:00	14%
Other	–	–	–	1	0:00:30	<1%	–	–	–
Advertisements	9	0:17:40	12%	6	0:15:10	10%	5	0:13:50	9%
Film	–	–	–	–	–	–	–	–	–

Source: Computed by authors.

Table 8.3
Network Coverage of the Republican National Convention

4-DAY TOTAL

Coverage	ABC N	Length	%	CBS N	Length	%	NBC N	Length	%
Anchor									
Alone	46	0:32:00	5%	58	1:54:50	20%	72	2:17:20	22%
Discussion	43	2:08:50	22%	16	1:10:20	12%	7	0:11:50	2%
Candidate	1	0:05:00	1%	1	0:05:10	1%	1	0:04:50	<1%
Congressman	–	–	–	–	–	–	2	0:09:00	1%
Senator	2	0:14:50	3%	1	0:05:10	1%	5	0:26:10	4%
Other	3	0:19:30	3%	5	0:25:30	4%	3	0:13:50	2%
Floor Correspondent									
Alone	22	0:45:50	8%	10	0:22:30	4%	15	0:25:40	4%
Delegate	8	0:10:50	2%	11	0:20:00	3%	14	0:23:40	4%
Congressman	4	0:06:30	1%	5	0:09:30	2%	6	0:11:30	2%
Senator	7	0:15:10	3%	2	0:03:10	<1%	12	0:24:30	4%
Other	2	0:06:00	1%	5	0:09:50	2%	11	0:19:50	3%
Podium									
Official	–	–	–	–	–	–	–	–	–
Delegate	–	–	–	1	0:07:50	1%	–	–	–
Candidate	2	1:11:30	12%	2	1:11:30	12%	2	1:11:30	12%
Congressman	1	0:09:30	2%	1	0:09:30	2%	1	0:09:30	2%
Senator	4	0:52:00	9%	5	0:56:00	10%	4	0:55:00	9%
Other	7	1:32:00	16%	7	1:33:50	16%	6	1:29:30	14%
Advertisements	32	1:08:30	12%	27	1:00:40	10%	29	1:07:20	11%
Film	2	0:08:50	2%	–	–	–	1	0:18:00	3%

Table 8.3 (Continued)

	ABC			CBS			NBC		
Coverage	N	Length	%	N	Length	%	N	Length	%
MONDAY									
Anchor									
Alone	3	0:00:50	<1%	11	0:09:10	7%	18	0:20:10	13%
Discussion	18	0:22:10	16%	3	0:10:00	7%	3	0:04:50	3%
Candidate	–	–	–	–	–	–	1	0:04:50	3%
Congressman	–	–	–	1	0:05:10	4%	–	–	–
Senator	–	–	–	–	–	–	2	0:14:30	10%
Other	1	0:07:20	5%	3	0:14:30	10%	–	–	–
Floor Correspondent									
Alone	4	0:09:10	7%	4	0:06:50	5%	1	0:04:20	3%
Delegate	4	0:05:00	4%	3	0:04:30	3%	3	0:04:20	3%
Congressman	1	0:01:30	1%	1	0:01:20	1%	1	0:02:00	1%
Senator	2	0:04:30	3%	–	–	–	4	0:10:10	7%
Other	1	0:02:40	2%	2	0:04:10	3%	3	0:05:20	4%
Podium									
Official	–	–	–	–	–	–	–	–	–
Delegate	–	–	–	–	–	–	–	–	–
Candidate	–	–	–	–	–	–	–	–	–
Congressman	–	–	–	–	–	–	–	–	–
Senator	1	0:10:00	7%	1	0:09:00	6%	1	0:10:00	7%
Other	3	0:58:20	42%	2	0:57:00	41%	2	0:57:30	38%
Advertisements	8	0:17:10	12%	8	0:18:00	13%	8	0:16:30	11%
Film	–	–	–	–	–	–	–	–	–

Table 8.3 (Continued)

TUESDAY

Coverage	ABC			CBS			NBC		
	N	Length	%	N	Length	%	N	Length	%
Anchor									
Alone	10	0:07:20	6%	21	0:15:40	12%	16	0:13:30	10%
Discussion	8	0:16:40	13%	3	0:20:30	16%	2	0:04:00	3%
Candidate	–	–	–	1	0:05:10	4%	–	–	–
Congressman	–	–	–	–	–	–	2	0:09:00	7%
Senator	2	0:14:50	11%	–	–	–	2	0:09:00	7%
Other	1	0:06:40	5%	1	0:04:00	3%	–	–	–
Floor Correspondent									
Alone	4	0:08:20	6%	1	0:01:10	1%	6	0:07:00	5%
Delegate	–	–	–	4	0:10:20	8%	7	0:12:20	10%
Congressman	2	0:04:40	4%	3	0:05:50	5%	2	0:04:10	3%
Senator	4	0:08:50	7%	–	–	–	2	0:03:10	2%
Other	–	–	–	1	0:02:30	2%	3	0:05:30	4%
Podium									
Official	–	–	–	–	–	–	–	–	–
Delegate	–	–	–	–	–	–	–	–	–
Candidate	–	–	–	–	–	–	–	–	–
Congressman	1	0:09:30	7%	1	0:09:30	7%	1	0:09:30	7%
Senator	1	0:06:00	5%	2	0:05:00	4%	1	0:05:00	4%
Other	2	0:29:40	23%	2	0:29:40	23%	2	0:28:00	22%
Advertisements	9	0:18:50	14%	8	0:19:00	15%	8	0:18:40	14%
Film	–	–	–	–	–	–	–	–	–

Table 8.3 (Continued)

WEDNESDAY

Coverage	ABC N	ABC Length	ABC %	CBS N	CBS Length	CBS %	NBC N	NBC Length	NBC %
Anchor									
Alone	18	0:12:30	7%	16	1:11:10	38%	29	1:28:00	43%
Discussion	9	1:12:10	40%	7	0:29:00	15%	2	0:03:00	1%
Candidate	1	0:05:00	3%	–	–	–	–	–	–
Congressman	–	–	–	–	–	–	–	–	–
Senator	–	–	–	–	–	–	1	0:02:40	1%
Other	1	0:05:30	3%	1	0:07:00	4%	2	0:07:30	4%
Floor Correspondent									
Alone	6	0:09:50	5%	4	0:05:10	3%	5	0:08:10	4%
Delegate	3	0:04:10	2%	1	0:01:20	1%	4	0:07:00	3%
Congressman	–	–	–	1	0:03:10	2%	3	0:05:20	3%
Senator	1	0:01:30	1%	2	0:01:20	1%	6	0:11:10	5%
Other	1	0:03:20	2%	1	–	–	5	0:09:00	4%
Podium									
Official	–	–	–	1	0:07:50	4%	–	–	–
Delegate	–	–	–	–	–	–	–	–	–
Candidate	–	–	–	–	–	–	–	–	–
Congressman	–	–	–	–	–	–	–	–	–
Senator	2	0:36:00	20%	2	0:42:00	22%	2	0:40:00	19%
Other	2	0:04:00	2%	2	0:03:40	2%	2	0:04:00	2%
Advertisements	8	0:16:40	9%	7	0:17:10	9%	10	0:20:50	10%
Film	2	0:08:50	5%	–	–	–	–	–	–

Table 8.3 (Continued)

THURSDAY

Coverage	ABC N	ABC Length	ABC %	CBS N	CBS Length	CBS %	NBC N	NBC Length	NBC %
Anchor									
Alone	15	0:11:20	8%	10	0:18:50	15%	9	0:15:40	12%
Discussion	8	0:17:50	13%	3	0:10:50	9%	–	–	–
Candidate	–	–	–	–	–	–	–	–	–
Congressman	–	–	–	–	–	–	–	–	–
Senator	–	–	–	–	–	–	–	–	–
Other	–	–	–	–	–	–	1	0:06:20	5%
Floor Correspondent									
Alone	8	0:18:30	14%	5	0:14:30	11%	3	0:08:30	6%
Delegate	1	0:01:40	1%	–	–	–	–	–	–
Congressman	1	0:00:20	<1%	–	–	–	–	–	–
Senator	–	–	–	–	–	–	–	–	–
Other	–	–	–	1	0:01:50	1%	–	–	–
Podium									
Official	–	–	–	–	–	–	–	–	–
Delegate	–	–	–	–	–	–	–	–	–
Candidate	2	1:11:30	52%	2	1:11:30	56%	2	1:11:30	54%
Congressman	–	–	–	–	–	–	–	–	–
Senator	–	–	–	–	–	–	–	–	–
Other	–	–	–	1	0:03:30	3%	–	–	–
Advertisements	7	0:15:50	12%	4	0:06:30	5%	3	0:11:20	9%
Film	–	–	–	–	–	–	1	0:18:00	14%

Source: Computed by authors.

9

Show Horses in House Elections: The Advantages and Disadvantages of National Media Visibility

Timothy E. Cook

A familiar complaint in current assessments of Congress has been to decry the preoccupation in both the House and the Senate with publicity. According to numerous scholars, beginning with Mayhew's (1974a) influential essay, Congress is nowadays organized less to address constructively public problems than to provide maximum opportunities for self-promotion. The "work horse," some say, has been succeeded by the "show horse," to the point that the mass media's effects on Congress include exacerbating the dispersion of power, increasing the dilemmas of coalition building in the institution, and contributing to the decline of Congress as a national policy-making body (see especially Robinson, 1981, Ornstein, 1983, and Ranney, 1983; a journalistic account that stresses this shift is Broder, 1986).

Evidence abounds that members of both the House and the Senate devote increasing resources to the search for publicity, not only through self-promotional efforts like trips home and mass mailings,[1] but also through the mass media. For example, the recent institutionalization of a designated press secretary position in House offices attests to the importance of the media as one focus for congressional activity. As of the Ninety-eighth Congress, in 1984, only 28 percent of House offices listed no staffers with press responsibilities—a striking shift from the Ninety-first Congress, in 1970, in which 84 percent of House offices had no designated press aide (Cook, 1985). Likewise, the national publicity accorded to House members has expanded during the same time period; whereas only 24 percent of House members were covered *at all* by the network news in 1970, more recent figures are as high as 55 percent in 1981 (Cook, 1986). Members may then be spending more time publicizing themselves and their activities, and they may be receiving more coverage, but it is less clear why they are doing so, how they are doing so, and with what effect.

The most common presumption has been that members of Congress pursue publicity to ensure reelection. There can be little doubt that the mass media play an important and growing role in congressional elections and reelections. Recognition of the competing candidates is a central determinant of voting decisions, and is highly affected by media coverage. As media advertising takes ever larger chunks of campaign finances, receiving free media exposure becomes crucial (see especially Goldenberg and Traugott, 1984). However, our knowledge approaches completeness only on the impact of local media coverage of the incumbent on congressional elections, where the symbiotic relationship of members and local media appears to work to the decisive benefit of the incumbent.[2] By providing newsworthy items to report, the members help the local media fill their newsholes; by reporting about the incumbents uncritically, the local media not only assure their own continued access to the newsmaking members, but also help to boost the incumbents' name recognition and favorable popular assessments of their activities.

The local media, however, make up only one part of what Robinson (1981) nicely terms the members' "media mix." We understand far less about the importance and impact of another component—national media visibility—on congressional elections, even though it is there that "show horses" often direct their attention. National media visibility has traditionally been assumed to be an advantage to members seeking reelection. For instance, Mayhew's (1974a) concept of advertising and Payne's (1980) consideration of "show horses" both suggest the national media as a key conduit of publicity with presumably beneficial effects on getting returned to Congress. Likewise, some members of Congress were initially prone to anticipate the incursion of national media into the House—especially the broadcasting of floor proceedings—as helping in reelection. In 1979 then-Representative John Anderson, a Republican from Illinois, called the nascent House television system "one more incumbent protection device at taxpayers' expense [that will] distort and prolong our proceedings by encouraging more and longer speeches for home consumption" (in Cooper, 1979, p. 252). On the other hand, there is reason to doubt that national media attention is seen to be as much of a plus for members in reelection as has been commonly assumed. Robinson (1981), for one, contends that most members of

Congress see the national media as being tougher and less fair to them than the pliant local media. And insofar as news coverage of Congress does tend to be more negative than positive (see Miller et al., 1979; Robinson and Appel, 1979; Tidmarch and Pitney, 1985), members may wish to avoid any guilt by association with the disdained institution far from the home district where the incumbent's support is best nurtured and reinforced.

It is then unclear whether the national media help or hurt the incumbents' pursuit of reelection, as the only examination of the value of national media visibility for reelection (Payne, 1980) is generally problematic.[3] There are intuitive reasons for each set of expectations. On one hand, coverage by the national news, particularly television's network news, could provide impressive indicators of members' value to constituents, not to mention to potential contributors who wish to invest their funds in important and salient candidates. Then again, such publicity could be less positive than that supplied by the local media; or, if it is taken as an indicator of importance, it could actually propel toward the challenger contributors and political action committees who wish to get the most for their money. In short, national media attention could plausibly be either a plus or a minus to members seeking reelection.

This chapter seeks to address these theses in two related ways. First, it considers the evidence from two recent (and much studied) congressional elections in 1978 and 1980 to ascertain the extent to which national media coverage in both print and network news can help or hurt incumbents' campaigns for reelection, either directly at the polls or indirectly through the candidates' relative strength. Two measures of national media visibility are used here—one from the nightly network news broadcasts, another from a national "newspaper of record," the *New York Times*. Second, it examines responses from two surveys of House press secretaries, both conducted in the fall of 1984, to gauge the attentiveness of House offices to the national media and their estimations of how well the national media aid their pursuit of the goal of reelection.

MEDIA VISIBILITY IN CONGRESSIONAL ELECTIONS: AN AGGREGATE ANALYSIS

As sketched above, national media coverage could empirically influence congressional election outcomes in interrelated ways. First, there could be a direct relationship between media visibility and the percentage of votes received by the incumbent; voters could respond directly, whether favorably or unfavorably, to noticing their representative in the national news. Because many fewer constituents read national newspapers than watch the network news, it is hypothesized that the relationship should be stronger with the latter than with the former. Second, and probably more likely, given the even chances that a representative will not be mentioned in the network news in a given year (Cook, 1986) and the general inattentiveness of the mass public to nightly network news (Comstock et al., 1977), there could be an indirect relationship mediated through the strength of the challenger as measured by the funds he or she is able to raise and spend (Jacobson, 1980). Here one would not expect the relationships with coverage in network news or the *Times* to differ, insofar as the coverage is taken as a surrogate for importance and/or notoriety on Capitol Hill.

To test these suggestions, data were collected for a variety of activities engaged in by members at least in part for electoral benefit (e.g., trips home, bills co-sponsored, district staff allocations), the member's position within the House (e.g., leadership status, seniority), and electoral liabilities (e.g., estimates of policy discrepancy from the district, ethical accusations), as well as indicators of partisan strength and the incumbent's past electoral performance in previous years, in order to assess the impact of media coverage over and above those variables more commonly thought to affect congressional elections. (For a fuller description and rationalization of these variables, see Ragsdale and Cook, 1987).

The media visibility variables are straightforward. For visibility in the network news, a count was made of the number of times each member was mentioned on any nightly network news broadcast according to the Vanderbilt Television News Abstracts and Indices; because this variable and a transformed variable (the square root of the actual mentions) were both collinear with the leadership status variable, the variable used in these equations is a dummy variable for whether or not the member was mentioned in any nightly news broadcast during a given year. For visibility in the national print media, a similar count was taken using the *New York Times Index*; here the variable is transformed by taking the square root in order to reduce the skewed distribution of the variable, and thus reduce the influence of isolated outliers on the regression equation results.

Table 9.1 reports the findings of an equation regressing a number of variables, including the network news visibility variable, on the percentage of the vote won by the incumbent. As can be seen, in neither 1978 nor 1980 did network news visibility have a significant direct effect on the vote totals; instead, the election returns were best explained by long-term and short-term partisan conditions, the challengers' expenditures and political experience, and accusations of ethical improprieties. Appearing on the network news had no independent impact on the vote totals. Similar results obtain if visibility in the *Times* is included in the equation in lieu of the media visibility variable. The coefficients for the

Table 9.1
Determinants of the Congressional Vote—Regression Estimates

Dependent Variable: Incumbent's Percentage of District Vote

	1978			1980		
	B	beta	t	B	beta	t
District trips[a]	.056	.069	1.843	-.015	-.016	-.415
Bills sponsored[a]	.002	.009	.213	.013	.051	1.379
National media	-.649	-.026	-.657	.509	.018	.466
District staff	2.601	.032	.839	2.985	.033	.863
Committee prestige	3.720	.053	1.417	4.343	.057	1.492
Tenure in office	.069	.051	.979	.036	.023	.464
Leadership	-1.586	-.050	-1.107	.845	.024	.498
Ethical problems	-8.697	-.171	-4.508**	-18.182	-.257	-6.824**
Policy discrepancy	-.035	-.053	-1.430	-.017	-.028	-.759
Incumbent money	-.006	-.051	-1.117	-.003	.051	1.086
Challenger money	-.045	-.394	-8.168**	-.032	-.431	-8.529**
Challenger experience	-3.03	-.102	-2.547**	-.515	-.032	-.849
Challenger prior run	.698	.021	.558	-.699	-.019	-.519
Primary opposition	-.080	-.100	-2.574**	-.084	-.098	-2.674**
Incumbent's party	-.356	-.016	-.412	3.468	.144	2.673**
Presidential vote	.317	.271	6.148**	.367	.439	7.990**
Past district vote	.185	.231	4.860**	.217	.278	6.307**
Intercept	35.373			67.432		

$R^2 = .651$ $R^2 = .664$

[a]Measure is the average of the election year and the year before.

** Coefficient significant at .01 level (t critical = 2.236).

Source: Ragsdale and Cook (1987, Table 7).

other variables do not change appreciably; the impact of *Times* coverage is slightly stronger but does not approach statistical significance even at a .10 level (beta in 1978 = .058; beta in 1980 = .030).

National media coverage would then initially seem to have little effect, positive or negative, on House elections. Such a conclusion, however, would have to be modified by the results in Tables 9.2 and 9.3, which regress variables measured in the year preceding the election year on challengers' expenditures in the two elections. The equations in Table 9.2 were constructed to give the best possible case to the impact of incumbents' activities on challengers' strength; those in Table 9.3 were set up to see the effect of the statistically significant variables from Table 9.2 over and above numerous other influences on challengers' funding levels.

Interestingly, media coverage in the network news did have an effect on challengers' strength as measured either by their expenditures or their political action committee (PAC) contributions. The effect is negative in 1978 but is not significant at a .05 level. In 1980, however, network news visibility *positively* predicted challenger moneys, and similar effects were in evidence on challengers' PAC contributions (see Ragsdale and Cook, 1987). Whether or not one was covered by the nightly news apparently increased one's chances of facing a strong opponent, even over and above the effects of variables that would best predict media visibility such as leadership status and ethical accusations.[4] Moreover, at the same time that incumbents' media visibility apparently assisted challengers in their abilities to raise and spend funds, it had no similar effects for incumbents attempting to match challengers' efforts. Network news visibility tended to positively predict incumbents' expenditures ($p < .10$ in both 1978 and 1980) but had no effect on incumbents' PAC contributions.[5] Again, similar but somewhat stronger effects were obtained, substituting the *Times* variable for the network news visibility variable. In sum, national media coverage either in print or over the air seems not to be, at best, a credible strategy for incumbents in seeking reelection, and, at worst, it may be a way to enhance the strength of one's opponent.

MEMBERS AND NATIONAL MEDIA: THE PRESS SECRETARIES' PERSPECTIVE

The results from the 1980 election show the perils of national media visibility. Members more visible in the national news were more likely to face credible opponents than those not covered. Receiving what "show horses" seek—coverage by the national media—not only seems not to pay dividends at the polls; it may actually hurt, indirectly but effectively, the member's chances for reelection.

Table 9.2
The Effects of Incumbent Resources on Challenger Strength—Regression Estimates

Challenger Expenditures

	1978			1980		
	B	beta	t	B	beta	t
District trips	.026	.004	.073	-.824	-.071	-1.182
Bills sponsored	-.053	-.051	-.837	-.070	-.036	-.616
National media	-15.133	-.083	-1.425	36.001	.116	1.906*
District staff	34.190	.049	.818	75.443	.062	1.011
Committee prestige	-16.903	-.028	-.478	-45.214	-.044	-.725
Tenure in office	1.118	.094	1.242	-.873	-.041	-.523
Leadership	15.440	.056	.815	20.958	.043	.576
Ethical problems	39.301	.089	1.584	-15.637	-.016	-.271
Policy discrepancy	.868	.150	2.695**	1.092	.133	2.274**
Past incumbent money	.349	.247	4.127**	.532	.319	5.100**
Intercept	-62.397			68.040		

$R^2 = .135$ $R^2 = .161$

Table 9.2 (Continued)

Challenger PAC Contributions

District trips	.036	.024	.453	-.275	-.091	-1.495
Bills sponsored	-.009	-.035	-.607	-.021	-.043	-.713
National media	-2.307	-.053	-.958	13.233	.164	2.710**
District staff	13.566	.081	1.429	14.048	.045	.716
Committee prestige	2.859	.020	.356	-16.940	-.063	-1.039
Tenure in office	.564	.199	2.896**	.135	.025	.317
Leadership	6.947	.105	1.621	1.927	.015	.202
Ethical problems	20.397	.192	3.631**	3.522	.014	.234
Policy discrepancy	.173	.125	2.375**	.248	.116	1.963*
Past incumbent money	.357	.331	6.191**	.362	.269	4.417**
Intercept	-46.797			-6.821		
	$R^2 = .223$			$R^2 = .145$		

* Coefficient significant at .05 level (t critical = 1.960)
** Coefficient significant at .01 level (t critical = 2.236)
Source: Ragsdale and Cook (1987, Table 1)

168

Table 9.3
Determinants of Challenger Money—Regression Estimates

	Challenger Expenditures			1980		
	B	beta	t	B	beta	t
Policy discrepancy	.862	.149	3.15**	1.065	.130	2.375**
Ethical problems	--	--	--	--	--	--
National media	--	--	--	44.799	.144	2.632**
Tenure in office	--	--	--	--	--	--
Past incumbent money	-.084	-.060	-.980	.262	.157	2.255*
Past challenger money	.459	.395	6.131**	.060	.043	.569
Past challenger experience	67.034	.043	.913	8.478	.019	.301
Challenger prior run	29.057	.102	2.118*	28.349	.057	1.033
Primary opposition	.154	.022	.443	.597	.051	.923
Incumbent's party	13.219	.069	1.383	38.632	.118	2.142*
Presidential vote	-2.417	-.236	-4.244**	-1.792	-.104	-1.670
Past district vote	-.820	-.117	-1.844	-2.690	-.253	-3.631**
Intercept	116.413			5.119		
	$R^2 = .370$			$R^2 = .255$		

Table 9.3 (Continued)

Challenger PAC Contributions

Policy discrepancy	.164	.118	2.539**	.396	.139	2.516**
Ethical problems	19.006	.179	3.738**	--	--	--
National media	--	--	--	11.150	.138	2.498**
Tenure in office	.176	.062	1.182	--	--	--
Past incumbent money	-.028	-.084	-1.372	.066	.153	2.181*
Past challenger money	.101	.363	5.690**	.002	.004	.055
Past challenger experience	46.843	.125	2.704**	-3.837	-.033	-.519
Challenger prior run	5.758	.085	1.739	9.931	.077	1.380
Primary opposition	.012	.007	.145	-.0009	-.0003	-.006
Incumbent's party	4.487	.099	1.986*	12.856	.151	2.718**
Presidential vote	-.407	-.166	-3.032**	-.209	-.047	-.742
Past district vote	-.324	-.193	-3.023**	-.849	-.308	-4.370**
Intercept	-1.250			-22.358		

$R^2 = .353$ $R^2 = .240$

* Coefficient significant at .05 level (t critical = 1.960)
** Coefficient significant at .01 level (t critical = 2.236)
Source: Ragsdale and Cook (1987, Table 2).

Yet, despite these empirical indicators and Robinson's (1981) contention that members and their staffs see the national media as tough and unfair, we know that members of Congress seldom hide from national attention. Of course, it may be that the national media may be worth the reelection risks in order to attain other goals—public policy accomplishments, influence in Washington, progressive ambition, or just plain ego gratification—but could there be subtle benefits from national news attention about which members and staffers are aware?

To estimate whether and why House press operations would pay attention to the national media, I proceeded in two complementary ways. First, I conducted forty semistructured interviews with a representative sample of press secretaries in the fall directly preceding the 1984 election. All interviews were held under "not-for-attribution" conditions in which strict anonymity for member and staffer alike was guaranteed. A semistructured format was chosen in order to ask particular questions while permitting the interviewee to digress into potentially important areas. Although this format does not permit easy quantification, it provides a rich basis for conclusions. Second, through the Association of House Democratic Press Assistants, a three-page questionnaire composed by myself and Lynn Drake, then-president of the association, was sent out in November 1984, after the election, to all Ninety-eighth Congress Democratic House offices, asking the press secretary to respond to questions pertaining to their media operations and their perceptions of a number of strategies and news outlets. The response rate was a reasonably strong 46 percent (N = 123), an acceptable percentage considering that numerous House offices do not have any one designated press aide.[6] Only Democrats were studied because of the importance of being able to determine the member for which particular press secretaries worked, and because of the sensitivity of press strategies. Although each of these approaches is imperfect, our ability to triangulate between the two studies enhances the confidence with which one can make conclusions. Moreover, although these surveys cannot give the perceptions of members themselves (or, for that matter, fellow staffers) on the presumed importance of the national media to congressional operations, they do provide solid indications of the strategies preferred by those most closely working with the press and the approaches that they bring to the relationship of Congress and the media.[7]

During the semistructured interviews I asked what the major focus of the press secretaries' jobs were, what they spent the most time doing, who they dealt with, and the strategies they used to get their members' names in the news. Questions about the national media were expressly reserved until later in the interview. Frequently, at this point, the respondents had mentioned nothing about the national media—either electronic or print. Moreover, to the pursuant question, "Do the national media help in getting the job done?" press secretaries were often incredulous, some indicating that nobody in the district read the *Washington Post* or the *New York Times*. National media do not seem to help most press secretaries in their daily work, as can be seen by the results from the questionnaires of Democratic press secretaries. Table 9.4 reports the mean ratings (on a scale running from a low of 1 to a high of 10) for various outlets and strategies that help to get the press secretaries' jobs done. There was strong consensus on the positive value of local newspapers—either dailies or, to a lesser extent, weeklies—and a slightly weaker agreement on the worth of local television news. However, the national media, whether electronic or print, are rated considerably lower in their value to press secretaries.[8] Although the higher standard deviations indicate more disagreement on the utility of the national media than that of the local press, the national media are simply not important to most House press operations.

Instead, there were strong indications that the local media came first. One press secretary said early on, "We'd rather get in the [hometown paper] than the front page of the *New York Times* any day," and only one press secretary among the forty semistructured interviews disagreed with that statement. Getting mentioned on the front page of the

Table 9.4
Democratic Press Secretaries' Evaluation of Media Outlets and Strategies

Q. "Please rate how valuable each is in getting your job done (on a scale of 1 to 10 with 1 being very low and 10 being very high)."

	Mean	S.D.
Local dailies	9.0	1.5
Local weeklies	8.2	2.0
Press releases	8.1	1.8
Newsletters	7.8	2.0
Local television news	7.4	2.6
Targeted mail	6.7	2.7
Radio actualities	5.6	3.3
Recording studio	4.9	2.9
Weekly columns	4.8	3.2
Washington Post	4.7	3.1
Network television news	4.4	3.2
New York Times	4.3	3.1
Televised floor proceedings	3.8	2.7

N ≥ 120

Source: Calculated by the author from Democratic press secretary questionnaire, November–December 1984.

Times is unlikely, and similar results obtain with a more realistic choice, as found in the questionnaire: only 15 percent disagreed with the statement "I'd rather get on the front page of my hometown daily than in the *New York Times* or the *Washington Post* any day," as reported in Table 9.5.

The national media are then not central to the aims of the vast majority of press secretaries, who generally see their task as getting the member's name and accomplishments publicized back home. The national media are not viewed as less fair to their bosses. Few emphasized that their member discouraged, explicitly or implicitly, national media attention in general. In the survey of Democratic press secretaries, asked to agree or disagree with the statement "The local media are fairer to my boss than the national media," the bulk (59 percent) neither agreed

Table 9.5
Democratic Press Secretaries' Attitudes on Local vs. National Media

	"I would rather get in the front page of my hometown daily any day than the <u>New York Times</u> or the <u>Washington Post</u>."	"The local media are fairer to my boss than the national media."
Agree strongly	45% (56)	7% (9)
Agree somewhat	26% (32)	19% (23)
Neither agree nor disagree	10% (13)	59% (73)
Disagree somewhat	12% (15)	9% (11)
Disagree strongly	3% (4)	6% (7)
NA	3% (4)	1% (1)
	99%[a] (124)	100% (124)

[a]Rounding error

Source: Calculated by the author from Democratic press secretary questionnaire, November–December 1984.

nor disagreed; only 26 percent agreed. Likewise, in Dewhirst's (1983) survey of sixty-two press secretaries in 1981–1982, thirteen rated the national media as fairer, fifteen rated the district media as fairer, and the remainder reported no difference (p. 142). The national media are thus less important to House press operations than local media, but they are not shunned as being unfair or negative.

To be sure, some press secretaries were suspicious of the national media, visualizing them as uninformed and uninterested in either the complete account or the member of the district. Such a view was epitomized by a press secretary to a three-term midwestern Republican who admitted becoming "gun shy" after a two-minute phone call from a well-known national columnist who then wrote an article describing the poverty of the district. That experience was echoed by the press aide to a two-term moderate southern Democrat: "The national media just aren't familiar with it, can't just move into the district and report it. The local media are already savvy about local issues . . . so the local nuances are picked up. You run the risk of being criticized by the national media and then having your opponents use this information." Others felt less than comfortable with the image projected by national media visibility that implicitly distances the member from district concerns. As a press secretary to a freshman western Democrat phrased it, "I'm not sure it [network news] can help but I think it can hurt. What the network news does to news is something like what the big screen does to TV movies—it's larger than life, it's not the same story."

However, no fewer press secretaries were inclined to point out the *advantages* of dealing with the national media both in terms of fairness and the overall positive effect. As the press secretary to a senior southern Republican noted, "It's funny—some of the national media are easier to work with than the locals, and friendly too. . . . The local media expect you to run around and do all the work for [them]; they don't know what the bill is or how something gets done." More typically, press secretaries prefer to have attention from both local and national media, and the two are not seen as mutually exclusive. The staffer who coined the phrase about preferring the local daily was quick to add, "Of course, we salivate to get on the national news."

Moreover, the advantages of national news attention are not perceived to exclude achieving the goal of reelection. Several press secretaries, among the forty interviewed, suggested that national media visibility is one way to convince constituents of the importance of the member in such a way that it can complement local coverage. The press secretary to a senior southern Democrat told about an instance in which his boss was quoted in a variety of national newspapers, providing the occasion to package a portfolio to show down home; as he went on, "Then you've got a guy out on Route 3 in Kazoo City who reads where his congressman is in the *Washington Post* and *U.S. News*. . . . If it starts at the national level, there's a big chance of trickling down." This "trickling down" is abetted by the attentiveness of local and wire service newspersons to national coverage, particularly that of "papers of record," to provide clues and cues on newsworthiness (see, e.g., Gans, 1979, pp. 180–81). Other press secretaries indicated that an appearance on a network program solicited a much greater reaction back home than if the member had been covered by a local television station.

Yet, despite these potential advantages of using the national media for reelection, not to mention other goals like internal influence and policy accomplishments, virtually all press operations in the House primarily focus on the local media.[9] However, the possible liabilities of national visibility that were apparent in 1980 do not seem to weigh heavily on press secretaries' minds. Instead, several other factors propel press operations to favor local over national media in the pursuit of reelection.

First, the local media are the main customers for their product. Not only do press secretaries find local outlets more valuable, but local reporters are generally in much closer contact, sometimes on a daily basis, than national reporters. Local media, after all, come to depend on individual members to regularly make news for them. In the words of the press secretary to a four-term midwestern Republican from a rural district, "journalists are glad to talk to a member of Congress. It's an easy story, it's good copy cause anything he says is news. It makes the day easier to fill twenty column-inches or thirty seconds that way instead of a leaves-turning-color story." Not only may representatives provide stories of grants being awarded or local heroes being recognized, their reactions can provide a local angle to a national story, making the event more saleable to editors and (presumably) audiences. Most interactions are then with local newspersons; Dewhirst found his sample of sixty-two press secretaries estimating on the average that 76 percent of their time was spent dealing with district media, as compared with 18 percent with national media and 11 percent with statewide media, even though the press releases sent out were approximated to be just about evenly divided between national and local issues (1983, p. 142). It is then difficult to establish rapport with national media, who have numerous reporters covering Congress, sometimes by issues rather than by beat, and with whom contact is sporadic. Keeping regular customers happy and willing to come back to buy a product again is something every enterprise aims for; congressional enterprises are no exception.

Second, even if the member is newsworthy to both local and national media, the latter has different needs, which places an angle on the story that deemphasizes the member's personal role in favor of the issue or controversy concerned. The national media cannot be expected to find

1 out of 435 newsworthy in the same way that the local outlets find the
lone representative important. Unlike in the local media, obtaining almost any member's reactions to some national event would not be considered nationally newsworthy unless that member had a base of legiti-
mation as an "authoritative source." The distinction is then not only
between local media attending to members versus national media ig-
noring, but also in what each level considers important,[10] especially since
what is newsworthy to the national media can often get covered without
covering the member pushing it. As the press secretary to a senior
southern Democrat on Appropriations put it, "anybody who calls, we'll
call back, whether it's a high school newspaper or NBC. We don't often
go to them [the national media] and say, 'We've got a story for you.'
Stories of national significance deal with his bills, and they're coming to
us, so we don't need to. [Q: Do they help in your job?] If it's positive
coverage, yeah. But they tend to focus on his legislation, his appropria-
tion rather than on him."

Consequently, as a result of these two factors, any national coverage
on one's own terms requires much more expenditure of resources than
it would cost to obtain an equivalent or greater amount of local coverage. This is especially true of network television news, the national medium most likely to directly reach the voters but where the vagaries of
the twenty-two minute constraints are unpredictable and where the
preparation involved is daunting. As the press secretary to a southern
Democratic committee chair concluded, "to do an interview here, it takes
up thirty or forty minutes just to get set up and then some more to do
it. And then he gets seven seconds of time. Sure seems like a lot of
trouble for not very much meat." Even success in breaking into national
news may not reap many rewards, as one of Dewhirst's informants, a
press secretary to a junior urban member, signaled through an anec-
dote of getting on a morning news show: "I talked with those network
people for more than a week convincing them that my boss really was
an expert in his subcommittee area. Well, they finally took him and his
chairman but we really got clobbered in the ratings. The other network
had Bob Keeshan and Suzanne Somers on during the same time slot"
(1983, p. 78).

In short, the national media are not closely attended to because their
interest in a member is unpredictable and likely to be ephemeral.
Alongside Tuchman's (1973) classic accounts of the centrality of routines to reporters so as to manage their workload, one could easily find
a parallel among press secretaries who must make sure that their members routinely get covered in as many media as possible. Given that
serving the needs of the local media could easily become a full-time job
in any media market, devoting resources to enticing the national media
with only uncertain prospects for beneficial results is not an efficient
way to ensure that the member almost continually makes news.

Thus dealing with the national media is seldom pursued for reelection purposes. Why, then, do members have any interest in national media visibility? One might hypothesize other goals besides district-related ones that might encourage attentiveness to the national media—such as raising the national salience of an issue, becoming a national spokesperson, or running for higher office. In the questionnaire of the Democratic press secretaries, the respondents were asked to rate the importance of five long-term goals in their work; these variables were then correlated with an index of the value of national media in general. This index was derived, for reasons of parsimony, from a varimax factor analysis on the variables of the stated utilities of different media and strategies.[11] Three important factors emerged, the first of which was defined by the perceived values of the *Washington Post*, network television news, and televised floor proceedings, all of which loaded on this factor at values well above .5.[12] The index was then constructed from these results as linear combinations of the variables weighted by their factor scores.

As reported in Table 9.6, the index of the value of national media was highly correlated with two goals: national spokespersonship and creating national constituencies for an issue. By contrast, the correlations were insignificant with the two constituent-oriented goals and only

Table 9.6
Correlates of Democratic Press Secretaries' Perceived Value of National Media

Importance of Long-Term Goals	Pearson's r with Index of Value of National Media
Building name recognition of member in district	.06
Creating national constituency for issue	.51**
Enabling member to run for higher office	.19*
Serving as liaison to different constituent groups	.05
Making member national spokesperson on an issue	.52**

* p < .05; all other coefficients not statistically significant at p < .05

** p < .001

Source: Calculated by the author from Democratic press secretary questionnaire, November–December 1984.

marginally significant with the goal of progressive ambition. Note that more constituent-oriented press operations are not significantly less inclined toward the national media, only that they are largely irrelevant to the variation in reelection goals. The national media, it seems, are largely important for national goals. Even considering a run for a more salient office only somewhat impels House press operations to find national media more useful, and they are seldom perceived as an effective way to gain the local benefits, which, more often, are, at best, a useful by-product.

CONCLUSION

Members of Congress have sought publicity throughout history. The show horse-work horse distinction is far from new to students or members of the national legislature. What is new are the allegations that the incentives and rewards for being a show horse now outstrip those for being a work horse. Yet the results here suggest that if being a show horse is primarily oriented toward national media visibility, the main incentives do not include winning reelection, the usual "proximate goal" (Mayhew, 1974a) of members of Congress. Aggregate analyses of election outcomes in 1978 and 1980 show that the aim of show horses, national media visibility, does not seem to help in reelection; the only significant effect was to bolster the campaign moneys and PAC contributions of challengers in 1980. Nor do the interviews with and questionnaires from House press secretaries in 1984 display any dependence on national media attention for getting reelected. Local media are seen as more reliable and predictable outlets, more eager not only to cover the member's activities, but also to stress the member's role itself as the most newsworthy aspect of a story. The national media, it appears, are seldom spurned, but they are not openly pursued in most House offices for reelection. Despite the frequently perceived advantages of the publicity that "trickles down" from national to local coverage, it is simply too costly to spend limited resources getting in the national news when other, less expensive means of publicity exist for the folks back home.

It may well be that more and more members of the House are courting national publicity in a manner once reserved for senators (see, e.g., Ornstein, 1981). However, it seems that national media visibility is sought for national goals that cannot be achieved through the local press— especially influence in Washington and attainment of public policy goals. In that sense, members' attentiveness to national media is much more an element exclusively of their Washington styles, not their home styles, to recall Fenno's (1978) crucial distinction. Particularly with the ascendancy of a president, much of whose power rests on the ability to control the agenda through the media (see, e.g., Sinclair, 1985), and with an exceedingly complex Congress in which consensus is difficult to achieve by the old rules of bargaining, members can find that strategies to work with and through the national media are central ways to attain goals inside the institution through such an outside strategy. If there are some slight advantages for reelection as a by-product, so much the better; if there are risks involved, as the aggregate findings from 1980 suggest there may be, most members do not apparently conclude that such risks rule out the importance and value of dealing with the national media.

"Show horses" in Congress are not, then, primarily receiving a boost for reelection, nor are they primarily getting ego gratification from their names in the national headlines and their facts on the nightly news. Even if they do not exploit such strategies much for reelection, being a show horse is rationally goal-oriented more than it is an effect of personality dynamics alone—oriented toward goals that make being a show horse and being a work horse more compatible than mutually exclusive. If members were interested only in reelection, we might not see them paying any attention to the national media. That the national media are not ignored is then testimony to two crucial arguments: members of Congress have important multiple goals beyond reelection and, just as important, media effects must be presumed to go beyond electoral politics in a way whereby the audience usually studied, the mass public, is not directly involved. Whether legislative styles geared toward and dependent on national media are effective ways to get things done in Congress cannot be answered here; all we can conclude is that such styles are not efficient tools for reelection. National media visibility is indeed a resource much more accessible to incumbents than to challengers. But, unlike its local counterpart, its effects as a key perquisite of office are mixed.

NOTES

My principal gratitude goes to two collaborators. Lyn Ragsdale generously allowed me to use data that we jointly collected and findings we present elsewhere; I thank her for her energy, perseverance, and hard work. Lynn Drake, former president of the Association of House Democratic Press Assistants, helped to assemble and distribute the questionnaire of Democratic press secretaries and graciously lent the imprimatur of her organization, without which the project would have been incomplete at best. Fellow participants in the Nebraska Wesleyan conference, especially John Peters and Michael Traugott, offered useful criticisms. My additional thanks to the Brookings Institution, where I served as Guest Scholar while conducting the semistructured interviews, and to the office of Representative Don Pease, Democrat from Ohio, where I was an American Political Science Association Congressional Fellow at the time of receiving and tabulating the questionnaires. Funding for the collection of data was provided by a research grant from the Dirksen Congressional Leadership Research Center and Division II grants from Williams College, and an Adsit Fellowship.

1. On trips home, see Parker (1986b); on mass mailings, see Blakely (1985). These trends match an apparent growth in the percentages of legislation passed that is of largely symbolic import; Peterson (1986) refers to a study conducted by the Senate Democratic Policy Committee that indicates a monotonic rise in "nonsubstantive or administrative" laws from 17 percent in 1977 to 70 percent in 1985.

2. Virtually every chapter in this book attests to the incumbent's advantage in news coverage. Book-length treatments that underscore this point include Clarke and Evans (1983) and Goldenberg and Traugott (1984).

3. Payne examined only show horses and work horses on two House committees in the early 1970s. His Table VII seeks to test the hypothesis that "electoral insecurity cause[s] publicity-seeking on the national level and hence national publicity" (pp. 446–47) and shows no linear relationship. However, his measure of publicity, being a compilation of the members' actual visibility in five newspapers, may or may not reflect whether or not the members sought such publicity, even though this assumption is key to the conclusion that show horses and work horses are distinguishable personality types. Members cannot manipulate media visibility as easily as Payne makes it sound, given that the media's judgments of newsworthiness may or may not coincide with those made by the member. Several pages later Payne, inquiring into the incentives for show horsing, hypothesizes electoral benefits and produces "tentative" (p. 454) findings that "suggest that being a show horse pays off electorally, while being a work horse does not" (p. 454). This conclusion is based on results on only six show horses, and four of them were freshman representatives prone to gain substantially from the "sophomore surge" from the last election. We need not investigate in depth other flaws in the analysis, but it is important to note that the empirical conclusion that show horsing and work horsing are mutually exclusive legislative styles is accurate only if one uses the mean as the cut-off point between low and high media visibility. If we construct a two-by-two table from Payne's data, the Yule's Q would be $-.82$ for both committees combined. However, because the measure of media visibility is highly skewed, the mean is inappropriate. But using the median as the cut-off point, the relationship between committee work and media visibility is *positive* for both committees (Yule's $Q = .40$). At the very least, being a work horse does not prevent one from succeeding as a show horse, and it may even be that the two styles are reinforcing rather than mutually exclusive.

4. It has been suggested that 1979 might have been a year of unusually bad news. Yet, despite the well-known tribulations of the Carter administration, 1979 was, in most ways, a typical news year for Congress. A review of the record shows that energy was the key issue, with the passage of the windfall profits tax being the most important news item. Moreover, the various scandals of incumbents that faced the voters in the following elections mostly occurred during 1980 itself—as was the case with Abscam and the sex solicitation charges of representatives Bauman and Hinson. One point should, however, be noted: the

approval rating of Congress hit a new low, 19 percent, in 1979. *New York Times*, June 21, 1979, part II, p. 10.

5. The Bs from the full equation for national media and incumbent expenditures were 14.83 in 1978 (t = 1.719) and 38.87 in 1980 (t = 1.799). For the full model, see Ragsdale and Cook (1987, Table 6).

6. These 123 include 5 questionnaires returned anonymously; if these are not included, the response rate falls to 44 percent. Questionnaires were also sent to the offices of the four nonvoting Democratic House delegates; one was returned. If that questionnaire is included, as in this analysis, the response rate is still 46 percent.

7. The two samples are fairly representative of the larger populations. In the sample of House press secretaries who were selected from semistructured interviews, Southerners are slightly underrepresented, whereas Northeasterners are slightly overrepresented; fortunately the biases were reversed in the questionnaire of Democratic press secretaries. The questionnaire also overrepresents press secretaries to freshmen representatives, although this bias will help us to distinguish more clearly the differences between those engaging in the "new apprenticeship" of the first term and those who have gotten past their first reelection.

8. If anything, these figures are somewhat inflated by the fact that both the *Times* and the *Post* are, after all, local outlets to members from, respectively, the New York and Washington media markets. If one adjusts these variables by substituting the perceived value of the *Post* for that of the *Times* among New York area press secretaries (from the states of Connecticut, New Jersey, and New York) and doing the reverse for Washington area press secretaries (from the states of Maryland and Virginia), the scores are even slightly lower.

9. Even in the Senate, long known for being a publicity chamber and president incubator, a recent study concludes that most senators' press operations are largely focused on the home state media (Hess, 1986).

10. Such discrepancies are often exploited by other national officials, especially the president, to get more positive coverage (see Grossman and Kumar, 1979).

11. We are presented with something of a dilemma in constructing this index, when one realizes the confounding effects of the *Times* and the *Post* being local papers for members from the New York and Washington metropolitan areas. When the factor analysis was performed including these cases, the perceived value of local dailies tended to smear across two factors, instead of the cleanness with these cases removed. If we wish to consider the *Times* and the *Post* exclusively in their role as national "papers of record," these cases are deleted. Alternatively, we may use one of the adjusted variables as described in footnote 8. By each procedure one loses information, either by reducing the size of the sample or by reducing the number of variables included in the scale, but the high correlation of the perceived utilities of the *Times* and the *Post* suggests that the latter approach is preferable; it has thus been followed.

12. There was no single factor for local media. Apparently members' strategies toward the local media are more complex and multidimensional than their approaches to the national press.

10

Media Coverage of Congressional Elections: An Ethical Perspective

Bruce Jennings

An ethical perspective on the role of the news media in congressional campaigns should do at least three things. First, it should enable us to critically evaluate the conduct of legislative candidates (both incumbents and challengers) in the light of certain ethical principles and the special role obligations that follow from them. Second, it should enable us to critically evaluate the conduct of journalists, again in the light of pertinent principles and role obligations. Finally, an ethical perspective should relate these principles and obligations to background considerations concerning the proper functioning of a system of representative democracy. Ultimately the significance of our concern with the ethical conduct of candidates and journalists depends on the fact that their conduct matters from a democratic point of view—when they play their roles responsibly, democracy is enhanced; when they don't, it suffers.

DEMOCRACY AND THE NEWS MEDIA

We might begin to take our bearings on what is at stake here by recalling the importance, and the fragility, of the underlying cultural prerequisites of a viable democratic political order. Democracy requires both institutional safeguards and, equally important, a widely shared commitment to fair electoral procedures. We should not forget how easily the desire to seize or retain political power can override that com-

mitment and threaten those safeguards. Being fond of sporting meta-
phors in our political discourse, we too easily say that in elections winning is not just the most important thing, it is the only thing. That is
neither a cliche nor a joke, much less a truism. If we really believed that
and acted on it, it would be the epitaph of democracy. What keeps us
from believing it are the countervailing commitments I mentioned,
commitments nurtured and sustained by the underlying values and ethos
of a democratic political culture. But what in turn sustains that political
culture? The answer to this question is most complex and multifaceted,
and has varied historically; but surely today one significant part of the
answer involves the role of the news media as an institution that both
reflects and helps to sustain basic democratic values.

Now the point of these rather abstract reflections is to broaden our
initial approach to the problem of the media's role in and effect on the
electoral process. Most discussions of this issue are preoccupied with
the question of whether or not news coverage affects the outcome of
elections, whether it distorts the way in which policy issues get debated
and perceived, whether it contains an illegitimate partisan or ideological bias, and the like.[1] These are important and interesting questions,
to be sure, but they need to be placed in a broader context. It is fair to
say that attempts to demonstrate these effects empirically have been
inconclusive. Indeed, political scientists who subscribe to the so-called
law of minimal consequences regard them as illusory.[2] Nonetheless,
whatever social scientists may say, political professionals believe in these
effects and, to a large extent, premise their electoral strategies on them.
For their part, professional journalists are deeply ambivalent about these
effects, believing both that they are real and that they subvert the ethical code of journalism.[3]

Concern about the negative effects of media coverage on public confidence in government has recently been expressed in the writings of
many political scientists and former public officials. Disillusioned by the
record of the Carter administration and the Congress in the late 1970s,
these critics believe that governmental institutions have become so frag-
mented by conflicting social pressures and so stymied by a lack of effective leadership that they are unable to make the hard decisions and
policy choices required to solve urgent social problems. Responding to
these concerns, some journalists have become more willing to raise issues of professional journalism ethics and to seek ways to increase responsibility and accountability in news organizations. For its part, the
general public is about as cynical about the news media as it is about
Congress.[4]

In many ways the current ferment and controversy have served to
reopen many of the questions that were posed by the work of the
Hutchins Commission in the late 1940s.[5] For example, in a controver-

sial address to the American Society of Newspaper Editors in 1982, Michael O'Neill, former editor of the *New York Daily News*, provocatively suggested that in pursuing its negative role as a critic of governmental activities, the press had lost sight of its equally important positive role as a constructive enabling force in the democratic process. O'Neill wondered aloud whether the time had come for the profession of journalism to rethink its democratic social responsibilities:

The mass media, especially television, are not only changing the way government is covered but the way it functions. The crucial relationship between the people and their elected representatives—the very core of our political system—has been altered fundamentally. . . . The media have . . . made a considerable contribution to the disarray in government and therefore have an obligation to help set matters straight. Or at least improve them. The corollary of increased power is increased responsibility. The press cannot stand apart, as if it were not an interested party, not to say participant, in the democratic process.[6]

This notion of the media's democratic responsibilities poses the basic questions with which I shall be concerned in this chapter. Is contemporary political journalism serving the needs of a healthy democracy well? What is the proper scope of the media's responsibility here, and how can that responsibility be fulfilled in practice? What relationship should obtain between those who hold political power and authority and the Fourth Estate? Is the political role of the media limited to providing a negative check on the abuse of power by elected representatives, or can the press also positively enhance the ability of conscientious officials to fulfill their ethical obligations and their public trust? And how, in particular, might these considerations bear on media coverage of congressional campaigns?

In meetings and interviews conducted with legislators, congressional staff, and journalists during a recently completed Hastings Center Project on Congress and the Media, my colleagues and I found that few on either side felt that "adversarialism" is an accurate characterization of the relationship between Congress and the press.[7] At the same time, neither side believed that adversarialism or its opposite—uncritical deference and cooperation—is an adequate notion to capture the ethical dimensions of that relationship: how Congress and the press as institutions, and how legislators and journalists as individual persons, should interact in a democratic system.

But if neither adversarialism nor its opposite is appropriate, what conception does capture the relationship between Congress and the media as it is and as it should be? I suggest that the appropriate conception is to be found in the notion of representation. My thesis can be stated as follows: Even though they occupy significantly different positions, have different institutional resources at their disposal, and function under different kinds of public expectations and demands, legislators and journalists are both essential actors in the overall process of democratic representation as it has evolved in the United States. For this reason, the moral duties of congressional journalists and legislators are not at odds, but flow from the same source. Both have parallel moral obligations that derive from the ethics of representation.

It has become common to think of the congressional media as outside the legislative and electoral process, as external observers who simply describe and explain what legislators and candidates do. This image is misleading. The media are an indispensable element in the broad pattern of institutionalized political representation. This is true not merely because the press serves as the principal medium for informing constituents about the activities of legislators, but also because what the press reports, and how the press reports it, affects the capacity and incentives of individual legislators to perform their representational functions and affects the capacity of Congress to function effectively as a representational institution. Similarly, the media help to shape the campaign process, and in this way, too, significantly affect the nature of representative democracy.

In short, although journalists may seem to be merely outsiders and spectators to the process of representation, in very real and important ways they are not outsiders, but de facto participants. As such, they, and their news organizations, bear a share of the ethical burden and responsibility for the success or failure of the process of representation in fulfilling its proper democratic mission.

Legitimate democratic representation requires that representatives embody three important moral or civic virtues. Representatives should be morally autonomous agents whose decisions are based on rational, informed, unbiased, and uncoerced judgments. Representatives should be accountable and responsive to constituents' interests, while at the same time informing and educating constituents about what reasonably can be accomplished. And finally, representatives should act in ways that help sustain or improve systems of representation and lawmaking that are responsive to the legitimate interests of all citizens and to the common good of the nation as a whole. The ethical duties that follow from these fundamental requirements of legitimate democratic representation are based on what I shall call the principles of autonomy, accountability, and responsibility. These principles constitute the generic framework for the ethics of representation. They define the basic obligations of all those who play a significant role in the representational process, and therefore apply to legislators, to congressional candidates, and to congressional journalists alike.

In the remainder of this chapter I shall offer a framework for the analysis of the ethics of representation by discussing these three principles, and I shall attempt to draw out some of the implications of these principles for the practice of journalism. Finally, I shall discuss the ways in which this framework can provide an ethical perspective on the role of the media in congressional campaigns.

THE ETHICS OF REPRESENTATION

When a private citizen steps into the role of representative, he or she takes on a second ethical identity, one composed of a structure of special obligations that are often more demanding and restrictive than the general moral obligations of private life. To assume the role of representative is to make a special promise to the rest of us, and to accept a special trust on our behalf.

What, precisely, is the content of that trust? Answering this question takes us to the heart of what we mean by representation in a democracy. As I understand them, the principles of representational ethics derive from our nation's democratic traditions and from our understanding of the political conditions necessary to sustain the legitimacy and health of the democratic way of life. The ethical duties of representatives that follow from these fundamental requirements of legitimate democratic representation are based on the principles of autonomy, accountability, and responsibility.

Autonomy

The principle of autonomy holds that representatives have an obligation to deliberate and decide, free from improper influence. In legislative life it is impossible to ensure that all decisions that representatives make will be wise ones. Representatives, like all other human beings, make mistakes, commit errors of fact and judgment, and have imperfect foresight into the consequences of their actions. But by taking steps to preserve the autonomy of their judgments, they can at least increase the probability that they will judge and decide correctly.

The idea behind the principle of autonomy is the assumption that representational decision-making is less likely to be intelligent and fair if representatives make decisions in an atmosphere of improper influence. The problem raised by the application of this principle in specific situations is to determine what counts as improper influence.

A representative's duty to act autonomously and to avoid factors that compromise autonomy does not mean that representatives should be isolated from all influences or that they should try to make decisions in some kind of vacuum. Isolating representatives from all influences would be both unworkable and unacceptable from the democratic point of view. Democratic representation clearly requires that representatives remain open to many kinds of outside influence, and that they remain accessible and responsive to constituent interest and the public interest.

These democratic requirements themselves provide the criterion that enables one to draw the line between proper and improper influences. Improper influences are ones that tend to distract representatives from their basic democratic responsibilities. They draw representatives' use of the authority and resources of their position away from the public ends—the representation of constituent interest and the promotion of the public interest—that these positions were created to serve in the first place.

In order to preserve their autonomy, congressmen as representatives must avoid becoming too dependent on any single source of information or analysis. In their political careers congressmen necessarily form close associations with the lobbyists, special interest groups, and certain sectors of their district constituencies. But these special associations must not become the exclusive source of a congressman's perspective and outlook; when they come to distract the congressman from his or her broader democratic responsibilities as a *public* servant, their influence becomes improper. Congressmen who, in the overall pattern of the roles they play, become simply the spokesmen for the narrow interests and objectives of specially favored groups violate the principle of autonomy as seriously as those who dispense legislative favors in return for financial benefits.

Similar considerations apply, *mutatis mutandis*, to journalists insofar as their judgments, influence, and exercise of power affect political representation. Journalists, in this sense, are also public servants, and they, no less than congressmen, occupy a position that entails an important trust.

Accountability

The principle of accountability holds that representatives have an obligation to provide constituents with the information and understanding those constituents require in order to exercise responsible democratic citizenship. Because democratic representatives have wide discretion in their activities, and because no theory of representation or representational ethics can prescribe all the choices they must make, the ultimate check against improper representational conduct and the ultimate support for proper representational conduct must come from the constituents—the voters in the case of congressmen—themselves. This is the core of the traditional democratic idea that the authority of those who govern rests on the consent of those who are governed. The idea behind the principle of accountability is that representatives themselves ought to take reasonable steps to ensure that democratic consent is fully informed and enlightened.

The problems of applying the principle of accountability arise in determining what kinds of information are integral to the constituents' exercise of responsible democratic citizenship. Where do we draw the line between what voters do and do not need to know if the outcome of elections is reasonably to be interpreted as an instance of informed democratic consent?

The duty of accountability involves many aspects of a representative's activities. Constituents need to be able to monitor representational activities so that they can provide feedback to representatives concerning needs and interests that have been neglected. Accountability is not simply a burden imposed on representatives by a long democratic tradition that has always been wary of anyone holding a position of political power. It also has a more positive and constructive rationale. When it gives citizens the information and understanding they need to become more thoughtful partners in the process of representation, accountability enables representatives to be more effective. They can provide intellectual and political leadership on important issues and, at the same time, they can benefit and learn from their constituents. Moreover, remaining accountable in this sense helps representatives to fulfill their duty to be open-minded, autonomous decisionmakers. Maintaining a well-informed, alert constituency is one of the representative's best protections against falling into an ethically dangerous dependence on narrow or biased advice, from whatever source.

Moreover, citizens need more than factual information; they need a context within which to interpret the significance of the information they receive about representatives. Accountability requires not only that representatives should *disclose* what they have done, but also that they should *explain* and *justify* what they have done. Here the principle of accountability has a double application to journalists. On the one hand, they should be accountable in their own journalistic activities, taking steps to ensure that their readers and viewers can intelligently respond to the information and interpretation the media provide. On the other hand, journalists are clearly integral to the accountability of congressmen, for it is through the media that information and understanding about congressional activity are largely conveyed.

Responsibility

The principle of responsibility holds that representatives have an obligation to contribute to the effective institutional functioning of the democratic representational process. Representation and lawmaking are collective processes; they rely on the cooperation and coordinated activities of many participants in an overall system. For example, individual congressmen cannot fulfill the ethical obligations of their office or role merely by attending to their own activities and their own relationship with their constituents. They must be concerned as well with the activities of other congressmen and with the functioning of Congress as a whole.

The problems of applying the principle of responsibility arise in determining what the "effective institutional functioning" of representational institutions requires in a democracy. In order to be responsible, congressmen must strike a delicate balance between accommodating themselves to the existing institutional and procedural arrangements of their chamber and pressing for organizational change through public criticism and institutional leadership. The principle of responsibility is not the ethical equivalent of Sam Rayburn's famous adage, "To get along, go along." It does not charge congressmen with an obligation to accept uncritically the institutional status quo. But it does require that they direct their efforts to bring about legislative reform in ways that will enhance the democratic character in the legislative process as a whole. At a time when several kinds of pressures are converging to make individual congressmen more entrepreneurial and less institutionally dependent than ever before, the principle of responsibility serves as an ethical caution to legislators against the temptation to use institutional procedures and resources merely as a means to advance their own personal or political ends.

REPRESENTATIONAL ETHICS AND JOURNALISTIC PRACTICE

Having outlined a generic framework for the ethics of representation, let me now attempt to spell out in more detail how these ethical principles might apply to journalistic decision-making and practices.

The principle of autonomy suggests that journalists should make reporting and editorial decisions free from improper influences. Journalists must strive to remain open-minded, and adequately and independently informed. They must avoid placing themselves or being placed in situations that would compromise their independent judgment through coercion, bias, or conflict of interest. The principle of autonomy is thus closely related to the modern journalistic norm of objectivity, but it suggests a much less passive and reactive image of the journalist as an ethical actor and decisionmaker. In this way the notion of autonomy incorporates and acknowledges the kernel of truth contained in recent critiques of traditional conceptions of objectivity. Journalists are not simply neutral conduits of information or facts. All reporting, let alone editing, analysis, and commentary, is an unavoidably active, selective, and interpretive process. This does not mean that there is no possible line to be drawn between journalism and fiction, as Janet Cooke and others have discovered. But it does mean that journalistic decision-making involves all the characteristic ingredients of human judgment—discernment, selectivity, setting priorities, and balancing conflicting values—and as such is subject to a broad range of influences.

Autonomy requires open-mindedness, listening carefully to all sides and reflecting on them. In the course of their work journalists necessarily form associations with people who have special interests and axes to grind. Autonomy means not being dependent on a single source of information and not allowing the value of the source of information to turn into an obligation to that source. It means separating professional and personal relationships, so that the interests of the latter do not undermine the responsibilities of the former. And it means remaining insulated from the business or economic interests of the corporate entity that owns the news organization. It is easy to see that pressures and influences that may undermine autonomy can be particularly intense in the context of congressional campaigns.

The principle of accountability suggests that journalists have an obligation to use sources of information and the resources of news organizations to provide readers and viewers with the information and understanding they require in order to exercise responsible democratic citizenship. Just as legislators have an obligation to take reasonable steps to ensure that the democratic consent and mandate they receive from constituents is fully informed and enlightened, so journalists too have an obligation to promote the same end.

Here, surely, the ethical connection between journalists and congressmen is most direct and telling. Congressmen cannot fulfill their duty to be accountable without using the media as a vehicle of communication between themselves and their constituents. In this sense the media provide a key element in making ethical legislative representation possible. At the same time, in a variety of ways, journalists regulate the use politicians make of the media and, through their own reporting and commentary, add to the political messages constituents receive. By using the media as a vehicle of democratic political education, journalists fulfill their obligation to be accountable, and thereby create a positive incentive for congressmen to fulfill theirs. Without a press that looks out after the quality and quantity of political information available to the citizenry, it is likely that congressmen would not be as open and forthcoming as they are. Thus applying the principle of accountability to journalists as well as to congressmen reminds us that Congress and the press are both integral elements in the system of political communication and dialogue that makes contemporary democracy possible.

When both sides fulfill their obligations under the principle of account-ability, the representational process can function as it was intended to. When one side falls down on the job, the other can compensate for that failing. If both sides fail, our democracy is in jeopardy.

What makes a journalist accountable? Part of this involves disclosure of financial interests, of entangling personal relationships, of an attitu-dinal bias one way or the other toward individual congressmen or pub-lic policies. Another reinforcement of accountability comes from access. Journalists should make themselves available to talk with readers and viewers, to answer questions, and to respond to criticism. News organi-zations should be open about their standards of editorial decision-mak-ing and news judgment.

The basic question for accountability, as I am using the concept here, is: What do citizens need to know in order to assess, evaluate, and use the information they are getting from the media? If we ideally expect congressmen not merely to disclose, but also to inform and to educate, however seldom this may actually happen, there is no good reason why we ought not expect the same of journalists.

The principle of responsibility suggests that journalists have an obli-gation to contribute to the effective institutional functioning of news organizations in order to make their role in the overall process of rep-resentation autonomous and accountable. Like individual legislators who serve in legislative institutions and must be responsible participants in a collective legislative process, and like congressional candidates who should be responsible participants in a democratic electoral process that does not exist simply to serve their own political self-interest and am-bition, individual journalists also have ethical obligations as members of news organizations and as participants in a process of reporting.

The principle of responsibility calls attention to the fact that any in-dividual journalist's ability to perform his or her role ethically is at least partially dependent on the conduct of other journalists and the ethical ethos or climate that is established within news organizations. Conscien-tious journalists have an interest in helping to maintain an organiza-tional ethos that supports autonomous and accountable journalistic de-cision-making; they also have an obligation to contribute to that ethos or to help create it when it does not exist. Although the burden of this responsibility falls on all journalists, it is especially significant for senior correspondents, editors, and publishers who are in a position to influ-ence policy and serve as ethical role models within news organizations.

The principle of responsibility suggests, moreover, that individual journalists should be attentive to the effects the policies and conduct of their news organizations are having on the public's understanding of the nature of the legislative process and of the strengths and weak-nesses of Congress as an institution. This is the corollary of their duties defined by the principle of accountability.

Finally, journalists as persons and news organizations as institutions have a responsibility to the electoral process itself. For all the drama, confusion, and uncertainty they may occasionally display, political campaigns are complex, institutionalized forms of political activity into which the press, and more recently the broadcast media, has been incorporated to play an integral role. Candidates and campaign managers increasingly plan the activity and strategy of their campaigns around anticipated media behavior and responses. And journalists, too, must strive to manage the difficult task of covering a campaign by reporting campaign activities and issues in a way that will be interesting to their readers and viewers and appealing to editors who allocate the scarce resource of air time or space in the "news hole" of the paper.

The journalistic norms of balance and fairness acknowledge that campaign coverage should not unduly favor one candidate in the electoral competition, and thereby provide tacit recognition of the fact that media coverage is a constitutive part of the institution of political campaigns. Balance is important because each candidate has a right to just or equitable access to the media and because the legitimacy of the democratic process requires that, in a meaningful and not simply a formal sense, the voters, not the media elites, determine who wins office. But the principle of responsibility goes one step further and requires not only that media coverage respect the fairness of campaign competition, but also that it serve to enhance the democratic purposes campaigns ought to serve. Thus the responsibility of journalists to the integrity of the campaign process and their responsibility to enhance the public's understanding of the legislative process are two sides of the same coin. That coin is their responsibility to the system of representative democracy itself.

What is the responsibility of journalists to the system of representative democratic government? Michael Schudson provides one answer to this question when he argues that journalists need to act as though they lived in two worlds: the world of the representative system as it might be in some realm of ideal democracy, and the imperfect world of representation as it exists in our actual democracy.[8] He wants the press to champion democracy as it might be, while responding to the realities of democracy as it is. In concluding, I suggest that this dual perspective may be particularly apt as a way of taking our moral bearings in the arena of media coverage of congressional campaigns.

CONGRESSIONAL CAMPAIGNS AND INFORMED DEMOCRATIC CONSENT

The ethical perspective one takes on the behavior of candidates and journalists in congressional campaigns depends, in large measure, on how one construes the democratic function and meaning of campaigns themselves. Here we may distinguish two fundamentally different ways of looking at campaigns. For want of better terms, I call them the economic interpretation and the ethical interpretation. Each of these accounts is useful for certain heuristic and analytical purposes, but they are not easily reconciled. Facets of the political and social reality of campaigns that the ethical interpretation highlights, the economic interpretation obscures; and vice versa.

According to the economic interpretation, campaigns are a kind of political bazaar in which competing candidates and their campaign organizations attempt to mobilize their political support as much as possible, short circuit the mobilization of political support for their opponents, and maximize votes. As a part of this process, concerted efforts are made to gain media access and shape news coverage by campaign journalists. Within the framework of this economic interpretation, journalists themselves play down their role as instruments for realizing the goals of the politicians and view themselves instead as particularly well-informed observers of a political drama involving the clash of conflicting personalities and alternative positions on policy issues.[9]

Now this perspective on campaigns and elections is quite familiar. Indeed, it bespeaks our conventional wisdom on these matters, reinforced not only by the discourse of mainstream academic political science, but also by the image of politics fostered by politicians and journalists themselves. Nonetheless, this perspective is incomplete because it neglects the underlying democratic values that campaigns ought to serve. Accordingly, the economic interpretation does not provide a robust moral vision of what campaigns ought to be. Apart from certain minimal side constraints—fight fair, obey the law, no dirty tricks—it articulates neither ethical standards with which to evaluate the conduct of key actors in the campaign process, nor ethical ideals those actors should strive toward.

Drawing on older democratic idioms and traditions in our political culture, the ethical interpretation of campaigns begins with the proposition that legitimate political authority rests on the regular, periodic renewal of a democratic mandate and the periodic giving and regiving of informed democratic consent. According to the ethical interpretation, campaigns and elections are reenactments of the political covenant between representatives and the represented. Campaigns are special moments of political time, moments when ordinary citizens turn from their normal preoccupation with private life and focus special attention on public affairs.

Viewing campaigns as especially significant moments in the political life of a democracy gives us an initial purchase on the ways in which the principles of representative ethics can be applied to the activities of candidates and campaign journalists.

Because the legitimating function of elections rests not on the expression of mere consent, but on the expression of informed democratic consent, the quality of the political education, broadly defined, contained in the campaign process is crucially important. Campaigns should be—and are to some extent—occasions for political teaching and political learning by both candidates and citizens. And the news media are one extremely important vehicle of that teaching and learning.

The principle of autonomy mainly pertains to the need for candidates to be learners. The principle of autonomy looks toward making representatives open and accesible to a broad spectrum of influences and viewpoints. Once in office a congressman is ethically required to represent all of his or her constituents, not just those persons and organizations that supported him or her during the campaign. During the normal course of legislative activity in Washington, a congressman is most likely to hear only from the highly motivated and well organized. However, the principle of autonomy requires that a congressman make special efforts to inform himself or herself about the interests of and to hear from the least well off and least organized members of the constituency. This is an ongoing ethical requirement, but campaigns provide a strategic opportunity for it to come to the fore.

With these considerations in mind, one might argue that the flow of information and opinion from constituents to candidates is as important as, if not more important than, the flow of information and opinion from candidates to constituents. Moreover, insofar as an open democratic dialogue provides an underpinning for the beneficent functioning of representation, that dialogue is likely to be most inclusive during campaigns, and the momentum it gains then may carry it through the subsequent legislative session. This looks forward to a situation in which there is more continuity in our political discourse than now obtains, for currently campaigns seem to be too often regarded as times when the serious business of governance is set aside in favor of high rhetoric, high posturing, and a general venting of frustrations. In order to enhance autonomy in the functioning of the representational process, campaign journalists should concentrate more than they do on (a) the ways in which their coverage might foster communication from constituents to candidates; (b) how coverage might establish better continuity between campaign and noncampaign political discourse; and (c) the ways in which the campaign process can be an occasion for autonomy-enhancing learning for candidates.

In a similar vein the principles of accountability and responsibility emphasize the role of candidates as teachers. For the principle of accountability, the implications of this perspective should be clear enough from what I said earlier about accountability. In the context of congressional campaigns, I would simply underline the point that accountability requires candidates not simply to disclose information about themselves and about their political views, but also to explain and justify through reasoned argument their record, their platform, and their vision of how they would use the authority and power of congressional office in the future. For journalists, the ethics of accountability suggests that they should use their role in congressional campaigns to facilitate the process of explanation and justification and prod candidates in these directions. It seems clear enough that without this kind of pressure from journalists, the kind of political education that comes from explanation and justification will languish in congressional campaigns.

Finally, there is also a connection between the principle of responsibility and the political education that campaigns ought to provide. Recall that responsibility, as defined here, means that representatives ought to promote the proper functioning of representational institutions. Part of that responsibility can be discharged internally through the activities of constructive, albeit critical, institutional membership. But the obligations that flow from the principle of responsibility must also be discharged, in part, externally by providing the public with a better understanding of Congress' institutional problems as well as its strengths.

Of all the ethical obligations of representatives that I have mentioned, this may be the one that congressmen most regularly and systematically fail to discharge. At a time when public confidence in Congress as an institution is low, congressmen find it politically advantageous to appeal to this anti-congressional sentiment and to distance themselves from the performance of the Congress as a whole. Reflecting on his experience of observing U.S. House members in their districts, Richard Fenno clearly describes this phenomenon:

Nothing . . . had prepared me to discover that each member of Congress polishes his or her individual reputation at the expense of the institutional reputation of Congress. In explaining what he was doing in Washington, every one of the eighteen House members [with whom Fenno traveled] took the opportunity to picture himself as different from, and better than, most of his fellow members of Congress. None availed himself of the opportunity to educate his constituents about Congress as an institution—not in any way that would "hurt a little." To the contrary, the members' process of differentiating themselves from Congress as a whole only served, directly or indirectly, to downgrade the Congress. . . . Members of Congress run *for* Congress by running *against* Congress. The strategy is ubiquitous, addictive, cost-free and fool-proof. . . . In the short run, everybody plays and nearly everyone wins. Yet the institution bleeds from 435 separate cuts. In the long run, therefore, somebody may lose.[10]

The principle of responsibility indicates the ethically troubling nature of this "ubiquitous, addictive, cost-free and fool-proof" political strategy. Responsible legislators certainly should criticize legislative procedures in an effort to mobilize public support for needed institutional reforms. The ethical justification of that activity is not in question. But running for the Congress by running against the Congress is not an ethically responsible activity and does not have the effect of enhancing the democratically sound functioning of Congress. If this practice is indeed as prevalent as Fenno claims, then it indicates that many legislators have allowed political expediency to override an important facet of their ethical duties. Instead of capitalizing on the low public confidence in Congress, and thereby perpetuating it in a vicious downward spiral, responsible congressmen should use the considerable resources of their special standing with constituents to create a more enlightened public understanding of the very real strengths that our congressional system has.

Concomitantly, if we take seriously the notion that journalists should promote the principle of responsibility in the representational process, we should consider how journalists might exert a countervailing pressure against the natural tendency of candidates to ignore their constituents' need to understand the institutional dimension of representation and lawmaking. From an ethical point of view, this is not merely an ancillary aspect of the broader democratic functions that campaign coverage ought to serve. On the contrary, it is central to the exercise of responsible democratic representation, and therefore of responsible democratic journalism as well.

NOTES

1. For discussions in this vein, see Robert MacNeil, *The People Machine* (New York: Harper and Row, 1968); Frank Mankiewicz and Joel Swerdlow, *Remote Control* (New York: Times Books, 1978); Edward Jay Epstein, *News from Nowhere* (New York: Vintage Books, 1974); Thomas Patterson, *The Mass Media Election* (New York: Praeger, 1980); and Thomas Patterson and Robert McClure, *The Unseeing Eye* (New York: G. P. Putnam, 1976).

2. Sidney Kraus and Dennis Davis, *The Effects of Mass Communication on Political Behavior* (University Park: Pennsylvania State University Press, 1976).

3. F. Christopher Arterton, *Media Politics: The News Strategies of Presidential Campaigns* (Lexington, Mass.: D. C. Heath, 1984).

4. Cf. Don Fry, ed., *Believing the News* (St. Petersburg, Fla.: The Poynter Institution for Media Studies, 1986); and American Society of Newspaper Editors, *Newspaper Credibility: Building Reader Trust* (Washington, D.C.: ASNE, 1985).

5. The Commission on Freedom of the Press, *A Free and Responsible Press* (Chicago: University of Chicago Press, 1947). For a contemporary discussion, see Keith S. Collins, ed., *Responsibility and Freedom in the Press: Are They in Conflict?* (Washington, D.C.: Citizen's Choice, 1985).

6. Michael J. O'Neill, "A Problem for the Republic—A Challenge for Editors," in *The Adversary Press* (St. Petersburg, Fla.: Modern Media Institute [Poynter Institute], 1983), pp. 4, 12.

7. Cf. Daniel Callahan, William Green, Bruce Jennings, and Martin Linsky, *Congress and the Media: The Ethical Connection* (Hastings-on-Hudson, N.Y.: The Hastings Center, 1985). This chapter draws substantially on this study. For related work on congressional ethics, see Bruce Jennings and Daniel Callahan, *The Ethics of Legislative Life* (Hastings-on-Hudson, N.Y.: The Hastings Center, 1985); and Bruce Jennings and Daniel Callahan, eds., *Representation and Responsibility: Exploring Legislative Ethics* (New York: Plenum Press, 1985).

8. "The News Media and the Democratic Process." A Wye Resource Paper (New York: Aspen Institute, 1983).

9. Cf. Arterton, op. cit., chapters 1 and 2.

10. Richard Fenno, *Home Style: House Members in Their Districts* (Boston: Little, Brown, 1978), pp. 164, 168.

11

Future Research on the News Media and Congressional Elections

Paul Bradford Raymond

This chapter outlines the direction future research should take on the relationship between the news media and congressional elections. It is argued that important research questions remain to be answered, but that new data sets will have to be collected before hypotheses are tested. Suggestions are made for studies that can be conducted with limited resources.

RESEARCH QUESTIONS

The growing literature on the relationship between the news media and congressional elections has identified and tested a number of hypotheses. Yet important questions remain to be answered. First, little attention has been devoted to studying differences in the way television newscasts and dailies cover congressional campaigns. Despite the wide audience for both national and local newscasts, research has focused almost exclusively on the print medium (for exceptions, see Cook, 1986; Katz, 1985).[1] The fact that those people who are most likely to be influenced by the news media (the poorly educated, for example) are as likely to watch a television newscast as to read a daily newspaper (Patterson, 1980, p. 61) makes the study of television newscasts particularly important.[2]

Of particular interest is whether the electronic media devote as little time as newspapers to congressional campaigns, and why some stations devote more attention than others. One might hypothesize that the proportion of the news devoted to congressional campaigns would be smaller on local TV newscasts than in dailies. Dailies often have difficulty in finding enough stories to fill available space and may welcome news about local congressional races, however dull they may be. Conversely, television news shows have limited time to devote to hard news and may feel pressured to devote virtually all of it to topics that entertain (rather than inform) their viewers (Ranney, 1983, p. 68).

A related question is whether there is an "incumbency bias" in television news. That is, it is important to know if incumbents receive more favorable coverage than challengers in TV news shows, as they apparently do in many dailies (Kelley, 1958; Clarke and Evans, 1983, pp. 35–50). Certainly one suspects that the competitive advantage representatives have in making their accomplishments newsworthy assures that they will receive more attention than challengers from both television reporters and newspapers. After all, representatives realize that many voters partially rely on television for local news, and actively solicit the attention of the electronic media (Robinson, 1982). On the other hand, in chapter 9, Timothy Cook offers some presumptive evidence that the national news media treat some incumbents unkindly. It would be interesting to see if local television coverage of congressional incumbents is sometimes negative. Although such a finding would fly in the face of conventional wisdom (which suggests that journalists feel obligated to cover events that inevitably place incumbents in a favorable light), it is possible that the competition for high ratings leads television news organizations to focus on the more controversial (and thus interesting) aspects of representatives' activities.

It is also important to learn if television newscasts are more or less guilty than dailies of reporting about campaign hoopla and candidate strategy rather than on substantive issues. Given local television stations' preoccupation with ratings, one might anticipate that they are more likely to emphasize hoopla and strategy than are newspapers. But Patterson's (1980) analysis of television and newspaper coverage of the 1976 presidential primary found relatively little difference in emphasis between network evening newscasts and dailies. Patterson examined coverage of *network* television newscasts in a high-visibility election. Because network newscasts contain more political information than local news shows, the extent to which Patterson's results are generalizable to local television newscasts in low-visibility congressional races remains to be demonstrated.

The extent to which journalistic norms and organizational processes shape how campaign news is reported is also an area in which additional work is needed. Scholars have emphasized the relevance of journalistic values and workways in predicting how campaigns are covered (Clarke and Evans, 1983; Goldenberg and Traugott, 1984). Yet it is still unclear which norms and organizational routines are most important.

For example, there are several possible reasons why challengers are less likely than incumbents to gain the attention of the press. One explanation focuses on the journalistic norm of fairness. Challengers' political attributes are downplayed, it is said, because editors do not want to appear to be unfairly stressing nonincumbents' weaknesses (Clarke and Evans, 1983, p. 45).

Other scholars argue that the journalistic norm of balance is important. According to this explanation, whether or not a challenger's campaign receives as much coverage as the incumbent's is determined by whether or not an editor believes this norm (which suggests that adversaries in a conflict should receive an equal amount of the news hole) should apply to the coverage of congressional campaigns (Goldenberg and Traugott, 1984, pp. 127–29).

It has also been suggested that incumbents' institutional position assures them of more coverage than does challengers'. Incumbents engage in behavior that the press feels obligated to report (introducing legislation, committee work, directing federal funds to the district) because they are "official" duties. Presumably such action would be reported whether or not the member was up for reelection. On the other hand, challengers' actions are considered newsworthy only if they are directly related to the campaign (Clarke and Evans, 1983).

And finally, challengers' lack of campaign resources has been cited as a reason why they are ignored. Many nonincumbents, so the argument goes, do not have the finances to hire experienced press aides who are skilled at getting their candidates in the news (Clarke and Evans, 1983, pp. 30–33). This explanation points to the importance of considering the technological constraints of the newsgathering process. Specifically, the pressure of deadlines and the limited time that news organizations can devote to congressional campaigns may give an advantage to those candidates who can make it easy for reporters to learn about them.

One or more of the aforementioned theories may explain why challengers receive less coverage than do incumbents. But their relative importance will not become known until additional research is conducted.

A third avenue for further inquiry concerns differences in how House and Senate campaigns are covered. There is now a substantial body of literature that suggests that House and Senate elections differ in important respects (Abramowitz, 1980; Mann and Wolfinger, 1980; Parker, 1981; Hinckley, 1981). Whereas members of the House seldom lose elections, senators are often defeated (Hinckley, 1981, p. 40). In the majority of House elections, voters learn little about challengers. Most Senate challengers become almost as well known as their opponents. And voters are more likely to take candidates' experience and issue positions into account in Senate than in House elections (Ragsdale, 1980).[3]

No doubt these findings are explained, in part, by differences in House and Senate candidates' campaign activity. Senate challengers spend a great deal of money on paid media and run well-organized campaigns. House challengers often have little money to spend and weak organizations. But the way news organizations report the races may also be important. The news media may contribute to representatives' victories and senators' defeats by paying more attention to Senate challengers or by being more critical of incumbent senators than members of the House. And candidates' issue positions and qualifications may be more important determinants of the vote in Senate races than they are in House contests simply because the news media pays particular attention to senators' issue orientations and political attitudes.

It is also important to learn more about the conditions under which congressional candidates are able to shape the content of the news. Although Vermeer (1982) supplies evidence that candidates can influence the way a candidate is covered, his study focuses only on press releases. It is also necessary to research whether or not candidates are able to affect the amount and tone of coverage through the orchestration of campaign events.[4]

We would also profit from studies that examined how news coverage influences candidates' campaigns. It is clear that press coverage has a substantial effect on high-visibility presidential campaigns (Arterton, 1984). Whether the press exerts this same power in low-visibility contests remains to be seen. For example, it would be interesting to know how variations in the amount (or tone) of press coverage affects the ability of congressional candidates to recruit volunteers and raise money.

Finally, there is a need to look more closely at the effect news coverage has on people's voting decisions. In the research reported in this book and in an earlier work (Goldenberg and Traugott, 1984; 1987), Goldenberg and Traugott demonstrate that voters' information and attitudes are influenced by the content of the news media. The quantity of the hard news coverage as well as endorsements are found to affect voting decisions independently of candidate-controlled communications. What is now needed are studies that extend this research (which has relied on inclusive measures of media content, such as the relative amount of news copy candidates receive) and specify the particular types of media communications that are most effective in influencing voters. For example, it would be instructive to learn if the news media are as successful in educating voters about candidates' qualifications or incumbents' constituency service as they appear to be in educating the public about the issue positions of incumbents who take controversial positions (Simmons, 1987).

DATA SETS

Efforts to answer the aforementioned research questions are hampered by the lack of appropriate data sets. To date, scholars have concentrated on gathering samples of daily and weekly newspapers.[5] Transcripts and videotapes of national newscasts exist, but they have not been coded with a view to answering questions about the role of the news media in congressional campaigns. Unfortunately no efforts have been made to systematically gather representative samples of local newscasts.

Crude measures of the relative emphasis given to congressional candidates in television newscasts and newspaper articles (such as the number of newscasts in which a candidate's name is mentioned) can be easily calculated with the aid of various indexes like the *Television News Index and Abstracts*, the *CBS News Index*, and the *New York Times Index*. A few local dailies also have indexes, such as *The San Francisco Chronicle* and the *St. Louis Post-Dispatch*. Coverage of congressional candidates in less traditional news media is indexed in the *Alternative Press Index* and the *Index to Black Newspapers*.

It is possible, for example, to use these indexes to research the relative visibility of Senate and House candidates, or to compare the amount of coverage in print mediums with coverage on TV newscasts. In Chapter 9 Cook measures the amount of national news attention given to members of the House by noting whether a candidate's name appeared in the *New York Times Index* or the *Television News Index and Abstracts*. These same indexes could be used to study the visibility of senators. But questions about the specific content and tone of national (and local) news coverage will have to await a content analysis of actual articles and transcripts. Fortunately archives are full of newspapers, and the transcripts of many national TV newscasts are available for analysis. Although copies of the local newscasts have not been systematically collected, some stations make available transcripts of their newscasts.

RESEARCH DESIGNS

Through careful selection of districts according to theoretically relevant criteria, it is possible to conduct preliminary tests of important hypotheses with limited resources. For example, a content analysis of a sample of newscasts and newspapers in just a few districts would enhance our knowledge of differences in the way print and electronic media cover congressional races. Of course, the media may treat the candidates differently when there is an incumbent in the race, or when the contest is close. And coverage may also be affected by the fit between media markets and House districts.[6] So districts will have to be carefully chosen on the basis of relevant candidate, district, and media characteristics.

Differences in how the news media cover senators and representatives can be examined through a content analysis of one or more news outlets (a network news program, a national newspaper, a local daily, etc.). As noted earlier, rough measures of the differences among media can be made by using indicators derived from various newspaper indexes and television abstracts. But it is also desirable to analyze actual articles and transcripts. This is the only way to determine the specific content and tone of the coverage. If only selected news outlets in a limited number of districts are studied, such a project becomes feasible.

A study that examines the values and workways of a small sample of editors and journalists through semistructured interviews (or participant observation) would shed some light on the relative importance of journalistic norms and newsgathering techniques in shaping coverage of candidates' campaigns. It is of particular interest to see if journalistic norms such as balance and fairness are more useful than the constraints imposed by the news production process. Particular attention will have to be paid to the selection of news outlets, however, since the standard operating procedures of news organizations may vary, depending on such factors as organization size and the type of media market.

It would be useful to study the effect of candidates' campaign communications on news coverage in a single race. By examining a candidate's campaign records, conducting interviews, and content analyzing paid and free media, it would be possible to determine the extent to which a candidate's campaign themes are reflected in news coverage. Of course, the generalizability of the findings from a single campaign would be limited, but such a study would suggest avenues for further inquiry. A similar design could be used to determine how news reports influence volunteer recruitment, campaign workers' morale, and financial contributions.

The effects of news coverage on voting decisions could be studied by conducting polls in one or more districts. Questions could be tailored to reflect the specific content of newscasts and paid media. And with a panel design, it will be possible to examine how changes in news coverage influence attitudes toward the candidates.

To be sure, the generalizability of the findings from any of the aforementioned research projects will necessarily be limited. Definitive tests of the hypotheses necessitate a large, representative sample of districts and media outlets. But before resources are devoted to a large national study, it would be useful to provide preliminary tests of the more important hypotheses on a more limited scale.

NOTES

1. Whether or not people receive more of their news from television than from dailies depends on how exposure is measured (Patterson, 1980, pp. 57–66). But there is no doubt that the public is exposed to a great deal of television news. And audiences for local news programs are often as large (or larger) than audiences for network broadcasts (Epstein, 1974a, pp. 94–96).

2. If one measures exposure by asking where people get most of their news rather than by using a measure that taps the regularity of exposure, poorly educated people are more likely than the well educated to use television as a source for news (Patterson, 1980, p. 61). Robinson (1977) argues that television news is a particularly important source of information for less informed voters. However, the effect of television news on even poorly informed voters may be more limited than is often supposed (Patterson and McClure, 1976; Clarke and Fredin, 1978; Patterson, 1980).

3. Westlye (1983) notes, however, that some Senate challengers have low visibility.

4. Most of the work that has been done on the effect of the press campaigns has focused on presidential contests. See, for example, Arterton (1984).

5. Two major collections of newspaper articles are available for analysis. One set was gathered as part of the 1978 American National Election Study. However, the clipping service employed to gather the data failed to clip two-thirds of the items appearing in the sampled newspapers. Consequently conclusions based on an analysis of the newspaper articles are problematic. A second set of newspaper clippings was gathered by Goldenberg and Traugott as part of their study of the 1978 elections (Goldenberg and Traugott, 1984). This data set includes sample articles from thirty-three newspapers that covered a total of forty-three House races.

6. See Goldenberg and Traugott (1984, pp. 124–31) for a discussion of how candidate status, competitiveness, and media markets influence coverage.

Bibliography

Abramowitz, Alan I. (1980). "A Comparison of Voting for U.S. Senator and Representative in 1978." *American Political Science Review*. 74:633–40.

———. (1983). "Candidates, Coattails and Strategic Politicians in the 1980 Congressional Elections: Explaining the Republican Victory." Paper presented at the annual meeting of the American Political Science Association, Chicago, Illinois.

Adams, William. (1985). "Convention Coverage." *Public Opinion*. 7:43–48.

Agranoff, Robert. (1976). *The New Style in Election Campaigns*. Boston: Holbrook Press.

Allen, Charles L. (1928). *Country Journalism*. New York: Thomas Nelson and Sons.

Alternative Press Index. Baltimore, Maryland: Alternative Press Center, Inc., 1969 to present.

American Society of Newspaper Editors. (1985). *Newspaper Credibility: Building Reader Trust*. Washington, D.C.: ASNE.

Arterton, F. Christopher. (1984). *Media Politics: The News Strategies of Presidential Campaigns*. Lexington, Massachusetts: Lexington Books.

Bagdikian, Ben H. (1974). "Congress and the Media: Partners in Propaganda." *Columbia Journalism Review*. 12:3–10.

Becker, Samuel L. and Elmer L. Lower. (1962). "Broadcasting in Presidential Campaigns." In Sidney Kraus, ed., *The Great Debates*. Bloomington: Indiana University Press, pp. 25–55.

Behr, Roy L. (1983). "The Effect of Media on Voters' Considerations in Congressional Elections." Paper presented at the annual meeting of the

American Association for Public Opinion Research, Hunt Valley, Maryland.

Bennett, W. Lance. (1980). *Public Opinion in American Politics*. (New York: Harcourt Brace Jovanovich.

Berelson, Bernard R., Paul F. Lazarsfeld, and William N. McPhee. (1954). *Voting*. Chicago: University of Chicago Press.

Blakely, Steve. (1985). "Congressional Franked Mail Untouched by Budget Ax." *Congressional Quarterly Weekly Report* (October 19):2109–11.

Blalock, Hubert M., Jr. (1972). *Social Statistics*, 2nd edition. New York: McGraw-Hill.

Brady, D. et al. (1979). "The Decline of Party in the U.S. House of Representatives." *Legislative Studies Quarterly*. 4:381–408.

Broder, David. (1986). "Who Took the Fun Out of Congress?" *Washington Post Weekly Edition* (February 17):9–10.

Brogan, Denis. (1954). *Politics in America*. New York: Harper and Brothers.

Cain, Bruce, John Ferejohn, and Morris Fiorina. (1984). "A Comparative Examination of Incumbent Visibility." Unpublished manuscript.

Callahan, Daniel, William Green, Bruce Jennings, and Martin Linsky. (1985). *Congress and the Media: The Ethical Connection*. Hastings-on-Hudson, New York: The Hastings Center.

Calvert, Randall and John Ferejohn (1983). "Coattail Voting in Recent Presidential Elections." *American Political Science Review*. 77:407–19.

Campbell, Angus. (1966). "Surge and Decline: A Study of Electoral Change." In Angus Campbell, Philip E. Converse, Warren E. Miller, and Donald E. Stokes, *Elections and the Political Order*. New York: John Wiley and Sons, pp. 40–62.

Campbell, James, John R. Alford, and Keith Henry. (1982). "Television Markets and Congressional Elections: The Impact of Market/District Congruence." Paper presented at the annual meeting of the Southern Political Science Association, Atlanta, Georgia.

———. (1984). "Television Markets and Congressional Elections." *Legislative Studies Quarterly*. 9:665–78.

Carey, John. (1976). "How Media Shape Campaigns." *Journal of Communication*. 26:50–57.

CBS News Index: Key to the Television News Broadcasts. Ann Arbor, Michigan: University Microfilms, 1975 to present.

Clapp, Charles L. (1963). *The Congressman: His Work as He Sees It*. Garden City, New York: Anchor Books.

Clarke, Peter and Susan H. Evans. (1982). "By Pen or By Pocketbook? Voter Understanding of Congressional Campaigns." In James S. Ettema and D. Charles Whitney, eds., *Individuals in Mass Media Organizations*. Beverly Hills, California: Sage, pp. 205–18.

———. (1983). *Covering Campaigns: Journalism in Congressional Elections*. Stanford, California: Stanford University Press.

Clarke, Peter and Eric Fredin. (1978). "Newspapers, Television, and Political Reasoning." *Public Opinion Quarterly*. 42:143–60.

Clausen, Aage R. (1973). *How Congressmen Decide: A Policy Focus*. New York: St. Martin's Press.

Collins, Keith S., ed. (1985). *Responsibility and Freedom in the Press: Are They in Conflict?* Washington, D.C.: Citizen's Choice, Inc.

Commission on Freedom of the Press. (1947). *A Free and Responsible Press.* Chicago: University of Chicago Press.

Comstock, George et al. (1977). *Television and Human Behavior.* New York: Columbia University Press.

Congressional Quarterly Special Report "Elections '84." Supplement to Vol. 42, No. 41 (October 31, 1984):2549–50.

Conover, W. J. (1971). *Practical Nonparametric Statistics.* New York: John Wiley and Sons.

Converse, Philip. (1962). "Information Flow and the Stability of Partisan Attitudes." *Public Opinion Quarterly.* 26:578–99.

———. (1966). "Information Flow and the Stability of Partisan Attitudes." In Angus Campbell, Philip E. Converse, Warren E. Miller, and Donald E. Stokes, *Elections and the Political Order.* New York: John Wiley and Sons, pp. 136–58.

———. (1975). "Public Opinion and Voting Behavior." In Fred I. Greenstein and Nelson W. Polsby, eds., *Handbook of Political Science: Nongovernmental Politics,* Vol. 4. Reading, Massachusetts: Addison-Wesley, pp. 75–169.

Cook, Timothy E. (1984). "Newsmakers, Lawmakers and Leaders: Who Gets on the Network News from Congress." Paper presented at the annual meeting of the American Political Science Association, Washington, D.C.

———. (1985). "Marketing the Members: The Ascent of the Congressional Press Secretary." Paper presented at the annual meeting of the Midwest Political Science Association, Chicago, Illinois.

———. (1986). "House Members as Newsmakers: The Effects of Televising Congress." *Legislative Studies Quarterly.* 11:203–26.

———. (1987). "Show Horses in House Elections: The Advantages and Disadvantages of National Media Visibility." Chapter 9 of this book.

Coombs, Steven Lane. (1981). "Editorial Endorsements and Electoral Outcomes." In Steven Lane Coombs and Michael MacKuen, eds., *More Than News.* Beverly Hills, California: Sage, pp. 145–230.

Cooper, Ann. (1979). "Curtain Rising on House TV Amid Aid-to-Incumbent Fears." *Congressional Quarterly Weekly Report.* (February 10):252–54.

Cover, Albert. (1977). "One Good Term Deserves Another: The Advantage of Incumbency in Congressional Elections." *American Journal of Political Science.* 21:523–43.

Cover, Albert and Bruce Brumberg. (1982). "Baby Books and Ballots: The Impact of Congressional Mail on Constituent Opinion." *American Political Science Review.* 76:347–59.

David, Paul T., Ralph M. Goldman, and Richard C. Bain. (1960). *The Politics of National Party Conventions.* Washington, D.C.: The Brookings Institution.

Davis, James W. (1983). *National Conventions in the Age of Reform.* Westport, Connecticut: Greenwood Press.

Denton, Robert E., Jr., and Gary C. Woodward. (1985). *Political Communication in America.* New York: Praeger.

Dewhirst, Robert E. (1983). "Patterns of Interaction Between Members of the

U.S. House of Representatives and Their Home District News Media."
Ph.D. dissertation, University of Nebraska-Lincoln.

———. (1986). Comment at the Dwight P. Griswold–E. C. Ames Conference
on Mass Media and Congressional Elections, Nebraska Wesleyan University.

Dodd, Lawrence C. (1981). "Congress, the Constitution and the Crisis of Legit-
imation." In Lawrence C. Dodd and Bruce I. Oppenheimer, eds., *Congress Reconsidered*, 2nd edition. Washington, D.C.: CQ Press, pp. 390–
420.

Donohue, George A., P. J. Tichenor, and C. N. Olien. (1972). "Gatekeeping:
Mass Media Systems and Information Control." In G. Kline and P. J.
Tichenor, eds., *Current Perspectives in Mass Communication Research*. Bev-
erly Hills, California: Sage, pp. 41–69.

Dreyer, Edward C. (1971). "Media Use and Electoral Choices: Some Political
Consequences of Information Exposure." *Public Opinion Quarterly*. 35:544–
53.

Dunn, Delmer D. (1974). "Symbiosis: Congress and the Press." In Robert O.
Blanchard, ed., *Congress and the News Media*. New York: Hastings House,
pp. 240–49.

Elazar, Daniel J. (1972). *American Federalism: A View from the States*. New York:
Thomas Y. Crowell Company.

Elebash, Camille and James Rosene. (1982). "Issues in Political Advertising in
a Deep South Gubernatorial Race." *Journalism Quarterly*. 59:420–23.

Epstein, Edward J. (1974a). *News from Nowhere*. New York: Random House Vintage Books.

———. (1974b). "Journalism and Truth." *Commentary*. 57, No. 4:36–40.

Erikson, Robert S. (1971). "The Advantage of Incumbency in Congressional
Elections." *Polity*. 3:395–405.

———. (1981). "Measuring Constituency Opinion: The 1978 U.S. Congressional Election Survey." *Legislative Studies Quarterly*. 6:235–46.

Fenno, Richard F., Jr. (1978). *Home Style: House Members in Their Districts*. Boston: Little, Brown.

———. (1981). *The U.S. Senate: A Bicameral Perspective*. Washington, D.C.:
American Enterprise Institute.

Fiorina, Morris P. (1974). *Representatives, Roll Calls, and Constituencies*. Lexington, Massachusetts: D. C. Heath.

Fry, Don, ed. (1986). *Believing the News*. St. Petersburg, Florida: Poynter Institute for Media Studies.

Gans, Herbert J. (1979). *Deciding What's News*. New York: Vintage Books.

Gitlin, Todd. (1980). *The Whole World Is Watching: The Mass Media in the Making
and Unmaking of the New Left*. Berkeley: University of California Press.

Goldenberg, Edie N. and Michael W. Traugott. (1984). *Campaigning for Congress*. Washington, D.C.: CQ Press.

———. (1985a). "Evaluating Models of Voting Behavior in U.S. Senate Elections." Paper presented at the annual meeting of the Midwest Political
Science Association, Chicago, Illinois.

———. (1985b). "The Impact of News Coverage in Senate Campaigns." Paper presented at the annual meeting of the American Political Science Association, New Orleans, Louisiana.

———. (1987). "Mass Media Effects on Recognizing and Rating Candidates in U.S. Senate Elections." Chapter 7 of this book.

Goldenberg, Edie N., Michael W. Traugott, and Frank R. Baumgartner. (1986). "Preemptive and Reactive Spending in U.S. House Races." *Political Behavior*. 8:3–20.

Graber, Doris A. (1970). "Presidential Images in the 1968 Campaign." Paper presented at the annual meeting of the Midwest Political Science Association, Chicago, Illinois.

———. (1971). "Press Coverage Patterns of Campaign News: The 1968 Presidential Race." *Journalism Quarterly*. 48:502–12.

———. (1972). "Personal Qualities in Presidential Images: The Contribution of the Press." *Midwest Journal of Political Science*. 16:52–63.

———. (1976). "The Effect of Incumbency on Coverage Patterns in the 1972 Presidential Campaign." *Journalism Quarterly*. 53:499–506.

———. (1984). *Mass Media and American Politics*. 2nd edition. Washington, D.C.: CQ Press.

Grossman, Michael Baruch and Martha Joynt Kumar. (1979). "The White House and the News Media: Phases of Their Relationship." *Political Science Quarterly*. 94:37–53.

Hale, Jon F. (1986). Comments at the Dwight P. Griswold–E. C. Ames Conference on Mass Media and Congressional Elections, Nebraska Wesleyan University.

———. (1987). "The Scribes of Texas: Newspaper Coverage of the 1984 U.S. Senate Campaign." Chapter 6 of this book.

Hart, Roderick P., Patrick Jerome, and Karen McComb. (1984). "Rhetorical Features of Newscasts About the President." *Critical Studies in Mass Communication*. 1:260–86.

Hershey, Majorie Randon. (1984). *Running for Office: The Political Education of Campaigners*. Chatham, New Jersey: Chatham House.

Hess, Stephen. (1986). *The Ultimate Insiders: The Senate and the National Press*. Washington, D.C.: The Brookings Institution.

Hibbing, John and Sara L. Brandes. (1983). "State Population and the Electoral Success of U.S. Senators." *American Journal of Political Science*. 27:808–19.

Hinckley, Barbara. (1980a). "The American Voter in Congressional Elections." *American Political Science Review*. 74:641–50.

———. (1980b). "House Reelections and Senate Defeats: The Role of the Challenger." *British Journal of Political Science*. 10:441–60.

———. (1981). *Congressional Elections*. Washington, D.C.: CQ Press.

———. (1983). *Stability and Change in Congress*. New York: Harper and Row.

Hofstetter, C. Richard. (1979). "Perception of News Bias in 1972 Presidential Campaign." *Journalism Quarterly*. 56:370–74.

Huckshorn, Robert J. and Robert C. Spencer. (1971). *The Politics of Defeat: Campaigning for Congress*. Amherst: University of Massachusetts Press.

Index to Black Newspapers. Wooster, Ohio: The Indexing Center, Micro Photo Division, Bell & Howell Company, 1977 to present.

Jacobson, Gary C. (1975). "The Impact of Broadcast Campaigning on Electoral Outcomes." *Journal of Politics*. 37:769–93.

————. (1978). "The Effects of Campaign Spending on Congressional Elections." *American Political Science Review*. 72:469–91.

————. (1980). *Money in Congressional Elections*. New Haven, Connecticut: Yale University Press.

————. (1983). *The Politics of Congressional Elections*. New Haven, Connecticut: Yale University Press.

Jacobson, Gary C. and Samuel Kernell. (1981). *Strategy and Choice in Congressional Elections*. New Haven, Connecticut: Yale University Press.

Jennings, Bruce. (1987). "Media Coverage of Congressional Elections: An Ethical Perspective." Chapter 10 of this book.

Jennings, Bruce and Daniel Callahan. (1985a). *The Ethics of Legislative Life*. Hastings-on-Hudson, New York: Hastings Center.

————, eds. (1985b). *Representation and Responsibility: Exploring Legislative Ethics*. New York: Plenum Press.

Joslyn, Richard A. (1980). "The Content of Political Spot Ads." *Journalism Quarterly*. 57:92–98.

————. (1984). *Mass Media and Elections*. Reading, Massachusetts: Addison-Wesley.

————. (1987). "Liberal Campaign Rhetoric in 1984." Chapter 3 of this book.

Katosh, John P. and Michael W. Traugott. (1981). "The Consequences of Validated and Self-reported Voting Measures." *Public Opinion Quarterly*. 45:519–35.

Katz, Karen L. (1985). "Television News Coverage of Incumbents and Challengers in Senate Elections." Unpublished manuscript, Ann Arbor, Michigan.

Keeter, Scott. (1985). "Public Opinion in 1984." In Gerald Pomper, ed., *The Election of 1984*. Chatham, New Jersey: Chatham House, pp. 91–111.

Kelley, Douglas. (1958). "Press Coverage of Two Michigan Congressional Elections." *Journalism Quarterly*. 35:447–49.

Kernell, Samuel. (1977). "Presidential Popularity and Negative Voting: An Alternative Explanation of the Midterm Congressional Decline of the President's Party." *American Political Science Review*. 71:44–66.

————. (1986). *Going Public: New Strategies of Presidential Leadership*. Washington, D.C.: CQ Press.

Kingdon, John W. (1973). *Congressmen's Voting Decisions*. New York: Harper and Row.

Kristol, Irving. (1967). "The Underdeveloped Profession." *The Public Interest*. No. 6:36–52.

Kostroski, Warren. (1973). "Party and Incumbency in Postwar Senate Elections: Trends, Patterns and Models." *American Political Science Review*. 67:1213–34.

Kramer, Gerald H. (1971). "Short-Term Fluctuations in U.S. Voting Behavior, 1896–1964." *American Political Science Review*. 65:131–43.

Kraus, Sidney and Dennis Davis. (1976). *The Effects of Mass Communication on Political Behavior*. University Park: Pennsylvania State University Press.

Ladd, Everett Carll, Jr., and Charles D. Hadley. (1975). *Transformations of the American Party Systems*. New York: W. W. Norton.

Lazarsfeld, Paul F., Bernard R. Berelson, and Hazel Gaudet. (1944). *The People's Choice*. New York: Duell, Sloan, and Pierce.

Leary, Mary Ellen. (1977). *Phantom Politics: Campaigning in California*. Washington, D.C.: Public Affairs.

Lewis-Beck, Michael S. (1983). "Economic Voting in France and Italy: What We Know." Paper presented at the annual convention of the American Political Science Association, Chicago, Illinois.

Luttbeg, Norman R. (1983). "Television Viewing Audience and Congressional District Incongruity: A Handicap for the Challenger?" *Journal of Broadcasting*. 27:410–17.

MacNeil, Robert. (1968). *The People Machine*. New York: Harper and Row.

Maisel, Louis Sandy. (1982). *From Obscurity to Oblivion: Congressional Primary Elections in 1978*. Knoxville: University of Tennessee Press.

Manheim, Jarol B. (1974). "Urbanization and Differential Press Coverage of the Congressional Campaign." *Journalism Quarterly*. 51:649–53, 669.

Mankiewicz, Frank and Joel Swerdlow. (1978). *Remote Control*. New York: Times Books.

Mann, Thomas E. (1978). *Unsafe at Any Margin: Interpreting Congressional Elections*. Washington, D.C.: American Enterprise Institute.

Mann, Thomas E. and Raymond E. Wolfinger. (1980). "Candidates and Parties in Congressional Elections." *American Political Science Review*. 74:617–32.

Marshall, T. R. (1981). *Presidential Nominations in a Reform Age*. New York: Praeger.

Matthews, Donald. (1960). *U.S. Senators and Their World*. Chapel Hill: University of North Carolina Press.

Mayhew, David R. (1966). *Party Loyalty Among Congressmen*. Cambridge, Massachusetts: Harvard University Press.

———. (1974a). *Congress: The Electoral Connection*. New Haven, Connecticut: Yale University Press.

———. (1974b). "Congressional Elections: The Case of the Vanishing Marginals." *Polity*. 6:295–317.

McNitt, Andrew D. (1985). "Congressional Campaign Style." *Legislative Studies Quarterly*. 10:267–76.

McWilliams, Wilson Carey. (1984). "The Meaning of the Election." In Gerald Pomper, ed., *The Election of 1984*. Chatham, New Jersey: Chatham House, pp. 157–83.

Medcalf, Linda J. and Kenneth M. Dolbeare. (1985). *Neopolitics: American Political Ideas in the 1980s*. New York: Random House.

Merriam, Charles E. and Harold F. Gosnell. (1924). *Non-Voting, Causes and Methods of Control*. Chicago: University of Chicago Press.

Miller, Arthur H., Edie N. Goldenberg, and Lutz Erbring. (1979). "Type-set Politics: The Impact of Newspapers on Public Confidence." *American Political Science Review*. 73:67–84.

Miller, Susan H. (1978). "Reporters and Congressmen: Living in Symbiosis." *Journalism Monographs*. 53:1–25.

Miller, Warren E. (1979). *American National Election Study, 1978*. Codebook, Vol. 1. Ann Arbor, Michigan: Inter-university Consortium for Political and Social Research.

Miller, Warren and Donald Stokes. (1963). "Constituency Influence in Congress." *American Political Science Review*. 57:45–57.

Nelson, Candice. (1978/79). "The Effects of Incumbency on Voting in Congressional Elections." *Political Science Quarterly*. 93:665–78.

New York Times Index. New York: The New York Times Company, 1851 to present.

O'Neill, Michael J. (1983). "A Proposal for the Republic—A Challenge for Editors." In *The Adversary Press*. St. Petersburg, Florida: Modern Media Institute (Poynter Institute), pp. 2–15.

Orman, John. (1985). "Media Coverage of the Congressional Underdog." *PS*. 18:754–59.

Ornstein, Norman J. (1981). "The House and the Senate in the New Congress." In Thomas Mann and Norman Ornstein, eds., *The New Congress*. Washington, D.C.: American Enterprise Institute, pp. 363–83.

———. (1983). "The Open Congress Meets the President." In Anthony King, ed., *Both Ends of the Avenue*. Washington, D.C.: American Enterprise Institute, pp. 185–211.

Ornstein, Norman J. et al. (1984). *Vital Statistics on Congress*. Washington, D.C.: American Enterprise Institute.

Ornstein, Norman J. and M. Robinson. (1986). "The Case of Our Disappearing Congress." *TV Guide*. 34(January 11):4–10.

Page, Benjamin I. (1978). *Choices and Echoes in Presidential Elections*. Chicago: University of Chicago Press.

Parker, Glenn R. (1980a). "Sources of Change in Congressional District Attentiveness." *American Journal of Political Science*. 24:115–24.

———. (1980b). "Incumbent Popularity and Electoral Success." *American Politics Quarterly*. 8:449–64.

———. (1981). "Interpreting Candidate Awareness in U.S. Congressional Elections." *Legislative Studies Quarterly*. 6:219–34.

———. (1986a). "Is There a Political Life-Cycle in the House?" Paper prepared for delivery at the annual meeting of the American Political Science Association, Washington, D.C., August 28–31, 1986.

Parker, Glenn. (1986b). *Homeward Bound: Explaining Changes in Congressional Behavior*. Pittsburgh, Pennsylvania: University of Pittsburgh Press.

Patterson, Thomas E. (1980). *The Mass Media Election: How Americans Choose Their President*. New York: Praeger.

Patterson, Thomas E. and Richard Davis. (1985). "The Media Campaign: Struggle for the Agenda." In Michael Nelson, ed., *The Elections of 1984*. Washington, D.C.: CQ Press, pp. 111–27.

Patterson, Thomas E. and Robert D. McClure. (1976). *The Unseeing Eye: The Myth of Television Power in National Elections*. New York: G. P. Putnam.

Payne, James L. (1980). "Show Horses and Work Horses in the United States House of Representatives." *Polity*. 12:428–56.

Peterson, Bill. (1986). "How Do You Stand on Sewing?" *Washington Post Weekly Edition.* (January 13), p. 15.

Peterson, T. (1956). "The Social Responsibility Theory of the Press." In F. Siebert, T. Peterson, and W. Schramm, eds., *Four Theories of the Press.* Urbana: University of Illinois Press, pp. 73–103.

Pindyck, R. F. and Rubinfeld, D. L. (1976). *Economic Models and Economic Forecasting.* New York: McGraw-Hill.

Pitkin, Hanna Fenichel. (1967). *The Concept of Representation.* Berkeley: University of California Press.

———, ed. (1969). *Representation.* New York: Atherton Press.

Polsby, Nelson W. (1976). *Congress and the Presidency.* 3rd edition. Englewood Cliffs, New Jersey: Prentice-Hall.

Polsby, Nelson W. and Aaron Wildavsky. (1984). *Presidential Elections.* New York: Charles Scribner's Sons.

Pomper, Gerald M. (1985). "The Presidential Election." In Gerald M. Pomper, ed., *The Election of 1984.* Chatham, New Jersey: Chatham House, pp. 60–90.

Pomper, Gerald M., with Susan S. Lederman. (1980). *Elections in America: Control and Influence in Democratic Politics.* New York: Longman.

Ragsdale, Lyn. (1980). "The Fiction of Congressional Elections as Presidential Events." *American Politics Quarterly.* 8:375–98.

———. (1981). "Incumbent Popularity, Challenger Invisibility, and Congressional Voters." *Legislative Studies Quarterly.* 6:201–18.

Ragsdale, Lyn and Timothy E. Cook. (1987). "Representatives' Actions and Challengers' Reactions: Limits to Candidate Connections in the House." *American Journal of Political Science.* 31:45–81.

Ranney, Austin. (1983). *Channels of Power: The Impact of Television on American Politics.* New York: Basic Books.

Raymond, Paul B. (1983). "When Politicians Talk, Nobody Listens: The Effect of House Candidates' Campaign Communications on Voting Behavior." Paper presented at the annual meeting of the Midwestern Political Science Association, Chicago, Illinois.

———. (1987). "Shaping the News: An Analysis of House Candidates' Campaign Communications." Chapter 2 of this book.

Robinson, Michael J. (1975). "A Twentieth Century Medium in a Nineteenth Century Legislature: The Effects of Television on the American Congress." In Norman J. Ornstein, ed., *Congress in Change: Evolution and Reform.* New York: Praeger, pp. 55–96.

———. (1977). "Television and American Politics: 1956–1976." *The Public Interest.* (Summer):64–90.

———. (1981). "Three Faces of Congressional Media." In Thomas E. Mann and Norman J. Ornstein, eds., *The New Congress.* Washington, D.C.: American Enterprise Institute, pp. 55–96.

———. (1985). "The Media in Campaign '84: Part II." *Public Opinion* (February/March):43–48.

Robinson, Michael J. and Kevin R. Appel. (1979). "Network News Coverage of Congress." *Political Science Quarterly.* 94:407–13.

Robinson, Michael J. and Maura Clancey. (1985). "General Election Coverage: Part I." *Public Opinion* (December/January):49–59.

Robinson, Michael J. and Margaret Sheehan. (1984). *Over the Wire and on TV.* New York: Russell Sage Foundation.

Rothenberg, Stuart, ed. (1985). *Ousting the Ins.* Washington, D.C.: Free Congress Research and Education Foundation.

Salmore, Stephen A. and Barbara G. Salmore. (1985). *Candidates, Parties, and Campaigns: Electoral Politics in America.* Washington, D.C.: CQ Press.

Schudson, Michael. (1983). "The News Media and the Democratic Process." *A Wye Resource Paper.* New York: Aspen Institute.

Scott, William A. (1955). "Reliability of Content Analysis: The Case of Nominal Scale Coding." *Public Opinion Quarterly.* 19:321–25.

Simmons, Robert O., Jr. (1984). "A Little Learning Is the Safest Thing: Causes and Electoral Effects of House Incumbents Holding Well Known Issue Positions." Paper presented at the annual meeting of the American Political Science Association, Washington, D.C.

———. (1987). "Why Some Constituencies Are Better Informed Than Most About the Positions of House Incumbents." Chapter 4 of this book.

Sinclair, Barbara. (1976). "Political Upheaval and Congressional Voting: The Effects of the 1960s on Voting Patterns in the House of Representatives." *Journal of Politics.* 38:326–45.

———. (1977). "Determinants of Aggregate Party Cohesion in the U.S. House of Representatives." *Legislative Studies Quarterly.* 2:155–76.

———. (1985). "Agenda Control and Policy Success: Ronald Reagan and the 97th House." *Legislative Studies Quarterly.* 10:407–13.

Stokes, Donald E. and Warren E. Miller. (1962). "Party Government and the Salience of Congress." *Public Opinion Quarterly.* 26:531–46.

Television News Index and Abstracts. Nashville, Tennessee: Vanderbilt Television News Archive, 1968 to present.

Thomson, Charles A. H. (1956). *Television and Presidential Politics: The Experience of 1952 and the Problems Ahead.* Washington, D.C.: The Brookings Institution.

Tichnor, Philip J., George A. Donohue, and Clarice N. Olien. (1970). "Mass Media Flow and Differential Growth in Knowledge." *Public Opinion Quarterly.* 34:159–70.

Tidmarch, Charles M. (1985). "Scribes, Touts and Pamphleteers: Press Coverage of the 1982/84 Election." Paper presented at the annual meeting of the Midwest Political Science Association, Chicago, Illinois.

Tidmarch, Charles M., Lisa J. Hyman, and Jill E. Sorkin. (1984). "Press Issue Agendas in the 1982 Congressional and Gubernatorial Election Campaigns." *Journal of Politics.* 46:1226–42.

Tidmarch, Charles M. and Brad S. Karp. (1983). "The Missing Beat: Press Coverage of Congressional Elections in Eight Metropolitan Areas." *Congress and the Presidency.* 10:46–61.

Tidmarch, Charles and John Pitney. (1985). "Covering Congress." *Polity.* 17:446–83.

Tuchman, Gaye. (1973). "Making News by Doing Work: Routinizing the Unexpected." *American Journal of Sociology.* 79:110–31.

Tufte, Edward R. (1975). "Determinants of the Outcomes of Midterm Congressional Elections." *American Political Science Review*. 69:812–26.

———. (1978). *Political Control of the Economy*. Princeton, New Jersey: Princeton University Press.

Uslaner, Eric M. (1981). "Ain't Misbehavin': The Logic of Defensive Issue Strategies in Congressional Elections." *American Politics Quarterly*. 9:3–22.

Uslaner, Eric M. and M. Margaret Conway. (1985). "The Responsive Congressional Electorate: Watergate, the Economy, and Vote Choice in 1974." *American Political Science Review*. 79:788–803.

Vest, Ken and Richard Paul. (1984). "A Tale of Two Press Secretaries." *Washington Journalism Review* (October):18–20.

Vermeer, Jan P. (1982). *"For Immediate Release": Candidate Press Releases in American Political Campaigns*. Westport, Connecticut: Greenwood Press.

———. (1984). "The Electoral Vulnerability of Congressional Incumbents: Another Perspective." *Arkansas Political Science Journal*. 5:86–92.

———. (1987). "Congressional Campaign Coverage in Rural Districts." Chapter 5 of this book.

Vermeer, Jan P. and Joseph R. Mouer. (1986). "Exon and Hoch in Nebraska Headlines: Name Prominence in the 1984 Campaign." *Northern Social Science Review*. 11:25–34.

Wahlke, John C., and Heinz Eulau, William Buchanan, and LeRoy C. Ferguson. (1962). *The Legislative System*. New York: John Wiley and Sons.

Wattenberg, Martin P. (1982). "From Parties to Candidates." *Public Opinion Quarterly*. 46:216–27.

Weissberg, Robert. (1976). *Public Opinion and Popular Government*. Englewood Cliffs, New Jersey: Prentice-Hall.

Westlye, Mark C. (1983). "Competitiveness of Senate Seats and Voting Behavior in Senate Elections." *American Journal of Political Science*. 27:253–83.

Wright, Gerald C. (1978). "Candidates' Policy Positions and Voting in U.S. Congressional Elections." *Legislative Studies Quarterly*. 3:443–64.

Wright, Gerald C. and Michael B. Berkman. (1985). "Candidates and Policy in U.S. Senate Elections: A Comparative State Analysis." Paper presented at the annual meeting of the Western Political Science Association, Las Vegas, Nevada.

Index

Abramowitz, Alan I., 3, 70n, 109, 201

Abscam, 180n

Accountability, 184, 186-89, 191-92, 195-96

Adams, William, 145, 146n

Adversarialism, 185

Advertisements, 7, 67, 78, 91, 102, 112, 129, 162; newspaper, 66, 73n, 110; radio, 5, 14; television, 4-5, 9-10, 14, 36-38, 40-46, 53, 55, 57-62, 64, 66-69, 70n, 73n-74n, 75n, 94, 97, 101-7, 110-12, 116-17, 121, 124-27, 129-30, 131n, 135, 142, 143

Agranoff, Robert, 4

Alabama, 144

Alaska, 144

Albosta, Don, 44

Alexander, Bill, 139

Alford, John R., 5, 74n, 78, 87

Allen, Charles L., 88

Alpena, Michigan, 124

Alpena (Michigan) *News*, 120

Alternative Press Index, 203

Amarillo Daily News and Sunday News-Globe, 95, 98, 103-4

"Amarillo difference," 10, 103-6

American Broadcasting Company (ABC), 134, 136, 141, 143-44

Americans for Constitutional Action (ACA), 53

Americans for Democratic Action (ADA), 36-37

American Society of Newspaper Editors, 185, 197n

Anderson, John, 162

Appel, Kevin R., 163

Arizona, 138, 140

Arkansas, 52, 139

Armed Services Committee (House), 43

Arterton, F. Christopher, 7-8, 88, 197n, 198n, 202, 205n

Associated Press, 103, 105, 134

Association of House Democratic Press Assistants, 171

Atlantic (Iowa) *News Telegraph*, 82

AuCoin, Les, 42

Austin, Texas, 95, 103
Autonomy, 186-91, 195

Bain, Richard C., 146n
Baker, Howard, 138-40, 144
Bauman, Robert E., 180n
Baumgartner, Frank R., 75n
Bay City (Michigan) *Times*, 120
Beatrice (Nebraska) *Sun*, 82
Becker, Samuel L., 146n
Behr, Roy L., 74n
Bennett, W. Lance, 49n
Berelson, Bernard R., 13
Berkman, Michael B., 109, 130n
Biden, Joseph, 38, 49n
Blakely, Steve, 180n
Blalock, Hubert M., Jr., 71n
Boston, Massachusetts, 96
Bradley, Bill, 38, 40, 49n
Brady, David W., 29n
Brandes, Sara L., 91, 110
Brinkley, David, 143-45
Broder, David, 161
Brogan, Denis, 134, 146n
Brokaw, Tom, 143-45
Brown, George E., Jr., 49n
Bush, George, 138, 140

Cable Satellite Public Affairs Network
    (C-SPAN), 136, 138, 141-42, 145
Cadillac, 125
California, 138, 140, 142
Callahan, Daniel, 198n
Campaign brochures, 9, 14, 26n,
    28n, 54, 64, 73n, 78, 110
Campaign financing, 3, 4, 67, 75n,
    77-78, 88, 94, 97, 110, 127, 163-64,
    166, 178, 181n, 202, 204
Campaign Group, The, 37, 48n
Campaign resources, 3, 8, 34, 124,
    127, 201, 204
Campaigns: competitiveness of, 22-
    23, 25, 28n-29n, 204, 205n; as edu-
    cation, 8-9, 11, 15, 34-35, 45-47,
    53, 74n, 196, 202
Campbell, Angus, 3
Campbell, James, 5, 74n, 78, 87

Candidates: characteristics of, 23-24,
    59, 92, 95, 97, 129; national visibil-
    ity of, 162-64, 166, 173-75, 177-78;
    visibility of, 52-53, 55, 59, 68-69,
    89n, 117, 135, 203, 205n
Carey, John, 106
Carter, Jimmy, 24, 32, 42, 135, 138-
    39, 180n, 184
CBS News Index, 203
Chaffee, John H., 28n
Challengers: House, 2, 5-9, 13-14,
    18-19, 21-22, 27n, 35, 37, 52-53,
    56-59, 62, 64, 66, 68-70, 73n-74n,
    75n, 77, 79-80, 82-88, 119, 129,
    163, 164, 178, 183, 200, 202; quali-
    fications of, 2-3, 7, 21, 24-26, 28n,
    34, 67, 77, 166, 201; Senate, 4,
    111, 113-15, 117, 119-20, 121, 127,
    129, 201-2; visibility of, 3, 78, 89n,
    114, 179, 201-2
Cheney, Richard, 81
Chicago, Illinois, 133-34
Clapp, Charles L., 5
Clarke, Peter, 8, 13, 18, 24, 27n, 53,
    67, 69, 73n, 80, 87, 119, 180n,
    200-201, 205n
Clausen, Aage R., 20, 29n
Cleveland, Ohio, 134
Cochrane, Thad, 140
Coelho, Tony, 142
Collins, Keith S., 197n
Collins, Martha Layne, 139
Colorado, 41, 43
Columbia Broadcasting System
    (CBS), 134, 136, 141-44
Columbus (Nebraska) *Telegram*, 82
Commission on Freedom of the
    Press, 197n. *See also* Hutchins
    Commission
Comstock, George, 164
Congressional districts: and media
    market fit, 5-6, 54, 56, 64, 66-67,
    69, 78-79, 87, 111, 120, 127, 204,
    205n; rural, 9-10, 79-81, 87-88, 93
Congressional Quarterly Weekly Report,
    37, 49n
Connecticut, 140-41, 181n
Conover, W. J., 71n

Conservatism, 41-42, 45, 47, 48n
Constituencies, 1
Content analysis, 15, 55, 117, 131n, 203-4
Conventions, national nominating, 10, 133-46
Converse, Philip E., 48n
Conway, M. Margaret, 3
Cook, Timothy, 6, 10, 67, 135, 161-62, 164, 166, 181n, 199-200, 203
Cooke, Janet, 191
Coolidge, Calvin, 134
Coombs, Steven Lane, 119, 131n
Cooper, Ann, 162
Cover, Albert, 2
Cronkite, Walter, 143
Cuomo, Mario, 141

Dallas, Texas, 93, 103, 140, 143-44
Dallas Morning News, 95, 98
David, Paul T., 146n
Davis, Dennis, 197n
Davis, James W., 135, 146n
Davis, John W., 134
Democratic Congressional Campaign Committee, 37, 142
Democratic theory, 2, 13, 17, 25, 34, 36, 183-97
Democrats. *See* Partisan affiliation (candidates); Party identification
Denardis, Larry, 38
Denton, Jeremiah, 144
Denton, Robert E., Jr., 92
Detroit, Michigan, 112, 124-25, 131n
Detroit Free Press, 112, 120
Detroit News, 112, 117, 131n
Dewhirst, Robert E., 67, 174-76
Dodd, Christopher, 140
Dodd, Lawrence C., 91
Dodge City (Kansas) *Daily Globe,* 82
Doggett, Lloyd, 93-94, 96
Dolbeare, Kenneth M., 31, 48n
Dole, Robert, 140, 144
Drake, Lynn, 171
Duluth, Minnesota, 121, 130n
Dumont (television network), 134
Dunn, Jim, 110, 119-20

Eisenhower, Dwight D., 133
Elazar, Daniel J., 22, 29n
Elebash, Camille, 91
Electoral choice, 6, 11, 35-36, 47, 92
Elkhart, Indiana, 130n
El Paso Times, 95, 100, 103
Emery, Jill, 44
Epstein, Edward J., 26, 197n, 205n
Erikson, Robert S., 2, 71n
Ethics, 11, 183, 185-97. *See also* Journalism: ethical considerations in
Evans, Lane, 42
Evans, Susan H., 8, 13, 18, 24, 27n, 67, 73n, 80, 87, 119, 180n, 200-201

Falls Township, Pennsylvania, 41
Feighan, Edward, 46
Fenno, Richard F., Jr., 27n, 29n, 53, 178, 196-97, 198n
Ferraro, Geraldine, 140-42
Fiedler, Bobbi, 140
Fiorina, Morris P., 70n
Foley, Tim, 138
Ford, Gerald, 42
Fort Worth, Texas, 103
Francis, Jim, 48n
Fredin, Eric, 53, 69, 205n
Fry, Don, 197n

Gans, Herbert J., 175
Garcia, Robert, 140
Garland, Ray, 144
Gaudet, Hazel, 13
Georgia, 144
Gephardt, Richard, 139
Gingrich, Newt, 144
Goldenberg, Edie N., 5-6, 10, 22, 27n, 52-54, 64, 67, 70n, 73n, 74n, 75n, 78, 87, 111, 114, 118, 135, 162, 180n, 201-2, 205n
Goldman, Ralph M., 146n
Goldwater, Barry, 140, 144
Gore, Albert, 142
Gosnell, Harold F., 2
Graber, Doris A., 26n
Grace, Peter, 46
Grace Commission, 42-43
Gramm, Philip, 93-94, 96, 139

Green, William, 198n
Green Bay, Wisconsin, 130n
Greenstein, Fred I., 48n
Grossman, Michael B., 181n

Hadley, Charles D., 48n
Hale, Jon F., 7, 9-10, 14, 54, 64, 67,
  71n, 75n, 135
Hance, Kent, 94
Harkin, Tom, 142
Hart, Gary, 140
Hart, Roderick P., 106
Hastings Center Project on Congress
  and the Media, 185
Hawaii, 139
Hays, Brooks, 52, 55
Helms, Jesse, 68, 94, 142, 144
Henry, Keith, 5, 74n, 78, 87
Hershey, Marjorie Randon, 4
Hess, Stephen, 181n
Hibbing, John, 91, 110
Hinckley, Barbara, 3, 13, 28n, 29n,
  34, 49n, 51, 77, 89n, 109, 201
Hinson, Jon, 180n
Holt, Marjorie, 140
Hommel, Ted, 81
Houghton (Michigan) Daily Mining Ga-
  zette, 120
Houston, Texas, 93, 103
Houston Post, 95, 100
Huckshorn, Robert J., 28n
Humphrey, Hubert H., 32
Hunt, Jim, 68, 142
Hutchins Commission, 184
Hyman, Lisa J., 92

Ideology, 9, 33-34, 36, 40-43, 45-47,
  73n, 94, 130n, 184
Illinois, 42, 138-39, 144, 162
Incumbency advantage, 2-3, 5-6, 9-
  10, 13, 21, 27n, 28n, 34, 77-78, 86-
  89, 111, 119, 162, 179, 200-202
Incumbents: House, 2, 4, 7-9, 14, 18-
  19, 22, 24-26, 34-35, 36-37, 43, 46,
  51-54, 55-57, 59-70, 72n, 73n, 74n,
  75n, 77-78, 79, 80, 82-89, 111,
  162-64, 166, 179, 180n, 183, 200-
  202, 204; Senate, 36, 111, 112,

  114-16, 119, 121, 126-27, 129,
  131n, 202
Index to Black Newspapers, 203
Indiana, 138
Information environments, for vot-
  ers, 110-11, 117-18, 120, 125-26,
  129
Inouye, Daniel, 139
Interest-Group Liberalism, 46
Iowa, 79, 82, 87-88, 142
Issues (in campaigns), 9, 13-23, 25-
  26, 27n, 28n, 33, 35, 51-53, 55, 58-
  61, 63-70, 73n, 75n, 92, 94-107,
  129

Jackson, Jesse, 139
Jacobson, Gary C., 3, 35, 49n, 70n,
  75n, 77, 88, 164
Jennings, Bruce, 11, 51, 198n
Jennings, Peter, 143-45
Johnson, Lyndon Baines, 32
Joslyn, Richard A., 9, 22, 27n, 48n,
  49n, 53, 67, 70n, 91, 135
Journalism: ethical considerations in,
  183-84, 186-97; norms of, 14, 25-
  26, 63, 65-66, 85, 92-93, 102, 106-
  7, 110, 176, 184-85, 190, 192-93,
  200-201, 204

Kansas, 79, 81-82, 87-88, 138
Kanter, Julian, 37, 49n
Kaptur, Marcie, 40-41
Karp, Brad S., 92
Kassebaum, Nancy, 138-39, 141
Katosh, John P., 72n
Katz, Karen L., 74n, 199
Keeshan, Bob, 176
Keeter, Scott, 48n
Kelley, Douglas, 200
Kemp, Jack, 139-40, 144
Kemp-Roth bill, 17
Kennedy, Edward, 138, 141
Kennedy, John F., 32
Kennelly, Barbara, 141
Kentucky, 17-18, 139
Kernell, Samuel, 3, 51
Kingdon, John W., 52, 55, 75n
Kostmayer, Peter, 40-41, 49n

Kramer, Gerald H., 3
Kraus, Sidney, 146, 197n
Kristol, Irving, 29n
Krueger, Bob, 94
Kumar, Martha J., 181n

Ladd, Everett Carll, Jr., 48n
Lance, Bert, 142
Lansing, Michigan, 125
Lautenberg, Frank, 139
Laxalt, Paul, 140, 144
Lazarsfeld, Paul F., 13
Leary, Mary Ellen, 91
Levin, Carl, 110, 112, 114-16, 119-21, 125-27, 130n
Liberalism, 31-33, 36-38, 40-42, 44-45, 47, 48n
Linsky, Martin, 198n
Lott, Trent, 138, 140, 144
Lousma, Jack, 110, 112, 114-16, 119-21, 125, 127
Lower, Elmer L., 146n
Lubbock, Texas, 94
Lugar, Richard, 138, 140
Lundine, Stan, 44

MacNeil, Robert, 197n
Macomb (Michigan) *Daily*, 120
Maisel, Louis Sandy, 27n, 28n
Manheim, Jarol B., 79-81
Mankiewicz, Frank, 197n
Mann, Thomas E., 3, 51, 53, 55, 77, 109, 201
Marquette, Michigan, 124-25
Marshall, T. R., 146n
Martin, Lynn, 139-40
Massachusetts, 134, 138, 144
Mayhew, David R., 2, 3, 20, 29n, 71n, 161-62, 178
McCloskey, Frank, 43-44
McCloskey Amendment, 43
McClure, Robert D., 69, 197n, 205n
McIntyre, Richard, 44
McKinney, Frank, 134
McMillan, Ken, 42
McNitt, Andrew D., 79
McNulty, Jim, 46
McPhee, William N., 13

McWilliams, Wilson Carey, 31, 48n
Medcalf, Linda J., 31, 48n
Media, electronic, 5-6, 171-72, 199-200, 203-4. *See also* Newspapers; Radio; Television
Media bias, 7-8, 10, 92, 184, 200
Media markets, 110, 121, 124-25, 130n. *See also* Congressional districts: and media market fit
Merriam, Charles, 2
Michel, Robert, 138-41
Michigan, 10, 110, 112, 114, 117, 119-21, 124, 127, 130n, 131n, 140
Miller, Arthur H., 163
Miller, George, 138
Miller, Warren E., 52, 55-56, 77
Mississippi, 138
Missouri, 139
Mochary, Mary, 144
Mondale, Walter, 32-33, 94, 138, 140-41, 143
Morrison, Bruce, 38
Morrisville, Pennsylvania, 41
Mouer, Joseph R., 80, 85
Mt. Pleasant, Michigan, 44
Moyers, Bill, 143
Mudd, Roger, 142

Name recognition, 2-3, 5-7, 77-78, 88, 110-15, 127, 129, 131n, 162
National Broadcasting Company (NBC), 134, 136, 141-44, 176
National Conservative Political Action Committee (NCPAC), 4, 66, 110
National Council of Senior Citizens, 40
National Election Study, 2, 14, 54, 71n, 109, 131n, 205n
National Republican Senatorial Committee, 110
Nebraska, 79, 82, 87-88
Nebraska City (Nebraska) *News-Press*, 82
Nelson, Candice, 2
Nevada, 140
New Deal Liberalism, 31-33, 36, 38, 46
New Jersey, 139, 144, 181n

New Mexico, 142
News coverage, 2, 5, 7, 8, 11, 26n,
  27n-28n, 29n, 51, 54, 57, 59-60,
  62, 63-65, 66, 68, 73n, 74n, 78-88,
  91, 92-93, 95-108, 109-10, 112,
  114, 116-21, 127, 129, 135, 162-64,
  172, 174, 176, 184, 200, 202, 204;
  local, 9-10, 83, 88, 104-6, 135, 162,
  172-73, 174, 176; national, 10-11,
  67, 135, 162-64, 166, 172, 174,
  176, 180n; print, 9-10, 27n-28n,
  57, 62, 64, 66, 71n, 79-88, 91, 92-
  93, 95-108, 110, 117-21, 127, 130,
  163-64, 172, 200, 203-4; radio, 91;
  television, 74n, 91, 110, 114, 135,
  163-64, 166, 176, 200, 203-4
Newspapers, 9, 10, 54, 72n, 74n, 81-
  83, 85-86, 88, 94-96, 98-100, 102-7,
  110, 114, 117-21, 129, 131n, 176,
  200, 203, 204, 205n; daily, 10, 79-
  80, 87, 91, 117, 119-20, 130n,
  131n, 172, 174, 200, 203, 204;
  readership of, 112, 129, 199; rural,
  9, 79, 81, 83, 87; urban, 120;
  weekly, 172
Newton (Iowa) *Daily News,* 82
New York City, 134, 181n
New York Daily News, 185
New York State, 139-41
New York Times, 163-64, 166, 172-73,
  181n
New York Times Index, 164, 203
Nimmo, Dan, 6, 10
Nixon, Richard M., 133
North Carolina, 142, 144
Norton (Kansas) *Daily Telegram,* 82

Objectivity, 92-93, 97, 103, 190
Oklahoma, University of, 49n
O'Neill, Michael, 185, 197n
O'Neill, Thomas P. (Tip), 138, 140,
  142
Open seat contests, 4, 14, 18, 25, 35,
  70n, 71n, 79, 92
O'Riordian, Margaret, 134
Orman, John, 54
Ornstein, Norman J., 146, 161, 178
Ortega, Kathryn, 138

Page, Benjamin I., 16-17, 22, 51
Parker, Glenn R., 109, 180n, 201
Partisan affiliation (candidates), 20-
  22, 24, 28n, 29n
Party identification, 2, 77, 127
Patterson, Thomas E., 69, 91, 96,
  197n, 199-200, 205n
Paul, Richard, 91
Payne, James L., 162-63, 180n
Pennsylvania, 114
Penny, Tim, 49n
Pentagon, 42
Percy, Charles, 144
Peterson, Bill, 180n
Peterson, Theodore, 29n
Petoskey News (Michigan) *Review,* 117
Phillips, Kevin, 143
Pitkin, Hanna F., 2, 7
Pitney, John, 163
Political Action Committees (PACs),
  4, 66-67, 110, 163, 166, 178
Political culture, 22-23, 25, 29n, 184,
  194
Political parties, 10, 18
Polsby, Nelson W., 28n, 48n, 53
Pomper, Gerald, 18, 27n, 32, 48n
Pratt, Judith, 142

Radio, 5, 91, 134
Ragsdale, Lyn, 109, 111, 164, 166,
  181n, 202
Ranney, Austin, 7, 161, 200
Rather, Dan, 142-43, 145
Raymond, Paul Bradford, 9, 11, 53,
  67, 70n, 73n, 88, 89n
Reagan, Ronald, 42-43, 46, 93, 133,
  140
Realignment: ideological, 33, 36, 47;
  partisan, 32-33
Representation, 1, 6-9, 11, 183, 185-
  90, 192-93, 195-97
Republican National Convention Net-
  work Service, 145
Republicans. *See* Partisan affiliation
  (candidates); Party identification
Responsibility, 184, 186-87, 189, 192-
  93, 195-96
Richardson, Eliot, 144

Robinson, Michael J., 67, 145-46,
    161-63, 171, 200, 205n
Rockefeller, Jay, 142
Roosevelt, Franklin D., 32
Rosene, James, 91
Rothenberg, Stuart, 49n
Royal Oak (Michigan) *Daily Tribune*,
    120

St. Louis Post-Dispatch, 203
Salmore, Barbara G., 28n, 81
Salmore, Stephen A., 28n, 81
San Antonio Express-News, 95, 99-100,
    103
San Francisco, California, 141, 143-
    44
San Francisco Chronicle, 203
Schudson, Michael, 193
Senate Democratic Policy Committee,
    180n
Senate races, 10, 38, 91-95, 109-11,
    117-21, 127, 131n, 135, 139, 201-2,
    204
Shamie, Raymond, 144
Shields, Mark, 143
"Show horses," 161-62, 166, 178-79,
    180n
Simmons, Robert O., Jr., 9, 51, 53,
    68, 203
Sinclair, Barbara, 20, 29n, 179
Smith, Larry David, 6, 10
Somers, Suzanne, 176
"Sophomore surge," 180n
Sorkin, Jill E., 92
South Bend, Indiana, 130n
South Carolina, 144
Sparkman, John, 133
Spencer, Robert C., 28n
Stevens, Ted, 144
Stevenson, Adlai E., 133
Stokes, Donald E., 52, 55-56, 77
Superior, Wisconsin, 130n
Swerdlow, Joel, 197n

Taft, Robert, 133
Television, 5-6, 10, 69, 92, 114, 134-
    36, 138-45, 174, 185, 204, 205n;
    advertisements, 4-5, 9, 14, 36-38,
40, 47, 53-55, 57-62, 64, 66-69,
    73n-74n, 94, 97, 101, 110-12, 116-
    17, 121, 124-26, 127, 130n, 135;
    local, 91, 112, 172, 199-200, 203;
    national, 10-11, 134-36, 138-45,
    163, 174, 176-77, 199, 203; news,
    69, 91, 101, 110, 112, 117, 127,
    130n, 163, 172, 174, 176-77, 199-
    200, 203, 205n
Television News Index and Abstracts,
    164, 203
Tennessee, 138, 142
Texas, 10, 91-94, 103, 139-41
Thomson, Charles A. H., 146n
Thurmond, Strom, 144
Tidmarch, Charles M., 54, 92, 163
Toledo, Ohio, 130n
Tower, John, 93, 140
Traugott, Michael W., 5-6, 10, 22,
    27n, 52-54, 64, 67, 70n, 72n, 73n,
    74n, 75n, 78, 87, 92, 111, 114, 118,
    131n, 135, 162, 180n, 201-2, 205n
Traverse City, Michigan, 124-25
Truman, Harry S., 32
Tuchman, Gaye, 176
Tufte, Edward R., 3

Udall, Morris, 138-39
Uslaner, Eric M., 3
U.S. News and World Report, 175

Valence issues, 43
Vander Jagt, Guy, 140
Vermeer, Jan P., 3, 9-10, 26n, 27n,
    54, 79-80, 85, 89n, 135, 202
Vest, Ken, 91
Virginia, 144, 181n
Voters: evaluations of candidates, 3,
    130; information levels in congres-
    sional elections, 14, 56, 58-60, 62,
    66, 72n, 73n, 75n, 78, 97, 99, 105,
    112, 114, 116, 120, 129, 201-2

Wahlke, John C., 1
Washington, D.C., 10, 181n
Washington Post, 172-73, 175, 177,
    181n

Wattenberg, Martin P., 71n
Weicker, Lowell, 144
Weissberg, Robert, 26n
Westlye, Mark C., 91, 109, 120, 205n
West Virginia, 142, 144
Wildavsky, Aaron, 28n
Wirth, Timothy, 41, 43, 46

Wolfinger, Raymond E., 3, 51, 53, 55, 109, 201
Woodward, Gary C., 92
"Work horses," 161, 178, 180n
Wright, Gerald C., 109, 130n
Wright, Jim, 141
Wyoming, 81

About the Contributors

TIMOTHY E. COOK is Assistant Professor of Political Science at Williams College. He has widely published articles in the fields of congressional representation, political communication, and political socialization. An American Political Science Association Congressional Fellow in 1984–1985, he is currently working on a book on media strategies in the House of Representatives.

EDIE N. GOLDENBERG is Professor of Political Science and Public Policy and a faculty associate in the Institute for Social Research at the University of Michigan. She is the author of a number of articles as well as a book on politics and the mass media, *Making the Papers*. She co-authored *Campaigning for Congress* with Michael W. Traugott.

JON F. HALE is a graduate student in the Department of Political Science at Indiana University, with interests in survey research as well as in the media and politics.

BRUCE JENNINGS is Associate for Policy Studies at The Hastings Center. His recent publications include *The Ethics of Legislative Life* and *Representation and Responsibility: Exploring Legislative Ethics*.

RICHARD A. JOSLYN is Associate Professor of Political Science and Associate Vice-Provost at Temple University. He is the author of *Political Science Research Methods* (with Janet B. Johnson) and *Mass Media and Elections*.

DAN NIMMO is a Professor in the Political Communication Center, Department of Communication, University of Oklahoma. His research interests and publications have been in the areas of politics and the media, campaign communication, and public opinion.

PAUL BRADFORD RAYMOND is an Assistant Professor at the University of Kentucky. His research focuses on campaigns and elections, political participation, and political tolerance.

ROBERT O. SIMMONS, JR., is an Assistant Professor of Political Science at the University of Texas at Arlington. His contribution to this volume was completed while he was a Ph.D. candidate at the University of Michigan, where he had also been an adjunct instructor. Before entering Michigan he wrote about Washington politics for newspapers and a variety of other organizations.

LARRY SMITH is an Assistant Professor of Political Communication at the University of Arkansas in Little Rock. His research interests include government-media relations, political advertising, and nominating conventions.

MICHAEL W. TRAUGOTT is a senior study director in the Institute for Social Research and an adjunct Associate Professor of Political Science at the University of Michigan. In addition to his writings on voting behavior and politics and the mass media, he conducts surveys for the *Detroit News* and writes a periodic column for them. He co-authored *Campaigning for Congress* with Edie N. Goldenberg.

JAN P. VERMEER is Professor of Political Science and Chairman of the Faculty at Nebraska Wesleyan University. He is the author of *"For Immediate Release": Candidate Press Releases in American Political Campaigns* (Greenwood Press, 1982).